Transnational Wom

Transnational Women's Activism

The United States, Japan, and
Japanese Immigrant Communities
in California, 1859–1920

Rumi Yasutake

NEW YORK UNIVERSITY PRESS
New York and London

NEW YORK UNIVERSITY PRESS
New York and London
www.nyupress.org

Library of Congress Cataloging-in-Publication Data
Yasutake, Rumi, 1958–
Transnational women's activism : the United States, Japan, and
Japanese immigrant communities in California, 1859–1920 / Rumi Yasutake.
p. cm.
Includes bibliographical references and index.
ISBN 0–8147–9703–2 (cloth : alk. paper)
1. Woman's Christian Temperance Union.   2. Women social reformers—
Japan.   3. Women social reformers—California.   4. Women missionar-
ies—Japan.   5. Women in church work—Japan.   6. Women in church
work—California.   7. Women—Japan—Social conditions—19th century.
8. Women—Japan—Social conditions—20th century.   9. Japanese—
California—Social conditions—19th century.   10. Japanese—California—Social conditions—20th century.   I. Title.
HV5247.J3Y37   2004
363.4'1'095209034—dc22   2004007944

Manufactured in the United States of America

10 9 8 7 6 5 4 3 2 1

To August,
  and
    to my parents Fumiko and Susumu

Contents

Acknowledgments

Without the help of many people, this book would never have come to be. My mentor, Ellen C. DuBois, provided me with inspiration and encouragement at critical junctures of this project and in my pursuit of a career as a historian. I was first introduced to the joy of writing by Bill Stott at the University of Texas at Austin, and began contemplating writing a dissertation on the WCTU movement while taking a course taught by Miriam Silverberg at UCLA. At various stages of this project, I also received valuable comments and guidance from Valerie Matsumoto, Mariko Tamanoi, Yuji Ichioka, Fred G. Notehelfer, Donna M. Binkiewicz, Rebecca Mead, Sue Englander, Lisa G. Materson, Anastasia Christman, Sharon Sievers, Virginia L. Brereton, Allison Schneider, and William Johnston.

My writing and rewriting were facilitated by discussions with members of a dissertation group guided by Ellen DuBois (with Maggie), as well as the Women and Twentieth-Century Protestantism project organized by Margaret L. Bendroth and Virginia L. Brereton. Three study groups led respectively by Ryō Yoshida, Makoto Tanaka, and Barbara B. Zikmund at Doshisha University also facilitated the writing process.

I am indebted to the expertise of Alfred Epstein at the Frances Willard Memorial Library in Evanston, Illinois, L. Dale Patterson of the United Methodist Church General Commission on Archives and History in Madison, New Jersey, Eugene M. Itogawa of the California State Parks and Recreation Department Historic Preservation Office in Sacramento, Charlene G. Noyes at the Sacramento Archives and Museum Collection Center, Sibylle Zemitis at the California State Library in Sacramento, Stephan E. Yale at the Graduate Theological Union Methodist Archives in Berkeley, Seizo Oka at the Japanese American History Archives in San Francisco, Karl K. Matsushita at the Japanese-American National Library in San Francisco, and Mihoko Miki at the UCLA East-Asian Library. I also thank the staffs at the UCLA Research Library, the Los Angeles Public Library, the Fuller Theological Union Library, the Huntington Library, the University of the Pacific Library, the University of California Bancroft Library, the Graduate Theological Union Library, the San Francisco Theological Seminary Library, Presbyterian Church (U.S.A.) Department of History and Records Management Services, Doshisha University, the International Research Center for Japanese Studies, the Yokohama Archives of History, and the Aoyama Gakuin University Library.

My heartfelt gratitude goes to Elisabeth Bowen Butler, Yoshie Togasaki, and Akiko Kubushiro, who talked to me about their family members; and Claudia J. Dobbs, Y. Casper Horikoshi, Lester Suzuki, Kikue Takahashi, Masanori Miyazawa, and Ryō Yoshida who graciously shared their materials and research results. I am also deeply grateful to the officers of the (National) WCTU, the California WCTU, and the Southern California WCTU for their assistance in locating their materials in California and for granting me permission to browse through them. Although I failed to find permanent depositories for their California documents, I sincerely hope that these records, especially those of the California WCTU that were stored in boxes at a warehouse in Modesto, will ultimately be archived.

Funding from the UCLA History Department, the UCLA Institute of American Cultures, the UCLA Center for the Study of Women, Phi Beta Kappa Alumni in Southern California, the Pew Charitable Trusts, the W. M. Keck Foundation, the Andrew W. Mellon Foundation, and Konan University allowed me to undertake research travel. I also thank the UCLA Women's Studies Program, the CSULB History Department, and the Konan University Faculty of Letters for providing me employment and my colleagues there for their friendship and support.

I would be remiss if I did not recognize my editor, Eric Zinner, and Emily Park of NYU Press for their extraordinary patience and skillful guidance in the publication of this book. I am also indebted to Despina Papazoglou Gimbel and her staff at the press for clarifying and polishing my writing.

Lastly, I must thank my parents for encouraging me to explore possibilities in my life, and my husband for his patience, support, computer wizardry, and love.

Introduction

The history of the reformer, whether man or woman, in any line of action is but this: when he sees it all alone, he is a fanatic; when a good many see it with him, they are enthusiasts; when all see it, he is a hero. The radiations are as clearly marked by which he ascends from zero to hero as are the lines of latitude from the North Star to the Equator.[1]

—Frances E. Willard, cited by Helen E. Tyler

This statement, said to have been made by the second president of the Woman's Christian Temperance Union (WCTU), Frances E. Willard, illuminates the strategy by which activist churchwomen in nineteenth-century America attempted to generate a mass movement and to gain influence. Defined as "dependents" of men and discouraged from demanding their religious, political, and economic rights, American churchwomen were subjugated to men. They endeavored to unite with one another and pool their limited power and resources so as to be influential enough collectively to change their lives and societies. Seeking mass support, their flexible and pragmatic but often expedient women's movements combined multiple causes and emphasized women's special ability and roles as prescribed by the ideology of Victorian womanhood. American churchwomen were in a sense "timid" about challenging the roles assigned to women by their society. Yet they tactfully accommodated their womanly causes to the social and political currents of a predominantly Protestant but rapidly secularizing late-nineteenth-century America. During this period, when increasing numbers of non-Protestant and non-Christian immigrants were arriving on U.S. shores and modern scientific knowledge was encroaching on the religious authority of Protestant churches, the WCTU enlisted the support of Protestant churchwomen by

1

phrasing its causes in religious, scientific, and even racist terms. Under skillful and feminist-conscious leaders such as Frances E. Willard, the WCTU effectively used the power of the masses to promote various women's causes, including women's suffrage, in turn-of-the-century America.[2]

This book examines the spread of nineteenth-century Protestant churchwomen's social activism in the United States, Japan, and Issei (first-generation Japanese American) communities in northern California, in the context of America's global expansion and Japan's imperialist aspirations between 1859 and 1920. The main subjects of this study are American Protestant foreign and home missionary men and women, American WCTU workers, and their Japanese male and female protégés, who participated directly and indirectly in the trans-Pacific expansion of the WCTU movement. Treating both Americans and Japanese as active agents, this study investigates the intentions and experiences of many of the participants and the transformation of WCTU activism as it accommodated itself to the sociohistorical contexts of Tokyo and California during the period. In the process, this work aims to illuminate the complexity of gender, race, class, culture, and nation in the trans-Pacific expansion of the WCTU movement that, from a macro viewpoint, can be described as an example of Anglo-American cultural imperialism.[3]

The spread of American churchwomen's social activism across the boundaries of race, class, and nation was rooted in their evangelism and their acceptance of the Victorian cultural hierarchy.[4] It went hand in hand with the global expansion of an American, or, from a Japanese view, "Western" system, through the American continent and across the Pacific to Asia. With the arrival of giant American warships and the roaring sounds of their cannons in Japan in the 1850s, the Tokugawa feudal government (1603–1867) reluctantly concluded treaties with the United States to open a few ports and cities to diplomatic and commercial activity. These treaties were "unequal" not only because Japan was deprived of reciprocal most-favored-nation status and tariff autonomy, but also because citizens of the signatory nations enjoyed unilateral extraterritorial rights at the Japanese ports and cities opened to them. The weak-kneed attitude of the Tokugawa government inspired low-echelon samurais from four powerful anti-Tokugawa domains to carry out a successful coup d'état, the "Meiji Restoration," in 1868, thereby bringing about an end to Tokugawa feudalism. The revision of the "unequal treaties" that had been concluded with the United States and other Western powers became the top diplomatic priority in new Meiji Japan. Meiji leaders recognized Japan's need to be "rich and strong" so that it could fend off foreign pressures, and to be "civilized" so that it could also have jurisdiction over the citizens of the signatory nations residing in Japan.

So started Japan's quest for "civilization" and modernization. As early as the 1860s, despite the Tokugawa ban on overseas trips and migration by the Japanese, progressive feudal lords began dispatching their vassals to the West for education. After the Restoration, the Meiji government continually sent its officials and students to the West and also hired foreign advisors to facilitate the process of importing Western institutions into the nation. Additionally, young individuals, mostly from the former samurai class, sought opportunities for Western learning at home and abroad to improve their fortune and that of their country in the new age. While some crossed the ocean, others went to open ports and cities where Western missionaries started to arrive upon the conclusion of the "unequal" treaties. In the 1870s and 1880s, Japan was eager to adopt things Western as a way to "civilize" and "modernize" the country.

American Protestant missionary women started to arrive in Japan at this historically specific moment in the 1860s and 1870s, and brought their first-hand experiences of the West to housebound Japanese women. Since the male-dominant American Protestant church structure limited American churchwomen to work for women and children, they sought female clients in their neighborhoods, cities, frontiers, and foreign fields, thereby crossing the lines of race, class, culture, and nation, but not of gender. Funded by contributions from a large number of grassroots women, American missionary women endeavored to promote Christian education among Japanese women, and produced a pool of Japanese women who could respond to the organizing efforts of World WCTU travelers who began visiting Japan in 1886.

While American Protestant missionary women were constrained by the gender hierarchy of their American male-dominated foreign missionary enterprises, World WCTU missionary women, who followed in their wake, acted on their own as representatives of an exclusively women's organization. The WCTU was built on the bitter experiences of missionary women divided along the lines of male-controlled denominational churches. To be liberated from the control of clergymen who ruled the religious affairs of each denominational church, the WCTU became an interdenominational churchwomen's organization governed by women for the secular cause of temperance. "Temperance" has been a respectable cause since the colonial period in America and was the essential component of "the spirit of Capitalism," in the words of Max Weber.[5] Under the brilliant leadership of Frances Willard, the WCTU hoisted "temperance" in addition to "Christian" as shields protecting women's activism from public criticism in culturally diversifying, decreasingly religious, and increasingly capitalistic turn-of-the-century America. The temperance cause was especially important in expanding the reach of the WCTU movement to non-Christian societies both in the United States and the world.

For a community and a country such as Japan that realized that it had to introduce capitalism, an essential ingredient of modern Western "civilization," if it was to survive and develop, a temperance movement, although advocated by women, appeared to be an important means of "civilizing" and "modernizing" itself. Because of national inequality and cultural differences, both American Protestant and WCTU missionary women, who embodied the "spirit of capitalism," circumvented the Japanese gender hierarchy. While American Protestant missionary women were placed under male control in their own gender system and could not freely interact with Japanese men, World WCTU missionary women, who acted on their own, were on friendly terms with progressive Japanese men who wanted to promote the "temperance" movement for the modernization and advancement of their community and nation.

Japanese churchwomen fell behind progressive Japanese males who had greater resources and more freedom to form close relationships with American World WCTU travelers visiting Japan between 1886 and 1894. Nonetheless, Japanese churchwomen, without fully understanding that the WCTU coupled the temperance cause with women's activism, associated themselves with the World WCTU network and began to work for their own causes. Having been introduced to Protestant notions of monogamy, companionate marriage, the "sin" of prostitution, and evangelical women's extradomestic activities at mission schools, they recognized the efficacy of these values and methods in casting off feudalistic expectations that Japanese women would be obedient daughters-in-law who served their in-laws, and "borrowed wombs" who secured an heir for their husbands' households. With little intervention from American World WCTU travelers, middle-class Japanese churchwomen formed a WCTU in Tokyo in 1886 and promoted their causes in their own way for several years until the inception of a Japanese women's national WCTU in 1893.

Japan's enthusiasm for westernization and the liberal political tide of the 1880s favored Tokyo WCTU women using "Western" and "civilized" ideas, and their activism leaped ahead of their Protestant missionary teachers. They gave speeches to gender-mixed audiences and openly demanded political and economic rights for women. Japanese middle-class churchwomen's WCTU activism and arguments, however, were class-specific, reflecting their elitism and rivalry with women from the pleasure quarters, namely, geishas, prostitutes, and concubines. The liberal political tide in Japan in the late 1880s saw the resurgence of the Movement for Freedom and Popular Rights (*Jiyū minken undō*). During this period middle-class Japanese wives and daughters explored various avenues to advance their status by borrowing both the vocabulary of middle-class American Protestant moral values and womanhood advocated by their missionary teachers and the Western liberal political theories promoted by popular-rights activists.

In the 1890s the strong intervention of a World WCTU traveler persuaded the Japanese women's union in Tokyo to become a national organization, but also invited its leaders to take their activism in a new direction. Simultaneously, the promulgation of the Meiji Constitution and Japan's growing imperialist ambitions in the 1890s caused a strong backlash against the rapid westernization of the previous era, which had allowed middle-class women to form their own voluntary organizations. The growing antiforeign and anti-Christian sentiments of the Japanese public made it especially difficult for Japanese WCTU women to continue their activism, and Japan's engagement in two imperialistic wars in the 1890s and 1900s subordinated women's causes to the good of the state and the nation.

To revitalize WCTU activism in Japan during this difficult era in the late 1890s and 1900s, World WCTU resident missionaries introduced organizational discipline and pragmatism, injected American funds, and facilitated cooperative relationships between Japanese WCTU members, Anglo-American Protestant missionary women, and Japanese male temperance workers. As a result, the Japan WCTU not only survived the conservative tide but also successfully transformed itself into an acceptable and "respectable" women's organization in Japan. However, it had improved its status and increased its influence at the cost of suppressing its feminist consciousness in favor of nationalism. Because of the conservative tide of the late Meiji period and the ideologically pliable nature of the WCTU intent on becoming a mass movement, the Japanese WCTU movement in late Meiji Japan accommodated itself to Japan's aspirations for imperialistic power and to the people's rising nationalism. By the time Japan won the Russo-Japanese war in 1905, both Japanese and American WCTU workers had turned into collaborators of the Japanese state. While promoting middle-class women's causes by borrowing the vocabulary of American Protestant moral and cultural values, both Japanese and American WCTU workers promoted Japan's war efforts and enforced a woman's role as "good wife and wise mother" to ensure her selfless contribution not only to the household but also to the nation.

Meanwhile, across the Pacific in northern California, middle-class Issei churchwomen's activism took a similar trajectory to that taken by the WCTU movement in Japan. Issei churchwomen, like their sisters in Japan, subordinated their feminist consciousness to the interests of their communities as the anti-Asian sentiments of the American public were transferred from the Chinese to the Japanese. Recognizing that American images of Japan and "Japanese" women in America were based on the high visibility of Japanese prostitutes, middle-class Japanese churchwomen in Japan and northern California, in collaboration with Japanese male leaders, attempted to counter the anti-Japanese campaigns by eliminating Japanese prostitutes. In their stead, they encouraged "respectable" Japanese women to join Issei communities as "picture brides." Since the sound development of Issei communities depended on the selfless contribution of these newly arrived brides from Japan, middle-class Issei churchwomen echoed male community leaders in urging them to become good wives and wise mothers while they grappled with their unknown husbands and the unexpected reality of their married lives in America.

Chapter 1 sheds light on American Protestant foreign missionary women's work in promoting female Christian education among Japanese women in male-controlled American missionary enterprises during the 1870s and 1880s, and speculates on the effect they had on their Japanese students and employees. This chapter also examines the changing roles and status of middle-class Japanese women as male Meiji leaders attempted to build a modern centralized state modeled after the Western powers and how American Protestant missionary women's efforts affected that process.

Chapter 2 covers the period from 1886 to 1894. The arrival in Japan of the World WCTU's first round-the-world missionary in 1886 led to the creation of Japanese local unions, including the Tokyo WCTU, among Japanese women teachers and graduates of female mission schools. From then until 1894—a year after these local unions coalesced into Japan's first women's national organization, the Japan WCTU—at least six World

WCTU missionaries toured Japan, each for a short period of time, interacting more closely with progressive Japanese males than with Japanese churchwomen. This chapter examines how activist Japanese churchwomen in Tokyo took advantage of the liberal political tide of the early Meiji period. They received little help from the World WCTU travelers but collaborated with popular-rights activists in generating a feminist and class-specific women's movement.

Chapter 3 deals with the conservative late Meiji era when five more World WCTU women came to Japan and lived and worked in the country to transfer WCTU methods and strategies simultaneously to Japanese WCTU women, and to American Protestant missionary women working in Japan who also formed their own national union in 1895. Facing a strong backlash, Japanese churchwomen's fledgling feminist movement suffered a setback and their newly nationalized organization faltered. But the World WCTU resident missionaries' ambition of generating a mass movement for the temperance cause saved the Japan WCTU at its most difficult moment and provided the organizational base which allowed it to become the respectable national organization that it continues to be today. This chapter also studies how WCTU's ideologically and organizationally pliable activism accommodated itself to the consolidation of state power in Meiji Japan and to the rising nationalism and imperialism of the public.

Chapter 4 examines the social activism of American and Issei church members in northern California between the 1870s and 1920. Their activism was loosely connected to the emergence of Issei churchwomen's WCTU activism on the American Pacific coast in the early twentieth century. This chapter illuminates the different attitudes of American missionary women and middle-class Japanese churchwomen toward Japanese prostitutes and picture brides. In the view of Japanese churchwomen, as in the view of Issei men, given the anti-Japanese sentiments of the American public, the survival and sound development of Issei communities in California depended on the good conduct of women in their communities.

1

Tilling the Ground

American Protestant Foreign Missionary Women in Early Meiji Japan, 1859–1890

Woman's Work for Women in Early Meiji Japan

In 1872, responding to an inquiry from the Board of Foreign Missions of the Presbyterian Church, U.S.A., about the possibility of American women missionaries working in Japan, Dr. James C. Hepburn, a Presbyterian missionary doctor, reported that Japanese were increasingly enthusiastic about female education, thus creating a need for American missionary women. Hepburn wrote:

> There is, at the present time, great opportunities for "woman's work" in this country, especially in our large cities. The Japanese have awakened to the necessity of educating their females, and have pressed almost every available [missionary] woman into this service. [I]f this zeal continues, which it is likely to do though perhaps somewhat moderated, there will be a fine field for female workers. And I think the Board would do well to engage in it.[1]

Two decades after the Tokugawa feudal government (1603–1867) reluctantly concluded treaties with the United States, Japan fervently began to emulate Western values and institutions, kindling Japanese women's desire for an education. To achieve equality with the technically more advanced West, the newly established Meiji government in the early 1870s was willing to learn anything from the Western powers, including their notions of family and womanhood. Thus, the government added five female students, including Umeko Tsuda, to its diplomatic delegation to the West in 1871, and assigned them the task of living with American families and attending American schools for ten years. Furthermore, to build an educational system based on the American model, the Meiji government began promoting public primary school education for boys and girls of all classes in 1872. The social tide of the early 1870s favored new changes and westernization, and the government even established several women's schools to provide women with Western learning or to train them to become teachers for the emerging public primary school system. The government counted on Anglo-American Protestant missionary women in Japan to assist it in these efforts.[2]

During this period, the so-called "enlightenment thinkers," the Japanese male elite who had been to the West during the late 1860s and the early 1870s, also advocated female education. These male thinkers recognized that the issues of gender relations and sexual morality were crucial measures of an "enlightened" civilization. Like the United States when it was forging a republic, they emphasized the need for female education because of women's influence on their children, the future subjects of "enlightened" Japan. For example, Masanao Nakamura, a former Confucian scholar who had been strongly influenced by Protestant values while studying in England in the late 1860s, insisted on the need for female moral and religious education in order to "create good mothers" and to ultimately "change the character of the people" for the new age. Masanao Nakamura founded Dōjinsha, a school of Western learning, in Tokyo in 1873, and opened it to women in 1874.[3]

Nonetheless, female education was a lower priority than that of men for government officials and progressive male thinkers. Thus, when the central and local governments faced financial difficulties in the late 1870s, they allowed female secondary schools—except those which trained female primary school teachers—to fold.[4] In contrast, American Protestant missionary women, funded by contributions from a large number of grassroots women's organizations in the United States, made a more persistent commitment to promoting Christian education among Japanese women. They filled the gap between the growing thirst of Japanese women for an education and the Japanese government's undependable response, especially until the 1890s when the government increased its efforts for and control over female secondary and higher education. Despite the turbulence of the Restoration and the ban on Christianity that was not lifted until 1873, a small number of missionary wives had begun conducting English classes at open ports and open cities as early as the 1860s.

Japan's first female mission school originated in a class initiated by Mrs. Clara Hepburn in Yokohama, the wife of Presbyterian missionary doctor

James C. Hepburn, both of whom arrived in Japan in 1859. However, her efforts were often hampered by her responsibilities as wife and mother. The work of developing a school from the single class started by Clara Hepburn required the strong commitment of Miss Mary Kidder (1834–1909) of the Reformed Church in America, the first single woman missionary who worked in post-Restoration Japan. By 1890, about forty female schools in over twenty different cities were under the influence of American missionary women and supported by American foreign mission boards.[5]

This work by American missionary women in Japan in the 1870s had been preceded by more than half a century of struggle by American churchwomen to establish and expand a women's sphere in the male-dominant structure of the foreign missionary enterprises of American Protestant churches. American churchwomen, who were defined as "dependents" of men in need of male protection and supervision, strove to prove that they were capable of being independent of men and of carrying out women's projects separate from men's. When the American Board of Commissioners for Foreign Missions (ABCFM), the first agency to send American missionaries abroad was formed in 1810, it began to dispatch missionaries overseas by collaborating with the Congregational, Presbyterian, and Reformed churches. It allowed only married women to sail for foreign fields as "assistant missionaries." It saw the primary roles of missionary wives as homemakers for their husbands, managing the household and bearing and raising children. Secondarily, they were expected to "assist" their husbands in missionary work by exercising their female Christian influence as "teachers" of indigenous women and children. Despite their dependent status, however, able female missionary workers demonstrated that they could be "useful" as teachers, nurses, and social workers in addition to capably fulfilling their domestic duties. These American missionary wives laid the groundwork for female mission schools throughout the world.[6]

Although American female missionary workers wanted to work for the spiritual conversion of "heathens" as much as their male counterparts did, women were hindered from being ordained, preaching, or serving as lay delegates in the church's governing body. Thus, they directed their extradomestic activities in the secular realm toward women and children. In claiming "Woman's Work for Woman and Children," American churchwomen sought female clients in their neighborhoods, cities, frontiers, and the world by crossing the boundaries of race, class, culture, and nation, but not of gender. Establishing a women's sphere in home-and-foreign missionary activities, American churchwomen insisted that they were engaging in work that only women could perform and made it clear that they did not intend to invade the male sphere. This strategy successfully appeased male denominational missionary boards, which wanted to dominate the "true missionary" work of preaching and ministering. Tolerated by the male authorities, American churchwomen's missionary endeavor drew support from large numbers of American churchwomen at the grassroots level.

By the middle of the nineteenth century, building female mission schools in foreign fields became the primary tasks of American missionary women. While the foreign mission boards such as the ABCFM permitted single women, but only exceptionally, to work in foreign fields in the early and mid-nineteenth century, the demand for unmarried women to work as teachers increased as female mission schools took hold in mission fields. At the same time, expanding educational opportunities for women in the United States had produced pools of well-educated young women who were eager to take on the work. Since the male authorities of the denominational foreign missionary enterprises were reluctant to send single women as missionaries to foreign fields, in 1860 churchwomen of various Protestant churches in America formed the first women's missionary organization, the Woman's Union Missionary Society of America for Heathen Lands (WUMS), under the initiative of Mrs. Sarah Doremus of the Reformed Church. Importantly, this was an interdenominational and ecumenical effort by churchwomen who wanted to enlist the contributions of the rank and file to assist in women's work for women and children in foreign fields.[7]

With WUMS's success in enlisting women for missionary work outside the churches, however, the general foreign missionary boards of various Protestant denominations began to encourage the formation of their own denominational women's missionary boards so as to keep women's contributions within their own churches. Thus, American churchwomen's missionary efforts were reformulated along denominational lines. American churchwomen, who wanted to be virtuous, selfless, and helpful, committed themselves to "double giving" by supporting the regular parish work and women's missionary work of their denominational churches. By 1880, single and married women composed about 60 percent of American missionaries working abroad.[8] Women's foreign missionary movements organized under women's boards in different denominational churches became one of the most popular women's activities in the late nineteenth century.[9]

To demonstrate the influence of American missionary women on their Japanese employees and students, who later played crucial roles as activists in Japanese women's WCTU, I examine the experiences of two American missionary women, Mary Kidder (1834–1910) and Maria True (1840–1896), in promoting Christian education among Japanese women. Their efforts produced the first generation of Japanese women converts, including Toyojyu Sasaki (1853–1901) and Kajiko Yajima (1833–1925), both of whom later played key roles in the Japanese women's WCTU movement. Toyojyu Sasaki attended Mary Kidder's school for about a year around 1872 and 1873.[10] Kajiko Yajima was hired by Maria True in 1878 to teach at a Presbyterian female mission school in Tokyo.[11]

Mary Kidder and Japan's First Female Mission School in the 1870s

Today the Japanese remember Mary Kidder fondly as the founder of a well-established institution of female education in Yokohama. Arriving in Japan in 1869, when sending a single missionary woman overseas was still uncommon, Kidder had to overcome American and Japanese conventions that treated women as subordinates to and dependents of men. Kidder arrived in Japan with Rev. and Mrs. Samuel R. Brown whom she had known for many years, having worked at Rev. Brown's school as a teacher and attended his church in Owasco Outlet in New York. The Browns had been working as missionaries in Japan since 1859, and strongly recommended Kidder, a pious Christian and an able teacher in her midthirties, to work as a missionary teacher to promote female Christian education in Japan. Since women in her denomination did not organize a women's board until 1875, Kidder was appointed by the general board, the Board of Foreign Missions, Reformed Church in America. Being unmarried at the time, she was placed under the protection and supervision of Rev. and Mrs. Brown.[12]

In the course of her lifelong missionary work in Japan, Mary Kidder wrestled with this dependent status, which curtailed her freedom in pursuing a career and personal happiness but was a widely accepted practice by American missionaries in Japan. Living with the Browns, it was Rev. Brown, not Kidder, who received her full salary from the board, and he handed over only a portion of it to her and that too only upon her request. Kidder had to struggle both with Rev. Brown and the mission board to gain economic independence.[13] At the same time, to avoid any misunderstanding over her status in Japanese society—an unmarried woman away from her family—Kidder was reported to the Japanese government as the Browns' daughter. Thus, Kidder taught Japanese girls at the Browns' residence while assisting Mrs. Brown with her housework in Niigata, a newly opened port in Japan where Rev. Brown had been appointed principal of a Japanese government school. When he was discharged on the grounds that he taught the Bible at his residence, Kidder also had to give up her class in order to follow the Browns to Yokohama where Rev. Brown became the principal of another government school.[14]

After moving to Yokohama in 1870, Kidder, while continuing to assist Mrs. Brown at home, began helping Mrs. Hepburn of the Presbyterian mission teach English and explored ways to work outside the Browns' residence. Clara Hepburn, who had almost completed her own child-rearing duties, had spent whatever free time she had teaching English to Japanese students at her husband's dispensary in Yokohama. However, when she became engrossed in taking care of a baby whose Presbyterian missionary parents had died in a ship explosion, she handed the class over to Mary Kidder without hesitation. In 1871, when Dr. and Mrs. Hepburn left Yokohama for an extended trip, Kidder also began to teach at the Sunday school for the children of foreign residents in Yokohama. By the summer of 1872, there were more than twenty-eight Japanese students at the day school, and about half of them attended the Sunday school with the area's foreign children.[15]

When the Hepburns returned to Yokohama, Kidder endeavored to secure a building for the expanding day school. Although Kidder could not obtain funding from the financially troubled Board of Foreign Missions, Reformed Church in America, she was able to use her personal networks to obtain assistance from Japanese and American men in Yokohama, who were sympathetic to her efforts, as well as church women and Sunday school children in New York. Although both American and Japanese societies believed in women being dependent on men, Kidder, a "teacher" from an advanced Western nation, was able to sidestep the Japanese gender hierarchy to access resources unavailable to Japanese women. In her pursuit of independence Kidder took full advantage of this status, and found her first crucial supporter in the Governor of Kanagawa Prefecture, whose wife attended Kidder's school. In 1872, he procured an official unit located in the native part of Yokohama for use as her day school. To facilitate her commute, he also provided Kidder, who still lived with the Browns in the foreign concession, with a rickshaw. The same year, Miss S. K. M. Hequembourg from Owasco Outlet arrived to lend assistance to Kidder's efforts.

While managing her growing day school, however, Mary Kidder soon realized that her evangelical endeavors were hampered by the dependent status of her students. Many of them were daughters and wives of officers in the emerging Meiji government, and they had to leave her school whenever their fathers or husbands were transferred to new sites of duty. Kidder was chagrined at seeing her students leave Christian instruction before conversion. To keep her students under her Christian instruction, Kidder realized that she needed a boarding facility for her school. Once again, Kidder sought assistance through her personal networks in Japan and the United States. Through the efforts of the local governor, his successor, and the U.S. consul general, Kidder managed to acquire a lease on a plot of land from the Japanese government in late 1874. In addition, she found another dependable supporter in Rev. Rothesay E. Miller, a Presbyterian missionary, whom Kidder had recently married. Using $5,000 donated by women and Sunday school children of the Reformed Church in America, plus $500 contributed by her newly wedded husband, Mary, now Mrs. Miller, built a school on the plot. The school was named Ferris Seminary after Isaac Ferris and his son John M. Ferris, who served as former and incumbent secretaries of the Board of Foreign Missions, Reformed Church in America, respectively.[16]

However, it was extremely difficult for Mary to maintain her hard-won independence due to her new status as a missionary wife. Her aggressive attitudes in both the private and public spheres had been closely watched by the missionary circle in Yokohama and the mission boards in the United States, which pressured the Millers to follow conventional norms. When a husband and wife belonged to different denominational churches, convention required that the wife join her husband's church. Mary, however, did not want to leave her mission at the crucial moment when the Ferris Seminary had just been founded, and transfer to the Presbyterian mission where she would not be able to avoid the intervention of Dr. and Mrs. Hepburn. Rothesay, who advocated interdenominational cooperation in the evangelization of Japan, openly supported his wife working for a different denominational mission board.[17] Soon the couple faced pressure from both the Presbyterian general and women's boards to make Mary change her mission board. When she received a welcome letter from Mrs. Graham of the Ladies' Board of Missions of the Presbyterian Church, New York, Mary reaffirmed her intention not to leave her own mission board.

It was Rothesay, not Mary, who ultimately changed mission boards. In September 1874, the Presbyterian Board notified Rothesay that his annual salary would be reduced from $1,000 to $300, arguing that if Mary's income of $700 was added it would equal his original salary. Rothesay and Mary took this as an insult and he resigned his affiliation with the Presbyterian mission board. However, the board countered his resignation letter with the reinstatement of his salary and an urgent plea to make Mary change her mind. In October 1874, Rothesay had stopped receiving any salary from the Presbyterian mission board, and joined Mary's school as an independent missionary until he was accepted by the Reformed mission board in July 1875.[18] Thus, Rothesay, not Mary, changed mission boards.

This anomalous situation became an issue in Protestant missionary circles both in Japan and the United States. In Yokohama, Mary and Rothesay were frowned upon by old-timers such as Dr. and Mrs. Hepburn of the Presbyterian mission, who firmly believed that the role of missionary wives was to "manage the domestic affairs of the household and [to] relieve their husbands of family cares."[19] At the same time, although J. M. Ferris, secretary of the Board of Foreign Missions, Reformed Church in America, did not object to retaining Mary and gaining a male missionary already stationed in Japan, he could not permit a woman stepping out of her place. Facing Ferris's criticism of her relationship with her husband, Mary did not confront him but made the excuse that it was a "providential arrangement" to allow her to continue teaching at the fledgling seminary. Mary conceded that:

> I exactly agree with you that the husband is head of the wife not only in theory but in practice, and we have exactly agreed in all our plans for missionary work. Mr. Miller told Dr. Hepburn plainly after his return to Japan that if I come over to their mission, I could not take the school, that he would not permit it for he did not think it right. However, although it was pleasant for me to remain in the school, we thought it not best and so concluded that as soon as some teachers are sent out, I should leave it and go with Mr. Miller.[20]

Furthermore, missionary conservatives criticized Mary's evangelical efforts, suspecting that she and her students were breaking away from the biblically sanctioned convention that prohibited women from preaching or praying in gender-mixed meetings. After receiving a letter from J. M. Ferris expressing his concern, Mary again refrained from challenging his idea of the proper female missionary role. Instead, she simply tried to stretch it to meet her needs. She wrote:

> Your views in regard to women speaking or preaching in mixed gatherings exactly coincide with my own and I am sure that none of my pupils have done anything that you should disapprove. When we were on a trip north in the summer we were staying with the relatives of some of my pupils. One of them, a girl of fifteen, often helped me in talking to natives mostly men who came where we were staying to ask about our religion. This was nothing like preaching, we all sat down, they asked me questions and we answered them, sometimes talking hours in this way. Some times there were just one or two present and at other times twenty or thirty. That is all the preaching either my pupils or myself [have] done.[21]

In pursuing a career as a missionary of the Reformed Church, Mary had to be on good terms with American missionary circles both in Japan and the United States. When the missionary circle in Yokohama became critical of Mary and her husband, and J. M. Ferris and the Board of Foreign Missions, Reformed Church in America became aware of it, both their careers were at stake. During the pioneering years of American female missionary work in Japan, Mary's struggle to be an independent missionary laid the foundation for the first female mission school in Japan. While her aggressive pursuit of women's work for women was tolerable as a single missionary, the same attitude was unacceptable when she became a missionary wife. Facing pressure from the secretary of her own mission board, Mary chose not to confront the conventional view of a missionary wife's role that the majority still adhered to, but gave up her school instead. She and her husband lived with the student boarders in a new school building and conducted classes from the time the Ferris Seminary began in 1875 until their return to the United States on furlough in 1879.

When they came back to Japan in 1881, the Millers did not return to the Ferris Seminary. The management of the Ferris Seminary was handed over to a married couple, Rev. and Mrs. Eugene Booth, and the seminary grew with the steady support of the Woman's Board of Foreign Missions,

Reformed Church in America. Mary finally agreed to be her husband's "helpmate," and accompanied him on evangelical work in Tokyo and in the interior of Japan. Without being ordained, Mary could only "assist" in her husband's evangelical work for the rest of her life. She organized women's meetings and Sunday schools, and published a Christian newsletter in Japanese with the help of a Japanese minister.[22] Thus, Mary lost her hard-won independence.

Maria True and Her Projects in the 1880s

> I am not anxious to see many women sent out as missionaries—especially where their being sent consumes funds that might be used in sending men. The men are the proper instruments in this great work. It is through preaching the Word [that] nations are to be converted. The women are useful as teachers in schools mainly. They are dependent, and not so reliable—for they will get married when they have a chance. I think the time is not far off when you will have trouble and have to stand up against an undue number of appointments of this kind.[23]

By the end of the 1870s, Dr. Hepburn of the Presbyterian mission, who in 1872 had encouraged the women of his church to work for women's education in Japan, was uneasy about the increasing presence of single women missionaries and their expanding school projects in Japan. Hepburn believed that women should not act by themselves but should assist men. In his opinion, the women's boards could "collect money" but men should be the ones to decide how to use it. Missionary women in the field could visit Japanese women at their homes, read and explain the Bible, and invite women and their children to church and Sunday school. But Hepburn was against female missionaries starting and managing schools for Japanese women, especially boarding schools that were, in his view, of little use and too costly. He argued that women missionaries could best work by assisting Japanese men to educate Japanese women. Since conversion could only be done by ordained men, Hepburn insisted that the limited resources of the Presbyterian foreign missionary enterprise should be spent mainly on educating Japanese men.[24]

Despite Hepburn's opinion, "Western" female education provided by American missionary women kept growing in popularity among the daughters and wives of the emerging Japanese urban middle class

throughout the 1880s. In 1883, Toshiko Kishida from Kyoto, the first celebrated female popular-rights activist, revealed her strong desire for education in a public speech entitled "*hakoiri musume* (daughters confined to
boxes)," which fanned young Japanese women's desire for education. The
phrase "boxed daughters" was commonly used in the Kansai region to
refer to the beloved daughters of the upper and middle classes who led
sheltered nonpublic lives until they got married. Kishida argued that parents should give their daughters freedom and education rather than these
"boxes" which, although lovingly created, constrained them.[25]

The times were propitious for such an argument, as the Japanese government's westernization efforts, which peaked in the late 1880s, made
Japanese women especially keen to learn English and Western manners. In
working to revise the unequal treaties, the Meiji government frequently
threw extravagant Western-style parties at the Rokumeikan, a magnificent
Western-style guest pavilion built specifically to entertain foreign diplomats and VIPs. As a result, fluency in English and skill in European danc-
ing became sought-after accomplishments among Japanese ladies of the
upper and middle classes,[26] creating a demand for Western-style female
education. To meet the growing demands of Japanese women, American
women missionaries not only expanded their schools but also promoted
Japanese efforts for female education in local cities in the interior. They
obtained special permission from the Japanese government to live there
since they, as foreigners, were not yet allowed to live or travel freely in the
interior.[27]

Alongside the expanding projects managed by American missionary
women in Japan, women's presence and influence in the Presbyterian foreign missionary enterprise increased steadily through the late nineteenth
century. By 1890 Presbyterian women had organized seven women's
boards in Chicago, Philadelphia, New York, Albany, San Francisco, St.
Louis, and Portland to engage in foreign missionary work.[28] Unlike the interdenominational WUMS, the denominational women's boards of the
Presbyterian Church were auxiliaries of the preexisting male-controlled
general board. Thus Presbyterian women's efforts to promote women's
work in foreign fields required the approval of the local committee in foreign fields and the General Board at home, both of which were male.

Rather than confronting the male-dominant structure, Presbyterian
women endeavored to "influence" the male authorities and to establish
the autonomy of the women's sphere. Although the women's boards were
unable to assert their moral authority when working with the male clergy

for "God's work," they successfully collected small sums of money from a large number of rank and file churchwomen. Encouraging "systematic" and "sacrificial" giving for women's missionary work in addition to parish work, the women's boards were expert at raising funds so as to exercise greater influence over the decisions made by the General Board.

Missionary women increasingly engaged in activities assigned to men, although they continually framed their ambitions in terms of their motto, "Woman's Work for Woman and Children" and emphasized women's special ability and separate spheres of work. In managing female mission schools, missionary women accurately read the social norms of the host society and deftly employed their business and management skills.[29] In the process, although some of them came to demand equality with men in the missionary enterprise, they did not easily abandon the middle-class ideology of Victorian womanhood and women's sphere, which defined women as morally superior to men and therefore entitled to exercise their moral authority but only as long as it was limited to domestic and subordinate roles.[30] While able and ambitious women missionaries became increasingly aware that this strategy fell short of making women's work fully independent of or equal to men's work, they maintained the separate-sphere strategy as far as possible. They were reluctant to break away from the ideology that was still unquestioned by male authorities and the majority of women in America. But while they were "timid" about taking radical action, they were "practical" in pursuit of their immediate goals on projects that they were involved in.[31] Expanding "Woman's Work for Woman" in the world required more support and contributions from women at the grassroots level. At the same time, missionary women also wanted to avoid any "unnecessary" conflicts with men so as to make swift progress in their chosen projects. Overall, stretching the women's sphere and role was less traumatic than a head-on confrontation.

Nonetheless, conducting women's projects under the supervision of men who wanted to subordinate them to their own male agenda was a truly onerous experience. The more dedicated and ambitious the women missionaries were, the greater their frustration and despair. While struggling to provide a fine Christian education to the ever increasing numbers of Japanese women asking for it in the 1880s, a group of Presbyterian missionary women, led by Maria True (1840–1896), eventually objected to their "unjust" treatment by the male-dominated foreign missionary enterprise. Comprising one of the most resourceful women's boards in the United States, the Presbyterian "Woman's Work for Woman and Children"

in Japan was extensive and involved not only gender conflict but also denominational, personal, and regional rivalries.[32]

Like Mary (Kidder) Miller, Maria True is fondly remembered by the
Japanese as the chief contributor to the establishment of a still-existing female school in Tokyo that resulted from the merger of two Presbyterian
female mission schools, Bancho School and Graham Seminary, and for
founding a short-lived training school for female nurses. Although Bancho School and Graham Seminary belonged to the same Presbyterian foreign missionary enterprise, Bancho School was supported by the Woman's
Foreign Missionary Society of the Presbyterian Church, Philadelphia
(Philadelphia Woman's Society) while Graham Seminary in Tsukiji was
funded by the Ladies' Board of Missions of the Presbyterian Church, New
York (New York Ladies' Board). The rivalry between the two women's
boards in Philadelphia and New York hampered the merger of the two
schools until 1890. Until then they competed rather than cooperated in
conducting "Woman's Work for Woman and Children" in Tokyo.[33]

Maria True, the widow of a Presbyterian minister, arrived in Yokohama
in 1874 as a missionary appointed by the interdenominational WUMS.
True changed her mission to take over a school started by Mrs. Julia Carrothers, a Presbyterian missionary wife. In the early 1870s, Julia Carrothers, without children of her own to take care of, committed herself to
instructing Japanese women in the area and founded a school by obtaining the support of the Philadelphia Woman's Society. However, her "difficult" husband could not get along with other members of the Tokyo Mission and decided to resign from the mission. Consequently, she had to
give up her school to follow him. Maria True was designated as the successor of Julia's school, but soon yielded Julia's students to new missionaries
sent from the New York Ladies Board.[34]

Instead, True channeled the Philadelphia women's resources that had
been supporting Julia's efforts to a school founded by Mrs. Chika Sakurai,
the wife of a Japanese Christian naval officer, in the Bancho district, a resi-
dential area for government officials. While learning English from American missionary teachers, Sakurai converted to Christianity and decided to
build a Japanese-run Christian school. Investing her personal funds and
obtaining assistance in English instruction from WUMS missionary
women, Sakurai successfully started a school in the late 1870s. Her school
soon came to need a larger facility and more teachers. With support from
the Philadelphia Woman's Society, Maria True began assisting Sakurai
with the school, and enabled her to add a department of higher primary

education in 1879 and a kindergarten in 1880. They ultimately grew into Sakurai Jogakkō (Sakurai Women's School) and moved to a new Western-style building in 1881. However, soon thereafter Chika Sakurai had to leave the school to follow her husband who had decided to engage in evangelical work in the frontier land of Hokkaido. Thus, management of the Sakurai Women's School virtually fell into the hands of Maria True and the Philadelphia Woman's Society supporting True. Because the school was located in Bancho outside the foreign concession and no foreigner was allowed to own land or engage in business there, Kajiko Yajima, who had been working under True, was registered as the principal to replace Mrs. Sakurai.[35]

As Japanese enthusiasm for "westernization and civilization" continued to rise in the 1880s, True and her right-hand missionary teacher, Anna Davis, endeavored to satisfy the ever-growing demand by Japanese middle-class women for female mission schools. To enlarge the facilities for the prosperous school in Bancho with limited resources, they put their business and management skills to work. However, all official actions required the prior approval of both the local mission in Japan and the general mission board in the United States, both of which were dominated by men. True and Davis had to overcome a series of exasperating hurdles ranging from red tape to gender, personal, and regional disputes in the Presbyterian foreign missionary enterprise.

One such trial occurred in 1884, when True was in the United States recovering from an illness. Anna Davis, who had been waiting for the right opportunity to purchase land for the growing Bancho School, came across an ideal plot complete with a building for sale. Not wanting to miss this opportunity, she requested approval for purchase of the plot. Despite strong opposition from Dr. Hepburn, in September 1884 the Standing Committee of the East-Japan Mission recommended that the General Board approve the purchase. However, the General Board deferred its decision on the grounds that the resolution was not accompanied by any statement of the case or reasons either pro or con. In the United States Maria True pleaded with the Board to "give a favorable answer promptly" before it became too late to purchase the land at its current price. True had already secured a promise of help from Anna Davis's father, an elder of the First Presbyterian Church in Pittsburgh, and other friends in the city to proceed with her project.[36]

Wanting to make the most of their resources, True was losing patience with the male authorities in Japan and the United States. Unable to per-

suade conservatives such as Dr. Hepburn in Tokyo, True, who firmly believed that the opportunity had been provided by God, became critical of
the General Board, the highest body of the Presbyterian foreign missionary enterprise, and its male-dominant structure. She criticized the General
Board for allowing the Standing Committee of the East-Japan Mission, a
local organization "composed entirely of gentlemen," to be solely "responsible for the expenditure of the funds." She also confronted the General
Board for requiring that women's projects first obtain a local committee's
recommendation before approving a project. According to True, it was un-
fair that "the ladies," who doubtless knew more about their work than the
men, had "no vote" on the matter. Furthermore, True criticized the General Board for inconsistency between its statement that it was "always glad
to hear the opinions of the ladies" and that women's view should "have
due influence" and its actions in this case. True argued that the General
Board hesitated to authorize the purchase of the land for Bancho School,
which was desired by all "the ladies" working at the school, because the
Standing Committee of the East-Japan Mission had not furnished the reasons or the plans for it. True continued:

> I think this proves that, while the Board desires to treat the ladies on the
> field with all due respect, the opinion of those ladies concerning the work
> committed to their hands, will count for nothing when contrary to the
> vote of the Standing Committee. In this case, a majority of the Committee
> [approves] but even that may not avail. My only reason for asking you to
> bring this matter again before the Board is that it illustrates a point of
> vital importance to the work to which we have given our lives.[37]

After this passionate plea from Maria True, the General Board finally
approved purchase of the plot. As it took considerable time for money to
arrive through official channels, Anna Davis went ahead and purchased
the plot by borrowing the necessary funds from two Tokyo-based male
missionaries who had been supportive of women's efforts. After True returned to Japan, the departments of primary school education and
kindergarten were moved to a new building on the new campus in 1886.
Miss Elizabeth Milliken, who had joined the Bancho School in 1884, took
charge of the kindergarten department with a newly added class to train
kindergarten teachers. In 1887, True reported that "three American and
five Japanese teachers, and six pupil assistants" conducted "the school
proper, the kindergarten with its normal class attachment, two Sunday

schools, a morning class for married women, and a training school for nurses" on the Bancho campus. At the center of these was the girls' school, which was divided into Japanese and English divisions, with the latter sub-divided into regular and preparatory departments. The total number of students exceeded 170. Of these, more than 60 were boarders.[38]

As the Japanese demand for English learning was reaching its peak in the late 1880s, the Bancho School, which had established a reputation for its English education, continued to grow. While True was pressed to fur-ther expand its facilities, she contemplated taking the opportunity to start a college for Japanese women. To bring more Japanese women under Christian influence and to increase the income from tuition, True ac-cepted as many applicants as possible. At the same time, her students were extending their stay in Bancho School and an increasing number were pursuing a six-year curriculum after completing their primary education. By September 1888, the number of students had reached 325, and two or three classes were being held in one classroom. To solve the problem of overcrowding and to provide a higher education, True asked the General Board if there was "a heart and purse ready to respond, and provide say $25,000 or $30,000 for the establishment of a Christian College for the young women of Japan." In True's estimate, the enlarged institution for higher women's education would be possible by uniting Bancho School and Graham Seminary, which was also overcrowded and thus compelled to refuse qualified applicants. According to True, after purchasing a "large and well-located ground" and putting up a building with initial funds, more money could be raised by selling some of the existing buildings and lands of the two schools to found a Christian college in Japan.[39]

But True's plan was far more innovative and expensive than the General Board and the Philadelphia Woman's Society had imagined.[40] As the Japanese desire for westernization was reaching its climax, Presbyterian women missionaries were striving to respond to the Japanese enthusiasm for female education in Osaka, Kanazawa, Sapporo, and Yokohama as well as Tokyo.[41] Bancho School was already the most expensive women's school in Japan, and given "the active mind of Mrs. True at its head" it gave con-servatives like J. C. Hepburn "more trouble than all the other female schools put together." Moreover, male mission members in the Tokyo-Yokohama area were demanding $50,000 to build a mission college and seminary for male education, a project that Dr. Hepburn considered far more important than female education.[42] Besides, Mrs. Hepburn's sister, Isabella Leete, who worked at Graham Seminary with the support of the

New York Ladies' Board, considered True's plan to be an attempt to absorb their Seminary into the more prosperous Bancho School backed by the Philadelphia Woman's Society, and thus she opposed it.[43]

However, True's plan to enlarge Bancho School won the support of the Standing Committee of the East-Japan Mission because of its future promise and the denominational rivalry between the missions in Japan. In November 1887, the East-Japan Mission recommended that the General Board grant $10,000 for Bancho School in order to secure a larger plot of land so it could increase its capacity. If the General Board could not do so, the East-Japan Mission asked that it allow Bancho School to raise the amount itself.[44] By then, the Methodist Episcopal mission had asked its board for $20,000 and sixteen women missionaries for its female school in Tokyo, and Rev. Booth of the Reformed mission's Ferris Seminary had returned with $15,000 from his fund-raising tour in America. To compete with these denominational missions' women's projects, the Presbyterian mission in Tokyo recognized the need to further expand Bancho's facilities to increase enrollment and make it self-supporting. It also saw the desirability of unifying Bancho School and Graham Seminary, if not at the present then sometime in the near future.[45]

More than six months later, in June 1888, the General Board of the Presbyterian Church, with the agreement of the Philadelphia Woman's Society, finally decided to grant $8,000 for Bancho School and True's other project of building a school to train female nurses. By that time, however, the desirable plots had come and gone from the market and land prices in the Bancho district had soared. Thus the money finally granted was insufficient for True's project.[46] Henceforth True relied increasingly on her own business skills and personal networks in Japan and the United States to pursue her goals. Relying on tuition at Bancho School to increase the school's income and disposable funds, she made it possible for financially troubled students to attend classes for half a day while working on campus for the other half of the day.[47] She also promoted female education in local cities where "the people were willing to meet the expenses of the school except for the salary of foreign teachers." True sent Anna Davis and Bancho's senior students out to local cities to teach preparatory studies. In this way, she reduced the number of boarders at Bancho School, for their costs were an economic burden both on the school and their parents. She thus made it possible to "give girls a good education at far less expense." True and Davis also made private fund-raising efforts both in Japan and in the United States.[48]

True's vision for an enlarged institution for female higher education finally materialized when the New York Ladies' Board accepted the merger of two Presbyterian female mission schools in Tokyo by moving Graham Seminary, whose old buildings were in need of renovation, out of the foreign concession to a better location in the Bancho district. In the fall of 1890, Bancho School, supported by the Philadelphia Woman's Society, and Graham Seminary, backed by the New York Ladies' Board, finally moved to the new location and officially became one entity named Joshigakuin. Bancho School obtained its new campus funded by the Philadelphia Woman's Society. Then, with financial support from the New York Ladies' Board, Graham Seminary purchased a plot of land adjoining the new Bancho campus. Graham Seminary and Bancho School built their own buildings carrying their old names, and boarders from the two schools lived separately. But the boarders and commuters studied together at classes conducted at Joshigakuin.[49] The management of Joshigakuin was placed under a board of directors composed of twelve female missionaries, six supported by the Philadelphia Woman's Society, and the other six by the New York Ladies' Board.[50] As the school was located outside the foreign concession, Kajiko Yajima was registered as principal. Although Joshigakuin was not a college, it was an enlarged institution of higher education for Japanese women built by Presbyterian women.

Presbyterian Women and Women's Right to "Vote"

Masking their ambitious goals in selfless service for God and adhering to the separate-sphere strategy, able missionary women such as Maria True aggressively pursued their educational projects in the male-dominated foreign missionary field. Since the Japanese enthusiastically welcomed Western civilization but were deeply hostile to Christianity, American women missionaries' secular efforts met the needs of Japanese society better than American male clerical endeavors. Furthermore, women missionaries were able to influence male decisions and advance their goals by working patiently within the exclusively male official decision-making procedures of the Presbyterian foreign missionary enterprise. Eventually this strategy caused the decision makers to review their procedures. In fact, men of other denominational churches also increasingly acknowledged women's effort and contributions. In the Methodist Episcopal

Church, for example, the national debate over ordination and lay rights took place in the late 1880s and early 1890s. For the ease of the ABCFM, missionary women were granted a vote on all mission matters in 1893.[51]

True had never demanded a woman's "vote" but had only complained about the unjust treatment of women by the General Board in 1884. Her passionate appeal, presumably similar to that voiced by Presbyterian foreign missionary women working in other fields, generated enough pressure in the women's boards to cause the General Board to start considering women's participation in the decision-making process of the local mission committee. In February 1887 the Standing Committee of the East-Japan Mission responded to the General Board's initiative by recommending the formation of two separate standing committees of male and female missionaries, with each committee allowed direct and equal communication with the General Board. But the General Board, expecting more "radical" changes, rejected the recommendation.[52] True had already been corresponding directly with the General Board, unlike many other missionary women. She took this opportunity to insist on a "united council" of men and women rather than two separate committees to make decisions at the local level.[53] Although True did not intend to affect men's work, she saw the limitations of the separate-sphere strategy for women because sympathizers for and opponents of her projects cut across gender lines.

In December 1889 the General Board adopted new revisions to its manual, granting single missionary women a vote on all issues at the mission level. Rule 30 of the revised manual stipulated:

> A Mission consists of all foreign missionaries under appointment by the [General] Board within specified territorial limits, who are all, including single women, entitled to vote. Wives of missionaries are regarded as advisory members of the mission, entitled to express [an] opinion on business before the body, but not to vote except where they devoted themselves exclusively to the work, as in the case of single women.[54]

While single missionaries such as True rejoiced and responded that the new manual gave "much satisfaction to the Bancho Family,"[55] the majority of East-Japan Mission members saw it as too "radical" and some emphatically opposed it. For example, Rev. George W. Knox of the mission represented men's fear of women's power and the feminization of Presbyterian foreign missionary efforts. According to Knox, there were only ten men but fifteen single women, and "two or three" married women "who [might] now claim their right of suffrage." Thus, male missionaries who were "required to study in college and seminary," "examined by Presbytery," and "solemnly set apart to the work of the ministry" would be "outvoted" by women, many of whom had only "the education of the academy and the Sunday School, that is to say, the management of the mission would be taken from men and given to women." Arguing that the General Board's decision resulted "not from reason but from pressure" from women who controlled funds, Knox claimed that the General Board's action constituted "the most extreme position, the radicalism of Mill and Spencer" and deplored that it granted "what the agitators [could] not get in the [United States] and what Miss Willard [had] vainly [asked] from the Methodist Church" for Presbyterian women.[56]

Missionary wives such as Clara Hepburn also expressed their opposition to the changes, which granted only "young ladies" the right to vote on all issues. Sympathizing with her husband who loathed female control, Clara Hepburn wrote:

> We are sorry about the new departure, that is of woman voting—We did not want that privilege—at least there are only two or three in the Mission that would care about it, and they always have their way and carry their plans whether the Mission approve or not—Our men are considerably stirred up—they see danger ahead where there are such large proportions of . . . female members.[57]

She was surprised and indignant that missionary wives were treated "as children" who lacked "maturity" and "a right to be consulted." Accusing the General Board of being "only arbitrary but entirely un-Presbyterian," Clara Hepburn insisted that "ladies ought to be compelled to manage their own affairs."[58]

Facing such opposition from members of the East-Japan Mission and quite possibly from other missions in the world, the General Board adopted another revision to Rule 30 by the end of 1890. Under it women missionaries, regardless of their marital status, "who actively engaged in mission work" were "entitled to vote" only on "what [was] known as Woman's Work."[59] To appease male fear of women's power, women's official say in the local decision-making body was limited to women's matters—just like their missionary work. Even with this change, however, it was an achievement for women in the Presbyterian foreign missionary enterprise to have an official say in their own projects.[60]

Influencing Japanese Students

When the first American missionaries such as Julia Carrothers and Mary (Kidder) Miller arrived in Japan, the feudalistic gender relationship established during the early Tokugawa era was undergoing a transformation. During the Tokugawa period between 1600 and 1868, the shoguns, drawing upon neo-Confucian ideology, had imposed a feudalistic, hierarchical social order in which distinctions between superior and inferior were strictly observed. The essentialist neo-Confucian view of gender characterized men as *yang* (positive) and women as *yin* (negative). Men were associated with the heavens and the sun, which are high, full of light, and hence superior; while women were linked to the earth and the moon, which were seen as humble, dark, and hence inferior. Thus it was considered "natural" for women to be ruled by men. To maintain social order, the Tokugawa authorities also emphasized the neo-Confucian values of "loyalty" and "filial piety." Among the ruling samurai class, local lords were required to be loyal to the shogun, as were vassals to their lord, children to their parents, and wives to their husbands.[61]

The Tokugawa shoguns and local lords ruled their vassals through the "*ie*" (house) system, which also restricted women's roles in society. The *ie* system only allowed men to become heads of households and entitled them to serve their lords for a stipend. The system also invested the household head with exclusive authority over the members of his household. This status and authority were passed down to a male heir through undivided inheritance and male primogeniture. Within an *ie*, the relationship between a father and his eldest son was central, and the Confucian emphasis on "filial piety" had absolute importance. Under the *ie* system, marriage was a household matter, arranged between two household heads to further the interests of their *ie*. Thus there was no room for romance or love between those who were to become husband and wife. According to Ekken Kaibara's *Onna daigaku* (Greater Learning for Women), a popular neo-Confucian text on Japanese womanhood during the late Tokugawa period, marriage for a woman meant entering the *ie* and contributing to its continuity and prosperity. Her primary roles were to be an "obedient daughter-in-law" who served her husband's family and a "borrowed womb" who gave birth to an heir to the *ie*. A man could divorce his wife for one of seven legitimate reasons, among them "disobedience to the parents-in-law," and childlessness.[62]

However, a childless wife could remain in the household as long as she was "right-minded" and "well-behaved" and raised the children born to her husband's concubines without jealousy. Among the ruling samurai concubinage was an essential means by which a household secured an heir in the event that the wife was barren, while allowing her to retain her status in the household. Since women were in theory "borrowed wombs," mere tools for the reproduction of sons, the children of a wife or concubine belonged equally to the husband's *ie*.[63] But the rigid social system prohibited marriage across class lines and there was a clear distinction between a wife who came from the respectable samurai class and concubines who came from the lower classes and were officially categorized as "servants."

In fact, sexual morality was only to assure social order under the Tokugawa rule, creating a sexual double standard in terms of gender and class. The Tokugawa rulers, in promoting an austere lifestyle, discouraged their vassals from engaging in extramarital sex for pleasure, but permitted them to take concubines so they could procreate, thus allowing men to have multiple relationships. In contrast, female chastity was stressed in order to secure the patriarchal bloodline and social order. Among the samurai, a philandering husband could legitimize his behavior, while a wife in an extramarital relationship was committing an offense punishable as adultery.[64] The Tokugawa rulers also prohibited women of the ruling class from engaging in the "humble" trade of prostitution,[65] but they permitted the daughters and wives of the lower classes to be indentured into the prostitution business as long as they had the consent of their parents or husbands. The feudal authorities often commended the daughters of poor farmers for improving their families' financial condition by working as prostitutes; these "filial" daughters normally married after finishing their indenture.[66] The Tokugawa shoguns and local lords created pleasure quarters to confine, regulate, and tax the licensed prostitution businesses.

After the Meiji Restoration, the gender hierarchy of the Tokugawa era was preserved, but the new government's efforts to establish a modern state system brought assorted changes to the lives of Japanese women. Ironically the new government's temporary efforts to transform a hierarchical human relationship into one that was more egalitarian—this being part of its effort to modernize and civilize Japan—negatively affected the status of samurai wives. In 1871 Meiji leaders abolished the feudalistic class system, thereby making intermarriage across class lines possible.[67] The emerging modern legal system of Meiji Japan, *Shinritsu kōryō* (General Principles of New Laws) of 1870, granted a wife and a concubine the same relationship with the husband. Furthermore, an ordinance issued by the Meiji government in 1871 formally endorsed polygamy by permitting the registration of a concubine as a spouse.[68] As a result, the distinction between the statuses of legitimate wives and concubines disappeared and lower-class women benefited at the cost of legitimate upper-class wives.

However, the Meiji government dropped its legal endorsement of polygamy in 1883 because of strong opposition from male enlightenment thinkers. Like the issue of female education, they debated question of marriage and sexual morality in the light of "civilization." While they disagreed about a number of women's issues, they agreed that concubinage and misogyny were "barbarian" customs which ran counter to "fundamental human morals" or the natural law that created an equal number of men and women.[69] These debates led the Meiji government to drop its legal endorsement of polygamy, although the custom continued to be practiced to the chagrin of legitimate wives. Furthermore because of the persistent sexual double standards of society only a wife's extramarital relationships were punishable as adultery.[70]

Striving to provide a Christian education to Japanese women, American missionary teachers, who insisted on the absolute importance of chastity, made their Japanese students more conscious about their "uncivilized" marriage and gender relationships. As the class line between concubines and legitimate wives was blurred in the 1870s, the students of American missionary women included both groups of women. In the eyes of the missionary teachers, Japanese concubines and legitimate wives were both "heathens" in need of salvation, and their egalitarian evangelical efforts allowed the two groups to study side by side.[71] In their daily interactions with these "Japanese" women, American missionary teachers dismissed women's positions and roles in the Japanese *ie* system and were horrified by the "unspeakable" custom of concubinage.

Surrounded by heathen customs, American missionary women idealized the Christian home where a husband and wife were bonded by love even though a wife was treated as a dependent of her husband. While conducting a female class in Tokyo in the early 1870s, Julia Carrothers was astonished to realize that the Japanese language had no word for "home," which American Protestants so revered, but only for "house" or "place of habitation." She frowned upon the Japanese *ie,* in which marriage between a husband and wife was contracted by the parents or go-betweens, and entered upon without love or even previous knowledge of each other. In the view of American missionaries, Japanese women, who were so easily divorced and who endured their feudalistic roles and the sexual double standard, were mere "playthings" of men, at the mercy of male desire and licentiousness.[72]

In 1883 Mary (Kidder) Miller presented a paper—which, following American church conventions, was read by her husband—at the interdenominational conference of Protestant missionaries working in Japan. In it she argued that there were only a few "chaste-minded Japanese women, as Christian women count chastity." According to her:

> women's position in Japan is emphatically dependent upon the marriage relation. She must at all times obey her lord, her mother-in-law, and, as far as possible, all her husband's family, without reasoning or question. This is not sufficient. She must not only obey, but absolutely please her husband. This covers all that words can express. If she fails in this, she may at any time be divorced; if she suffer[s] beyond the power of endurance from the exactions of her husband or his family and leave[s] of her own accord, she cannot take her children or her clothing with her, and in the eyes of the Japanese world she is disgraced.[73]

American missionaries wanted to "purify" the Japanese "house" and transform it into a "Christian home." In the Christian home, the marriage bond, entered into by husband and wife of their own free will, was "sacred" and lifelong. In this environment, the "pious" and "pure" wife gained moral authority. Many women in nineteenth-century America had thus been empowered by the institution of marriage.[74] For this reason, they believed, Japanese women must be Christianized so that they would understand the importance of "purity" and the "sacredness" of marriage. Mary Miller continued:

> By a knowledge of the pure teachings of Christ, our women and girls would learn that they must not live only to minister to the selfishness and sensual gratification. . . . [T]hey would learn that the marriage ties are sacred and should be as enduring as life. We would be compelled to make new marriage laws, and we are not ready for this.[75]

To give her students first-hand experience of her ideal of a Christian marriage, Mary Miller invited all her students to her wedding.[76] By endeavoring to bring as many Japanese women as possible under her Christian influence, she believed she was offering them the means of "elevating and purifying the character of [Japanese] women, and thus purifying the homes." Mary Miller argued that until the homes were made "pure," one could not expect "any great radical change" in women's status in Japan.[77]

American missionary women also recognized the need to Christianize Japanese women in order to transform them into "noble consecrated women with strong will and self-control." Assisting Japanese women to know "Him as Savior" and "to have experience of His power working in them," American missionary women assumed that they could make their students "strong and assertive" in their pursuit of divine causes by the conviction of God's truth.[78] Their deep sense of religious "mission" propelled them to engage in an aggressive social activism that they believed to be altruistic. At the same time, claiming that they were conducting their selfless efforts for the sake of God, American churchwomen and their missionaries successfully expanded their sphere of activities outside their homes in predominantly Protestant nineteenth-century America. There, being a Christian gave women a deep sense of social responsibility and a good excuse to leave their homes for the sake of an activism consecrated to God.

However, in anti-Christian Japan, being a Christian was to be a blatant social rebel. Thus, Japanese women had to be "strong-willed" to convert to Christianity and to remain Christians. In the early 1870s, Julia Carrothers was well aware of the trouble her students would face when "the seed sown in the girls' hearts . . . sprung up and bore fruit." Those of Julia's students who sought baptism met with strong opposition from their fathers, families, and relatives. Julia refrained from advising "the girls to go [against] their fathers," but did not hide her joy in seeing them baptized since she was convinced that she was spreading "the truth" of God.[79] Thus, under the influence of Christian missionary teachers, some Japanese women learned how to be "strong-willed" in their actions and perhaps even rebel against the orders of their parents, husbands, and teachers, as well as the social constraints of Japanese womanhood.

Furthermore, American missionary teachers formed networks and groups among Japanese Christian women to help them remain Christians and to guide them to be useful for sacred causes. They organized their

Christian students and graduates to help them keep their faith in anti-Christian surroundings and to encourage them to promote evangelical and philanthropic causes. In this process, missionary teachers introduced their students to American churchwomen's skill at fund-raising, and at organizing and managing women's separate societies. As early as 1878, Kate Youngman, a Presbyterian missionary who initiated the Graham Seminary, formed Kōzensha (Friendship and Goodness Society) among her ten Japanese Christian students at the Seminary. Its members assisted in Youngman's evangelical work by teaching Sunday school, conducting classes for the poor, and holding evangelical meetings. To raise funds for their work, they asked for contributions at Sunday schools and church meetings, and held bazaars to sell their handmade products.[80] In 1881 when Mary (Kidder) Miller left Ferris Seminary and began evangelical work with her husband in Tokyo, she formed a similar network among former students of hers who had converted to Christianity.[81]

In the 1880s, a number of student organizations were formed at female mission schools. For example, senior students at Bancho School in Tokyo founded Eionsha (Glory and Affection Society) in 1883. Once a week, the students knitted under the supervision of missionary teachers, and received half of the profits resulting from the sale of their products while donating the other half to charity. And in 1888, ten students working for their own educational and philanthropic goals formed a group called King's Daughters at Ferris Seminary in Yokohama. The King's Daughters later developed into an all-female students' organization in the Tokyo-Yokohama area, made up of students from different mission schools.[82] American missionary teachers, while propagating the ideals of American middle-class Victorian womanhood and the concept of the Christian home among their students, also encouraged them to engage in social service outside their homes and to seek higher education, so they could pursue careers as evangelists, teachers, nurses, or social activists.

Using skills and knowledge acquired from their American missionary teachers, Protestant mission school graduates extended their networks to other Japanese women, both Christian and non-Christian, for ecclesiastical and secular purposes. *Jogaku zasshi* (Women's Education Magazine), one of Japan's first women's magazines started in 1885, carried notices about women's meetings of various kinds. In the national drive to be "westernized" and "civilized," female mission school students and graduates, who had acquired a taste for the lifestyle and thinking of their missionary teachers, organized not only to spread the Gospel, but also to teach knitting, Western table manners, Western hairdos that allowed frequent washing, and other Western customs that they viewed as more "civilized." By the time the first World WCTU organizer, Mary C. Leavitt, arrived in Japan in 1886, American missionaries had produced a pool of Japanese churchwomen who were capable of sympathizing with WCTU causes and carrying out its agenda by working among less "westernized" Japanese women. Among them were Toyojyu Sasaki, who attended Mary (Kidder) Miller's class, Kajiko Yajima and Saku Asai, both of whom worked as teachers at Presbyterian female mission schools in Tokyo, and Chiseko Ushioda, who studied at Presbyterian and Methodist Episcopal schools and became a "Bible woman," a native woman hired for direct evangelical work by M.E. missionaries.

2

Sprouting a Feminist Consciousness
Japanese Women's WCTU Activism in Tokyo, 1886–1894

The Founding Mothers: The WCTU and the World WCTU

The organization of the WCTU in 1874 grew out of the bitter experiences of American churchwomen in their male-dominated denominational missionary enterprises. Its members were drawn from the same pool of churchwomen who participated in other women's causes, and depended on the leadership of "distinguished" women who were "well known in church circles." To avoid being controlled by male clergy who dwelled on theological differences and were split along denominational lines, the WCTU was a "nonsectarian" or interdenominational women's organization. Anne Wittenmyer, a founder of the Woman's Home Missionary Society of the Methodist Episcopal Church (WHMS), and Frances E. Willard, an influential member of the same church, were elected as its first two presidents. The WCTU was thus under strong Methodist influence, but it drew support from women from a number of denominational churches and managed to become a churchwomen's organization governed solely by women. In the WCTU, men could address meetings and were encouraged to make financial contributions as "honorary members," but they could not vote, hold office, or participate in official debates.[1]

Although Protestant missionary societies had been working in secular fields, their official goal, namely, the Christian "salvation" of "heathen women," could not be accomplished without ordained men. Thus, Protestant missionary women could only play secondary roles and had to be under the supervision and control of clergymen. The WCTU, on the other hand, emphasized secular causes, especially temperance. By emphasizing temperance, a respectable, patriotic, and Protestant cause since colonialism in America, the WCTU successfully sidestepped involvement by clergymen and legitimized social activism by women "For God and Home and the Native Land." In addition, by adopting the cause of temperance, the WCTU was able to use the language of science at a time when the revivalist fever was waning in a rapidly secularizing, industrializing, and increasingly multicultural America.

Liberated from the direct control of clergymen, the WCTU was able to enlist not only women but also men and boys in its effect to influence male behavior. Frances Willard, who became self-reliant and economically independent of men like single missionary women working in the field, envisioned men and women working as equals in the Christian social reform movement. To tackle issues that middle-class churchwomen saw as problems in American society, under Willard's leadership the WCTU was willing to work to reform women's conventional roles and sphere as well as the larger society in America. Unlike women's foreign and home missionary movements in which churchwomen's "selfless" contributions supported numerous projects located outside their communities on the frontier, in immigrant slums, and in foreign lands to save "heathen women," the WCTU left a good percentage of local members' dues in each local union so that they could reform their own communities and neighborhoods. The WCTU invested its resources in political campaigns to advance women's status and to realize a more woman-friendly environment. The WCTU was innovative and even took a revolutionary direction under the skillful leadership of Frances Willard.[2]

Despite WCTU activists' differences with the Protestant women's missionary movement, they retained the latter's fundamental strategy of stretching but not breaking the women's sphere by emphasizing women's special ability and nature. It was Willard's "manipulation" of rhetoric that transformed the radical demand for woman suffrage, which potentially challenged the Victorian ideology of womanhood and women's sphere, into a "safe" and "respectable" cause for women who adhered to that ideology. By coining the phrase "Home Protection Ballot," Willard justified women's vote as necessary to protect the home and the women and children within it. Willard's demand for woman suffrage won the official endorsement of the WCTU in 1881 and gradually drew the support of the rank and file, transforming the woman suffrage movement from a small-scale phenomenon into a mass movement. Moreover, by advocating "White Life" for men and women, Willard promoted a puritanical sexual relationship in which a morally superior wife could gain authority and the ability not only to avoid unwanted pregnancies but also to engage in various forms of social activism. Under her "Do Everything" policy that emphasized temperance, Willard attempted to stretch women's sphere in every direction without confronting the Victorian ideology of women's special ability and nature.[3]

Willard's genius in organization and management also quadrupled the WCTU's membership and increased its national budget tenfold during the 1880s, the first decade of her presidency. Arguing that to "agitate, educate, and organize" were "the deathless watchwords of success," Willard traveled extensively to speak for women's causes and to attract members by cutting across sectional, ethnic, and racial lines.[4] In addition, Willard facilitated the flow of income from local unions by basing a local union's representation at the national convention upon its paid membership. In return, she secured the autonomy of each local union. According to Willard, "We 'Liberals' interpreted the constitution of our society on the laissez-faire principle. . . . If they paid their small dues and signed the total abstinence pledge, we asked no more, believing that the less we asked the more we should get." This organizational scheme not only increased the national budget but also facilitated the formation of separate WCTU unions among blacks, Indians, immigrants, and foreigners, each enjoying autonomy under the WCTU's umbrella.[5]

Growing out of denominational home and foreign women's missionary movements, the WCTU inherited its assimilationist and universalist tradition and envisioned the world as the field for its activism. As early as the late 1870s, the WCTU, under Wittenmyer's presidency, began Anglo-American and trans-Atlantic cooperation.[6] When Willard took office, she turned to the West and to the Pacific as well and accelerated this expansive trend by forming the World WCTU in 1883. On her organizing tour to the American Pacific Coast, Willard visited San Francisco's Chinatown escorted by Rev. Otis Gibson, the Superintendent of the Chinese Mission of the Methodist Episcopal Church. Witnessing opium smoking and prostitution among Asian immigrants, Willard reported:

> We there saw the opium den in all its loathsome completeness, and next door stood the house of shame. Respectable Chinese women were not allowed to accompany their husbands to California, but here were Chinese girls, one in each of many small cabins with sliding doors and windows on the street, constituting the most flagrantly flaunted temptation that we have ever witnessed.

Willard interpreted the conditions in Chinatown not as "their" problem but as "our" problem, and was inspired to extend the WCTU's influence across the Pacific to the world. Willard continued:

> In presence of these two object lessons, the result of occidental avarice and oriental degradation, there was borne in upon my spirit a distinct illumination resulting in this solemn vow: But for the intrusion of the sea the shores of China and the Far East would be part and parcel of our own. We are one world of tempted humanity; the mission of the White Ribbon women is to organize the motherhood of the world for the peace and purity, the protection and exaltation of its homes. . . . We must be no longer hedged about by the artificial boundaries of states and nations; we must utter as women what good and great men long ago declared as their watchword: The whole world is my parish and to do good my religion.[7]

In her presidential address at the 1883 annual convention in Detroit, Willard proposed the organization of the World WCTU to "belt the globe and join the East and West." To realize this vision, Mary C. Leavitt of Boston, a divorcee, former schoolteacher, and a national WCTU organizer, was appointed as the World WCTU's first "round-the-world missionary." By the end of 1883, Leavitt headed west for the Pacific Coast, and in 1884 began her westward voyage from San Francisco.[8] Raising funds for her trip at each destination, Leavitt continued her organizing tour for eight years, visiting such places as the Sandwich Islands, Australia, New Zealand, Japan, China, Thailand, Burma (Myanmar), Singapore, India, Ceylon (Sri Lanka), Africa, and Europe before returning to New York in 1891.[9]

To follow in the footsteps of Mary C. Leavitt, the World WCTU sent two classes of workers across the oceans—"one on tours of inspection and inspiration," and "the other to specified countries to remain as long as seemed mutually desirable."[10] At least seven World WCTU women, who fell into the first category, traveled to Japan for short periods of time between 1886 and 1894, and another five, who constituted the second group, lived in the country for a few years. Among those in the first group were Mary C. Leavitt (who visited Japan in 1886), Pandita Ramabai and Dr. Emma B. Ryder (1888), Jessie A. Ackerman (1890 and 1901), Mary A. West (1892, died in Japan), and Elizabeth W. Andrew and Kate C. Bushnell (1894). Leavitt, Ackerman, West, Andrew, and Bushnell were the World WCTU's "round-the-world" missionaries.[11] Pandita Ramabai was an Indian educator who received the strong support of Frances Willard and

American churchwomen in her project of building a school for high-caste Indian widows, and Dr. Ryder was the World WCTU's "organizer and lecturer for India" appointed to assist in Ramabai's project.[12] On their way to India, Ramabai and Ryder also spent about ten days in Japan to study female education.

Mary C. Leavitt and the Founding of the Tokyo WCTU

While pioneering WCTU activism abroad, Mary C. Leavitt sought the support of preestablished English-speaking communities in the world. Anglo-American foreign missionaries had been active abroad since the early nineteenth century, and their nations had established colonial governments or diplomatic relationships with a number of countries around the world. In Japan, female and male Anglo-American Protestant missionaries and their government representatives assisted Leavitt in her organizational tours. Upon landing in Yokohama on June 1, 1886, Mary Leavitt visited a post office, a bank, the American Consulate, and missionaries' residences for errands, before heading to the Bible Society Room managed by an interdenominational group of American male missionaries. Once there, she introduced herself to a circle of American missionaries working in the city, including Dr. and Mrs. Hepburn. In Yokohama, Leavitt stayed with single women missionaries at WUMS's Doremus Seminary and in Tokyo, at Presbyterian Graham Seminary.[13] Leavitt also traveled to Kyoto, Osaka, Kobe, Wakayama, Okayama, and Nagasaki, where American missionaries had established stations or satellite stations, and gave lectures on the cause of temperance. American Protestant missionaries in these cities assisted Leavitt by providing accommodations, obtaining Japanese government permission to travel beyond the ports and cities open to foreigners, and gathering foreign and native audiences for her lectures. Through her lecture tours, Leavitt reported that she was able to find "a band of fine [Japanese] Christian women trained by missionary ladies to take up any work which needs to be done."[14] Leavitt's organizational efforts led to the establishment of several unions among Anglo-American missionaries and Japanese men and women. One of them was the Tokyo WCTU.[15]

While assisting Leavitt in her lecture tours on temperance in Japan, American missionary women in Tokyo, many of whom were still constrained by Paul's injunction that women be silent in church, hesitated to help her organize Japanese churchwomen in the city. Leavitt lectured to

Western and native, male and female, and Christian and non-Christian audiences, but in so doing transgressed the behavior codes of the American missionary circle in the city, which discouraged women from preaching among gender-mixed audiences. Although I am speculating, it is possible that Leavitt's unconventional attitude made it difficult for Presbyterian missionary women such as Maria True, whose Japanese protégés later came to play key roles in Japanese WCTU activism, to openly support Leavitt's endeavor. Observing American missionary circles in the Tokyo-Yokohama area, Leavitt commended missionary women for providing Japanese women a "good education," but commented that their efforts to preach "ought to have more encouragement . . . from their missionary brethren than they [got]."[16]

Along with Leavitt's unconventional practice of lecturing to gender-mixed audiences, the cultural gap between Leavitt and Japanese women further distanced her from the Japanese employees and students of American missionary women. Leavitt delivered a speech to Japanese women in Tokyo on July 17, 1886, which was interpreted by a Graham Seminary graduate on account of her firm insistence on using a woman as an interpreter.[17] According to Kajiko Yajima, however, the poor interpretation made Leavitt's talk even more difficult to understand than it would otherwise have been.[18] From Leavitt's viewpoint, speaking through unprepared interpreters in general was stressful. She wrote that "with the best interpreters it [was] much more difficult and tiresome speaking than in the home manner, but with a poor interpreter it [was] more wearing than anything else I [had] ever done."[19] Early World WCTU missionaries were not familiar with Japanese language and customs, and elite Japanese women had much less opportunity to study English and Western learning in Japan and abroad than their male counterparts. Consequently, for the rest of her tour through Japan, Leavitt was usually accompanied by Japanese male interpreters, who possessed a better command of English and more freedom and resources to travel with Leavitt than Japanese churchwomen.

Many of these progressive Japanese men were under the strong influence of Christianity. Japanese Christians in the early Meiji era came largely from the samurai class, having been intellectuals and bureaucrats in Tokugawa Japan. Having lost their hereditary ruling-class privileges and the stipends given to each patrimonial household after the Meiji Restoration, these déclassé samurais enthusiastically acquired Western knowledge to improve their own job opportunities as well as to aid their fledgling country. In their pursuit of Western education, some crossed the ocean while others went to the cities and open ports of Japan where American Protestant missionaries and other hired foreigners, some of whom were pious Christians, conducted classes. Especially susceptible to the Christian faith were the samurais of the pro-Tokugawa clans, the losing side in the 1868 Restoration, for whom knowledge of Western institutions was crucial if they were to improve their fortunes in Meiji Japan. After the Meiji government lifted its ban on Christianity in 1873, Protestant missionaries began leading evangelical tours into the interior. There they successfully converted the classes of *gōno* (influential farmers) and *gōshō* (influential merchants), who became another important group of Christians in early Meiji Japan. Japanese churchwomen who responded to Leavitt's call constituted one segment of the Japanese Christian population. They had adopted not only the Christian religion but also Western values and institutions and had established themselves as members of the emerging urban middle class as Japan proceeded on its path of economic development in the expanding world capitalist system.[20]

The reluctance of American missionary women to fall behind Leavitt distanced her from their Japanese protégés at female mission schools. Thus, the initiative to realize her vision had to come from Japanese churchpeople who were closely associated with a Japanese-run women's school, Meiji Jogakkō (Meiji Women's School), in Tokyo. The school was founded in 1885 by Rev. Kumaji Kimura, a minister ordained in the Reformed tradition during his twelve-year stay in the United States. Since the foreign missionary enterprise of the Reformed Church refused to support another female school in the vicinity of Ferris Seminary, Meiji Jogakkō was built with funds raised by Japanese Christians to provide Japanese women a Christian education. Toko Kimura, Rev. Kimura's wife, took charge of the daily management of Meiji Jogakkō. She enthusiastically responded to Leavitt's call. Her effort was faithfully backed by Yoshiharu Iwamoto, who had been supporting Rev. and Mrs. Kimura in building and managing Meiji Jogakkō.[21]

Yoshiharu Iwamoto, the son of a samurai family, came under Christian influence while studying at schools run by Japanese who supported female education. In the late 1870s, Iwamoto attended Dōjinsha, a school established by enlightenment thinker Masanao Nakamura. Advocating the need for women's education, Nakamura had opened his school to women in 1874 where such books as John S. Mill's *The Subjugation of Women* were used as textbooks.[22] After studying at Dōjinsha in the early 1880s, Iwamoto studied at Gakunōsha, an agricultural school founded by Umeko Tsuda's father, Sen Tsuda, who also supported American Methodist missionary women's efforts to promote women's education in Japan. Influenced by these Japanese teachers, Yoshiharu Iwamoto endeavored to promote women's education and women's causes in Japan. While assisting Rev. and Mrs. Kimura in founding Meiji Jogakkō, he published *Jogaku zasshi* (Women's Education Magazine), one of the few magazines that featured the writings of Japanese women activists, both churchwomen and female popular-rights activists, in the 1880s.[23]

The meeting on July 17, 1886, at which Leavitt addressed Japanese women in Tokyo, was sponsored by *Jogaku zasshi*. Only open to women, it was attended by more than six hundred women. In her talk Leavitt discussed the evils of drinking and smoking and the need to reform Japanese dress, housing, and marriage practices. At the end of the event, it was decided to hold a future meeting to organize a women's union in response to Leavitt's call.[24] In late July, after Leavitt's departure, the first follow-up meeting was held at Meiji Jogakkō and was attended by two men, Yoshiharu Iwamoto and Sen Tsuda, and fourteen Japanese churchwomen. Toko Kimura took the leading role by drafting the bylaws and deciding on the new organization's membership requirements. However, she contracted cholera and died suddenly in August 1886. This in turn led to a setback to the organization of a WCTU union in Tokyo.[25]

Yoshiharu Iwamoto endeavored to give concrete shape to Leavitt's call and continue the late Mrs. Kimura's efforts. In *Jogaku zasshi*, he published Japanese translations of Leavitt's lectures and writings and excerpts of the World WCTU's bylaws, and advocated the need for a viable women's organization to "correct" Japanese domestic and sexual customs in his editorials. He urged Japanese churchwomen, especially those who were working at women's schools, to organize in order to promote women's education; to find ways of providing educated women with careers; to reform marriage and divorce laws for the benefit of women; and to eliminate geishas and prostitutes. Iwamoto went further by discussing women's rights, and called on Japanese women to establish a law that would allow women to inherit property.[26]

Simultaneously, supplementing Iwamoto's efforts, Japanese ministers who had been working for the temperance cause by founding a male-led reform society, *kyōfūkai* (reform society) and its subsociety *kinshukai* (temperance society) prior to Leavitt's visit, came into play to fully realize Leavitt's vision.[27] In November 1886 another meeting was convened under the auspices of two Japanese ministers' wives to complete the organization of a woman's union in Tokyo. Rev. Motoichirō Ōgimi, president of the *kyōfūkai* and a close friend of Rev. Kimura, presided over the meeting, which was attended by forty-three women. Yoshiharu Iwamoto served as the secretary.[28] At the meeting, twenty-two Japanese churchwomen agreed to be founders of the women's union in Tokyo and seven of them formed a committee to work for the organization.[29]

As a result, the Tokyo WCTU came into being on December 6, 1886. Its Japanese name was Tokyo Fujin Kyōfūkai, which, literally translated into English, means Tokyo Women's Custom Correcting Society or, more loosely, Tokyo Women's Reform Society. In the presence of about one hundred churchwomen of various denominations in Tokyo, the creation of the Japanese women's union in Tokyo was publicly proclaimed, an election of officers was conducted, and finally two Japanese ministers spoke about the "responsibilities of Christian women." Kajiko Yajima, who had been working under Maria True as acting principal of the Bancho School, became the first president, and Toyojyu Sasaki, former student of Mary (Kidder) Miller and wife of a Christian doctor, became the secretary. Fifty-one Japanese churchwomen became members. The bylaws of the new organization declared that its goals were "to correct social customs, to purify morality, to prohibit drinking and smoking, and to promote women's dignity."[30]

Before we continue, a few points need to be clarified about the name of this local union of Japanese women in Tokyo and the future Japanese women's national union, both of which were affiliated with the World WCTU. First, the fact that the Japanese women's union was named Fujin Kyōfūkai (Women's Reform Society) indicates that male Christians assisting in its inception expected it to function as a female auxiliary of the male-led kyōfūkai (reform society). They expected its churchwomen members to assist male-led reform efforts, just as American missionary women were assisting American clergymen's evangelization efforts. Second, the fact that it became Fujin Kyōfūkai but not Fujin Kinshukai (Women's Temperance Society) shows that Japanese churchwomen intended to engage in social reform in a broad range of areas.

The World WCTU missionaries who came to Japan after the foundation of the new Tokyo organization, soon learned that the Japanese "had changed the name of the W.C.T.U."[31] In referring to the Japanese women's society, these World WCTU missionaries used names derived from those they were familiar with, for example, "W.C.T.U. of Tokyo," "the Tokyo

Woman's Society," or "Japan union." Although this book will call the Tokyo Fujin Kyōfūkai the Tokyo WCTU and the future Nihon Fujin Kyōfūkai will be referred to as the Japan WCTU, I wish to emphasize the difference in the meanings of the English and Japanese names of the Japanese women's society. Japanese churchwomen made their society an independent women's organization, and deliberately dropped the words "Temperance" and "Christian" from their organizational name.[32]

Breaking the Silence of the Tokyo WCTU

For a year after its inception, the Tokyo WCTU spent most of its time conducting public meetings. Since the Japanese ministers and churchwomen engaged in Tokyo WCTU activism were under the strong influence of American missionaries who observed Paul's teachings, only male speakers addressed the Tokyo WCTU's first three public meetings—although the meetings were presided over by the Tokyo WCTU president Kajiko Yajima.[33] The speakers were Japanese ministers of Protestant churches and male temperance activists in Tokyo who looked up to Western civilization and the Anglo-American missionary practice of women engaging in social activism under the supervision of clergymen. These Japanese male Christian elites had been exposed to Western enlightenment theories and discussed women's "rights" and "equality," but their interest in improving women's status was secondary to their concern that Japan be recognized as a "civilized" nation. Taking the gender relationships among Anglo-American missionaries as their model, in their lectures the Japanese Christian men emphasized women's special ability, roles, and sphere in encouraging Japanese women to be socially active. For example, a Japanese minister, Takayoshi Matsuyama, argued that women's activism should not be based on the concepts of "right" or "reason" but on "love," and that women should work for charity and benevolence. Another minister, Kajinosuke Ibuka, supported women's activism to improve their status based on the Christian teachings of "monogamy," "sacred marriage," and "equality." In his understanding, however, although men and women were "equal" they were naturally "different," and so were the roles they played in society.[34] These men wanted to promote social activism among Japanese women but only under the guidance of men.

Nonetheless, the fact that Mary Leavitt had traveled all the way from the United States by herself and had spoken to crowds of both men and women offered Japanese churchwomen a somewhat different lesson. Although interaction between Leavitt and Japanese churchwomen was limited and they had not fully comprehended her July 17 speech, which was open only to women, she had left a written message to further articulate her position. The message translated in Japanese was entitled "*Nihon no shimai ni tsugu*" (Talking to [my] Japanese Sisters) and appeared in Iwamoto's magazine in the late fall of 1886. In the message, Leavitt argued that women were only responsible to God, and that Providence does not require a woman to ask for male approval to use her God-given talent. She legitimized women receiving a higher education, pursuing a career, and speaking in public. According to Leavitt, if one interpreted the Bible correctly one would see that it did not prohibit women from speaking in public. Leavitt insisted that under no circumstances should a woman who spoke in public to praise God, to protect the home, and to advance humanity be accused of stepping out of her place, given that a woman opera singer was allowed to entertain the public while "exposing her shoulders and arms."[35]

However, many of the Japanese churchwomen who led the new organization were under the strong grip of American missionaries, who still hesitated to speak in public, especially to gender-mixed audiences. Their attitudes influenced even female popular-rights activists who had spoken in public in the early 1880s. The Popular-Rights Movement, another movement initiated by déclassé samurais in western and southern Japan, challenged the Meiji oligarchy by using Western liberal political theories and calling for the establishment of a national assembly. The first phase of the movement in the late 1870s and early 1880s successfully persuaded the Meiji government to publicly announce its intention in 1881 of drafting a constitution and establishing a national assembly by 1890.[36] However, the movement was at a low ebb in the mid-1880s due to its radicalization, as numerous peasant uprisings were followed by government suppression and divisions among the leaders of the movement who came from the former samurai class.

During this era, Toshiko Kishida, once an eloquent public speaker, moved to Tokyo following her love marriage to Nobuyuki Nakajima, a fellow activist who had earlier served as governor of Kanagawa and who had assisted Mary Kidder in obtaining a plot of land for her school. Toshiko was baptized in 1885 following her husband, and taught Chinese classics at Presbyterian Graham Seminary in Tokyo and at Ferris Seminary in Yokohama in the late 1880s. After joining the churchwomen's circle in the

Tokyo-Yokohama area, however, Toshiko Kishida stopped appearing in public, although she contributed articles to Iwamoto's *Jogaku zasshi*.[37]

Instead, Toyojyu Sasaki, secretary of the Tokyo WCTU, followed Leavitt's path by breaking women's silence through both the written and the spoken word. Sasaki had intended to express her opinion at the founding meeting of the Tokyo WCTU on December 6, 1886, but had decided against it because of the tight schedule, the day being packed with speeches by eminent male ministers and the election of officers. So she contributed an essay to *Jogaku zasshi* in early 1887, in which she argued that women should break away from what had been considered female virtues but were in fact "evil," "obsequious," and "barbarian" customs. These customs included women's silence, samurai-class women giving up their lives to save their chastity, lower-class women sacrificing their chastity to improve the financial condition of their family, and married women shaving their eyebrows and dyeing their teeth black.[38] In March, Sasaki contributed another article which argued specifically that women needed to express their opinions. While recognizing the importance of co-operating with men, Sasaki insisted in this article that the Tokyo WCTU should not be a men's but a women's organization and that "men would never know women's pain and troubles unless women spoke out."[39]

Sasaki's call received the support of several American missionary women, including Maria True, who had been struggling with the male-dominant structure of the Presbyterian foreign missionary enterprise. In May 1887, just before the Tokyo WCTU held its third public meeting with only male speakers, Sasaki, True, and two other women finally broke the silence of Tokyo WCTU women by delivering their speeches at a lecture meeting sponsored by Iwamoto's magazine.[40] However, the audience at the meeting was limited to women because Iwamoto was reluctant to violate the convention observed by Western women.[41] While Sasaki and her fellow Tokyo WCTU members who spoke at the meeting were indignant about the arrangement, Maria True probably was not. True was willing to assist Japanese women in their activist agenda but also wanted to avoid any "un-necessary" conflict with men in order to secure their cooperation in the expansion of the Bancho School. Addressing the exclusively female audience, True encouraged them to set "noble goals" and to acquire power but also advised them to use a "*hashigo*" (ladder) when they faced hindrances in their way.[42] Striving to realize her goals in the male-dominant Presbyterian foreign missionary enterprise, True believed it was prudent not to confront the male authorities but to circumvent them by using the "ladder" of her own efforts, networks, and patience.

For Sasaki, whether Tokyo WCTU members could address only women or both men and women became an important issue symbolizing women's freedom and the independence of the Tokyo WCTU from male control. When the Tokyo WCTU held its fourth public meeting at the end of 1887, Sasaki and two other Tokyo WCTU members went further by addressing the gender-mixed public, along with two male speakers.[43] In the spring of 1888, when the Tokyo WCTU started publishing its own official journal, Toyojyu Sasaki became its joint editor along with Saku Asai, who had previously worked as a teacher of Chinese classics under Chik Sakurai and Maria True but was currently running her own female school.[44] In her articles in the new Tokyo WCTU's magazine, Sasaki elaborated on her opinion about women's public speech and writing. Explaining why the Tokyo WCTU had to have its own official magazine that published women's "thinking," Sasaki argued that "all the women in the East" were enclosed within the "fence" of men's thought. According to her, even if women had opinions on matters outside the "fence," they were required to keep their thoughts to themselves because the public did not allow them to do otherwise. Because they were silent, men became esteemed as the "heaven" and the "lord" while women were compared to lowly "earth" and "slaves." The Tokyo WCTU's magazine enabled women to "proceed to the level of civilization" by "freely voicing their thoughts," "by expressing their pent-up complaints," and by releasing themselves from the shackles imposed by society.[45] For Sasaki, "civilization" would free Japanese women from its social restraints.

To further encourage Japanese churchwomen to speak out despite their missionary teachers' reluctance, Sasaki translated a WCTU article, which appeared in *Union Signal,* the WCTU's official publication. In an article entitled "Let Your Women Keep Silence in the Churches" that also became a WCTU leaflet, an American author had reproduced her husband's speech protesting the views of a young minister who required women to be silent at church. The husband spoke:

Why . . . does anyone object to having women speak or pray? Why invite them to a meeting of soul with soul, and then forbid them to say anything? . . . I think it started with a distorted conception of Paul's direction, "Let your women keep silence in the churches." And I think your time will be spent to good advantage if you would give a little of it to the examination of the matter from an intelligent and common sense standpoint. Mr. Preacher, I am not speaking against you personally, but against the schools that made you.

Arguing that Paul's injunction was directed to the Corinthian Christians quarreling over the question of buying meat from heathen dealers and that it was only valid in that particular situation at that particular time, the husband persuaded the minister that it was preposterous to apply Paul's words literally to the present and that women were entitled to speak in church and to the public.[46] Sasaki published her translation with a new title, *Fujin genron no jiyū* (Women's Freedom of Speech) in August 1888. She commented in the preface that it was the advancement of knowledge that had allowed "the mistaken interpretation" of biblical teachings to be discovered, thus granting women "freedom of speech."[47] Despite the Japanese clergy's opposition and the American Protestant missionary teachers' reluctance, Sasaki, by following the WCTU, won the Tokyo WCTU's independence to pursue women's causes selected by women.

Toyojyu Sasaki, Kajiko Yajima, and Middle-Class Tokyo WCTU Women's Causes

Mary Leavitt's message had a strong impact on Sasaki's activism, but Leavitt and other World WCTU travelers who visited Japan between 1886 and 1894 were not in close touch with Japanese churchwomen. This fact provided an opportunity for the newly established Tokyo WCTU to generate a Japanese women's movement independent of the World WCTU. During this period, Kajiko Yajima (1833–1925), the president, and Toyojyu Sasaki (1853–1901), the secretary, despite the differences between them in terms of generation, personality, background, and political propensity, made an effort to work together to improve the status of women in Meiji Japan and played crucial roles in the development of the Tokyo WCTU women's movement. Outspoken and provocative, Toyojyu Sasaki was more willing to confront the social constraints imposed on women than any other member of the Tokyo WCTU.[48] She played a crucial role in generating a women's movement that embraced the vocabulary not only of American middle-class Protestant values but also that of Western liberal political theory. Patient and pragmatic, Kajiko Yajima allowed Tokyo WCTU members with different opinions and personalities to engage in a variety of women's causes under her presidency. As the acting principal of one of the most prosperous female mission schools in Tokyo, Yajima exercised considerable influence over its Japanese teachers and students. At the same time, she also had an extraordinary family network with connections to a band of early Christian converts in Kumamoto, which produced some notable Christian ministers and activists in Meiji Japan.[49]

Both women moved to Tokyo and came under the influence of American missionary women in the 1870s, but American middle-class Protestant values and standards affected them differently. Toyojyu Sasaki was a student of Mary Kidder's only briefly around the time of Kidder's romance and love marriage to Rev. Rothesay Miller. Then Sasaki attended Dōjinsha, which opened its doors to women in 1874. There she met and fell in love with Motoe Sasaki, a married doctor from her hometown who was teaching English at the school. Motoe had converted to Christianity in 1872 when it was still prohibited in Japan, and Toyojyu did the same in 1874. For this couple, the ideology of a Christian home justified dissolving Motoe's marriage arranged by his parents and their pursuit of love. Toyojyu gave birth to a daughter out of wedlock in 1878, and officially married Motoe after he had divorced his wife, who was believed to have been critical of his conversion to Christianity. Toyojyu bore Motoe four more children after her marriage to him and never worked for a salary. But she continued to be socially active with the support of her understanding husband. Studying at Dōjinsha, Toyojyu Sasaki was also exposed to Anglo-American liberal political ideas. Coming from a pro-Tokugawa samurai family, the losing side of the Restoration, she was critical of political and social developments under the Meiji oligarchs. She sought alliances with male and female popular rights-activists so that the Tokyo WCTU could carry out its activist agenda on its own terms.[50]

In contrast, Kajiko Yajima, who had divorced a drunkard, came under the strong influence of American missionary women and their institutions. Since teaching was one of the few jobs available to women at the time, after her divorce in Tokyo, Yajima became a teacher for the newly established public school system. But she also gave birth to a daughter out of wedlock. Unlike Toyojyu Sasaki, Yajima never married the child's father nor did she reveal the fact of the birth. Instead she raised the child as her adopted daughter with her own salary.[51] Yajima transferred to the Presbyterian female mission school because it offered her twice the salary as her previous job. At the school she came under Maria True's influence, converted to Christianity, and was appointed acting principal in 1880. Coming from an influential farmer's family connected to an ideologist for the Restoration, Kajiko Yajima was loyal to the Imperial couple. This made her less critical of political developments after the Restoration than Sasaki. At the same time, because of her career and economic status, it was difficult for her to devote herself entirely to the activities of the Tokyo WCTU and to go beyond the conventional churchwomen's roles adhered to by Anglo-American missionary women. But her sisters and nieces took the lead in the Japanese WCTU women's movement on the issue of doing away with sexual double standards.[52]

While Sasaki wanted to address broader issues, including the expansion of women's rights, Yajima emphasized the single cause of temperance due to her brief marriage to a drunkard. The two women agreed to work together for the "correction" of feudalistic customs that subjugated Japan to the West and women to men.[53] However, Tokyo WCTU activism under Sasaki and Yajima's combined leadership for Japan and "Japanese" women was class-specific. It reflected the interests of women from the emerging urban middle class and was directed at both the upper and lower classes. After discussing a broad range of issues requiring social reform at the Tokyo WCTU's gathering in April 1887, the members agreed with Sasaki that combating and eliminating geishas, prostitutes, and concubines was the most pressing task for the new organization.[54] In May 1887, when Sasaki first spoke at the previously mentioned public meeting sponsored by Iwamoto's company, she expressed her indignation at the "Occidental" perception of "Japanese women," which failed to distinguish between Japanese prostitutes and middle-class women like herself. Sasaki argued that in Japan, where prostitution was publicly licensed, the "elimination" of geishas, concubines, and prostitutes was a more urgent task than temperance. The new women's organization should therefore endeavor to abolish brothels, geishas, prostitutes, and concubines, and their overseas migration.[55]

As middle-class Japanese women the members of Tokyo WCTU felt threatened by women from the pleasure quarters, because the end of the feudalistic caste system had obscured the class line between legitimate wives and concubines. Although the government had ceased to endorse polygamy, marriage in Japan was still a means of uniting two households. Thus the parents' opinions outweighed those of the marrying son or daughter, and only a husband, if desired, could explore love and sexual pleasure outside the conjugal relationship. A prostitute or geisha could become a concubine by winning a man's favor, and a concubine could bear children for his household. If his legitimate wife failed to have a son and if the concubine had a baby boy, the concubine's son would succeed to the status of household head and be recognized by the father.[56]

A second source of grievance for middle-class churchwomen was the fact that Anglo-American missionary teacher at the female mission schools which they attended in the 1870s alongside women from the pleasure quarters—who became wives and concubines of the new Meiji leaders—spoke of unchaste "Japanese" women and the "unspeakable" "Japanese" conjugal relationship in the same breath, making no distinction between the two. Furthermore, when these middle-class churchwomen left their homes to be socially active, they encountered female professional entertainers who had been working in the male sphere for centuries. During the Tokugawa era, women of the ruling samurai class had been confined to their domestic quarters while women of the lower castes labored in the pleasure quarters to serve and entertain men, facilitating male social exchanges and providing romance. When Meiji oligarchs held extravagant balls to impress Western diplomats with Japan's "civilization" as part of their effort to facilitate the revision of the unequal treaties in the late 1880s, some of them—such as future prime minister Hirobumi Ito—brought their able and charming wives from the pleasure quarters to the balls. These women came to play important roles in Japanese high society.[57] Tokyo WCTU members as well as the Japanese public were critical of this phenomenon and resented the rise to power of female entertainers in the public sphere, especially as foreign diplomats and VIPs thought they represented "Japanese" women.

Members of the Tokyo WCTU sympathized with male activists working for the abolition of licensed prostitution and for the curtailment of prostitution overseas to uphold Japan's national reputation. In the early 1870s, the so-called Maria Luz incident, in which the Japanese government attempted to free Chinese indentured servants on a Peruvian ship, the *Maria Luz*, drew the public attention to Japan's trafficking in women.[58] Furthermore, as Japan's engagement with capitalism grew, Japanese laborers (including prostitutes) migrated overseas to earn foreign exchange. International networks of Western missionaries, journalists, and reformers began to problematize the increasing visibility of Japanese prostitutes overseas and Japan's system of licensed prostitution.[59] Despite the Meiji government's efforts to modernize its system to resemble, for instance, the French and British systems,[60] when Josephine Butler and her sympathizers held their second international conference in Geneva in 1880 to oppose the state regulation of prostitution,[61] they urged Japan to abolish the government licensing and taxation of prostitution businesses and prostitutes, and its requirement of mandatory physical inspections of prostitutes. In the 1880s, the abolition of the system of licensed prostitution advocated by progressive politicians became a political issue. Jirō Yuasa, a Christian politician and the husband of Yajima's niece, Hatsuko Yuasa, passed an abolition bill in the Gunma prefectural assembly in 1882, but resistance from the prostitution business and the Meiji government suspended its enforcement.[62]

Jirō and Hatsuko Yuasa had moved to Tokyo in 1885. Hatsuko Yuasa was present at the inception of the Tokyo WCTU in 1886 and collaborated with Toyojyu Sasaki in breaking the silence of Tokyo WCTU women at the public meeting sponsored by *Jogaku zasshi* in May 1887. In the late 1880s and early 1890s, Hatsuko Yuasa led the Tokyo WCTU movement in abolishing Japan's system of licensed prostitution and sexual double standards. Sasaki and Yajima supported Yuasa by encouraging the cooperation of male progressives and popular-rights activists who had stood by their side with their movement. In February 1888, they mailed two letters of appreciation from the Tokyo WCTU jointly signed by Yajima and Sasaki praising two men for their antiprostitution work.[63]

One of the letters was addressed to Tarō Andō, Japanese Consul General in Hawaii, who was promoting the temperance and antiprostitution movement in Hawaii with Kanichi Miyama. The latter was a Japanese minister sent to the islands by Japanese Christians in San Francisco to improve the "degrading" condition of Japanese immigrant laborers.[64] The Tokyo WCTU's letter thanked Andō for taking steps to benefit the Japanese both in Hawaii and in Japan, and asked Andō to cooperate with the WCTU in prohibiting drinking and controlling prostitution. The other letter was addressed to Emori Ueki (1857–1892), a popular-rights activist from Kochi Prefecture who was a representative to the Kochi prefectural assembly at the time. Ueki had introduced a petition in the Kochi prefectural assembly in January 1888 to abolish the system of licensed prostitution. The Tokyo WCTU letter praised Ueki for making Japanese men aware of the shame of allowing their sisters to engage in prostitution publicly.[65] Emori Ueki, Tarō Audō, and Kanichi Miyama later played important roles in WCTU activism in Meiji Japan.

While Tokyo WCTU members endeavored to establish the primacy of middle-class women over women from the pleasure quarters both in the public and private spheres, they soon emulated American missionary women in working to "rescue" and "reform" the latter. To raise funds for their work, Sasaki and her close friend Chiseko Ushioda (1844–1903) held a three-day fund-raising public meeting under the auspices of the Tokyo WCTU's East Branch in April 1888.[66] After Chiseko Ushioda was widowed, she studied at the Presbyterian Bancho School and the Methodist Episcopal (M.E.) Bible School for Women and became a Bible woman.[67] Matilda A. Spencer and other M.E. missionary women in Tokyo had been trying to provide a vocational education to poor Japanese women, including prostitutes, in response to the earnest pleas of Flora B. Harris, a fellow M.E. missionary wife who had left Japan to work among the Japanese on the American Pacific Coast.

Presumably through Ushioda, members of the Tokyo WCTU's East Branch learned of Spencer's efforts to influence would-be as well as "rescued" prostitutes and the American missionaries' methods of fund-raising. Using a slide machine called a "Magic Lantern" and materials borrowed from American missionaries, Ushioda and Sasaki organized a meeting where temperance stories were told in the Japanese language. Because the Magic Lantern was novel to the Japanese, the meeting attracted such big crowds that the police were called on to ensure that it was orderly.[68] After their successful fund-raising meeting, they donated forty yen to the WCTU's Temperance Building in Chicago, and used the rest to provide an education to "poor women." Cooperating with Spencer and other American missionary women, Ushioda, Sasaki, and other Japanese East Branch members taught classes to "correct the vocation and customs" of the poor as part of their attempt to abolish the system of licensed prostitution.[69] However, lacking systematic support and commitment, this work by Sasaki's group continued only intermittently.[70]

Facing Criticism: Sasaki Toyojyu and Pandita Ramabai

Ironically Sasaki's group's overwhelming success at the fund-raising meeting made Sasaki an easy target for criticism by conservatives. Further aggravating the situation was Sasaki's demand for women's "rights." Having imbibed the lessons of Western enlightenment philosophy and liberal political thought, and embraced the popular-rights activism of the 1880s, Sasaki became conscious of women's "rights," a concept difficult for Japanese whose lives had been shaped by feudalistic human relationships to understand. In July 1888 Sasaki published an editorial in the Tokyo WCTU magazine demanding economic rights for Japanese wives.[71] In her editorial she condemned the "evil custom" of the hierarchical relationship between husband and wife and argued that the first step to correcting this feudal human relationship was for wives to gain the right to half the household property. According to her, men and women's roles were fundamentally different but equally important and although a wife's contributions to the household did not bring in cash income like a husband's, she should be entitled to a 50 percent share of the household property.[72]

The conspicuous social activism of Sasaki's group followed by her radical demands provoked a strong reaction from conservative Japanese Protestant ministers and more moderate members of the Tokyo WCTU. According to Ushioda, the group's views were repudiated by male ministers who held that a "woman's true vocation was to keep house and to assist her husband and that it was inexcusable to engage in public affairs" through speeches and writings.[73] Criticism of Sasaki and her group was also voiced by Saku Asai (1843–1906) who shared the joint editorship of the Tokyo WCTU magazine with Sasaki.[74] Asai regarded Sasaki's outspokenness and public activism as a selfish and imprudent course of action that would harm society.

In June 1888, Asai wrote in an editorial that prostitution, drinking, and smoking were on the rise, but the Tokyo WCTU "lacked unity" because its members were concerned about "their own petty business" and only a few were eager to take on the challenge of "noble and useful" work. According to Asai, Tokyo WCTU members did not have to be highly educated or talented but needed to "cultivate a gentle but indomitable will."[75] She also argued that pressing for reform without due consideration of Japanese customs and the status of women would cause a public uproar.[76] According to Asai, the ideal woman was one who quietly executed her duties in her household. Sensible people had been aware of the harmfulness of drinking and smoking and of the immorality of prostitution even before Tokyo WCTU members began "boisterously" and "theoretically" preaching about it. In order to make people act on knowledge they already had, Asai felt strongly that Tokyo WCTU women and their families should seek to "influence" society through their good behavior.[77] Because Asai's version of ideal womanhood received more support from Tokyo WCTU members than Sasaki's, Sasaki was forced to resign as secretary of the Tokyo WCTU in August 1888.[78]

Although Sasaki resigned as secretary, she did not withdraw her membership from the Tokyo WCTU under Yajima's presidency. She continued to express her views and opinions in Iwamoto's *Jogaku zasshi* instead of the Tokyo WCTU's public organ. In light of the strong criticism of the Japanese Christian circle in Tokyo, it became important for her to expand her network beyond this circle so as to generate a women's movement and secure the leadership of the Tokyo WCTU. Sasaki corresponded with Frances Willard and learned from her about the prospective visit of Pandita Ramabai and Dr. Emma B. Ryder to Japan in December 1888.

Ramabai was an advocate of female medical training for Indian women who were neglected by male doctors, and of female education for young high-caste Indian widows to turn them into teachers. As an activist Ramabai had fought against the power of both Indian male elites and British missionary women, but her independent views on the status of Indian women were criticized by both groups. Ramabai's conversion to Christianity had met with harsh criticism from Indian reformers, while her resistance to certain aspects of Anglican orthodoxy created a rift with her Anglican benefactress. After giving up on her dream of a medical education in England, Ramabai returned to India.

While visiting the United States to attend a distant relative's graduation from the Woman's Medical College of Pennsylvania in 1886, Ramabai received strong emotional and financial support from churchwomen of various denominations for her project of building a home for high-caste widowed women. In 1887, the Ramabai Association was established in Boston and Ramabai circles were formed in various cities to raise funds for her project. One of the strongest supporters of Ramabai's cause was Frances E. Willard, who invited Ramabai to attend the WCTU conventions in Nashville in 1887 and Philadelphia in 1888. In 1888 the World WCTU appointed Dr. Emma B. Ryder to assist Ramabai in India in building a hospital attached to a home for the widowed.[79]

Presumably through her correspondence with Willard, Sasaki received leaflets about the Ramabai Association and Ramabai circles and two of Ramabai's writings: *The High-Caste Hindu Woman,* and a transcript of Ramabai's speech, the title of which was translated in Japanese as *Ryōhankyū no hinan* (Criticisms in the Two Hemispheres).[80] When Sasaki was criticized by male and female conservatives in Japanese Christian circles in Tokyo, she found solace and inspiration in Ramabai's writings. In anticipation of Ramabai and Ryder's visit to Japan, she wrote an article

A world WCTU network of women. Frances E. Willard, *top right*; Togoju Sasaki, *bottom left*; Mary C. Leavitt, *bottom center*; Pandita Ramabi, *bottom right*; Reproduced from Frances E. Willard, *Glimpses of Fifty Years: The Autobiography of an American Woman* (Chicago: Women's Temperance Publication Association, 1889). *Courtesy of the Frances E. Willard Memorial Library.*

about Ramabai's struggle to build a school for high-caste Hindu women, and translated Ramabai's account of opposition to her work in India and England. Both publications appeared in Iwamoto's *Jogaku zasshi* in September 1888.

In *Criticisms in the Two Hemispheres,* Ramabai problematized the Indian custom of early marriages arranged by parents and the existence of young high-caste widows who were not allowed to remarry or to have contact with society. Ramabai also expressed her distress at criticism directed at her from two different sources: fellow Indian reformers were critical of her conversion to Christianity, while her "Western" Christian sisters resented her attempts to maintain her independence from Christian denominational organizations.[81] Ramabai was trying to build a home for young high-caste widows that would be acceptable to high-caste Indian society, which was distrustful of Christianity. Ramabai's problems resembled those faced by Sasaki and other Tokyo WCTU members who were trying to create an independent movement of "Japanese" women in collaboration with Anglo-American Protestant and World WCTU missionary women.

Although Ramabai and Ryder spent only about ten days in the Tokyo-Yokohama area en route to India, Ramabai's resolute defense of her cause strongly impressed Sasaki and her friends. Articles in *Jogaku zasshi* that had reported Ramabai's arrival described Ramabai as a "short" and "dark-colored" Asian woman in "simple" native costume but one who expressed her beliefs in a "stately" fashion.[82] In interviews, Ramabai said that American churchwomen who engaged in interdenominational activism were more willing to respect her autonomy in her efforts on behalf of Indian women than their British Anglican sisters. Ramabai argued that she found more "help" and "sympathy" in the United States than in Britain where people showed only "pity" for Indian women. Asked if she would like to raise funds in Japan, she answered that she would do so only if the contributions were based on "mutual interests" and not on "pity."[83] Iwamoto invited Ramabai and Ryder to speak at the third in a series of lecture meetings sponsored by his *Jogaku zasshi,* and advertised her writings for sale in the magazine. The Tokyo WCTU, the male-led Yokohama Temperance Society, and female mission schools in Yokohama also arranged public meetings where Ramabai could talk about her work and raise funds.[84] Encouraged by Pandita Ramabai's indomitable will, Toyojyu Sasaki held a gathering at her house for Ramabai and Ryder before their departure. Among those invited were Kajiko Yajima, Sen Tsuda, Yoshiharu Iwamoto, Matilda A. Spencer, and others whom Ramabai and Ryder had met with.[85]

The Popular-Rights Movement and the Japanese Women's Movement

While the woman suffrage movement in mid-nineteenth-century America developed in conjunction with Garrisonian abolitionists against slavery,[86] the politically conscious women's movement that emerged in late-nineteenth-century Japan was closely allied with the radical wing of the popular-rights movement. As mentioned earlier, the rising tide of the movement in the early 1880s had produced female activists who appeared and spoke in public. While the Tokyo WCTU was affected by Anglo-American missionary women and the World WCTU, it was also influenced by the popular-rights activist Emori Ueki.[87] Like other male popular-rights activists, Ueki frequented the pleasure quarters for alcohol and romance but unlike other ideologists of the movement, he extended the concept of human rights to women. Although he had never been to the West, Ueki avidly read books on Western liberal political theory as well as religious and moral issues, in Japanese translation.

Ueki's home prefecture, Kochi, was the mecca of the liberal faction of the popular-rights movement, where Kita Kusunose, a legendary widowed woman registered as a household head demanded the right to vote in exchange for payment of the household tax in the 1870s. When the people's assembly was organized at the ward, town, and village levels by government order in 1880, two villages in Kochi prefecture granted women the right to vote and to contest elections for representatives in their village assemblies.[88] Working for the formation of the Liberal Party, the political party led by the Kochi popular-rights activists, Ueki openly declared his support for woman suffrage in Osaka in September 1880. He argued that although America and Europe were considered highly "civilized," women had not yet gained their suffrage in those nations because they had not worked for it hard enough when their nations were establishing political democracy. He thus urged Japanese women, whose country was about to establish a people's assembly, to endeavor to achieve their enfranchisement. Returning to Kochi, Ueki rallied the women of the two villages who had gained woman suffrage to demand their franchise at the prefectural and national levels.[89]

But the women in the two villages soon lost their rights in 1884 when the Meiji government stripped the local assemblies of their autonomy. Although the popular-rights movement temporarily lost momentum at the national level in the mid-1880s, it successfully reversed this downward trend in the late 1880s by attacking the Meiji government, which was still unable to revise the unequal treaties concluded with the Western powers. In addition, when the Meiji government was drafting the Constitution, the popular-rights activists also made a number of trial drafts of the Constitution. Unlike other drafts produced during this era, Ueki's draft barred criminals, non-taxpayers, and government officials—but not women—from the right to vote and to be elected as representatives to the national legislature.[90]

In the summer of 1888, Sasaki contributed to the preface of a book entitled *Women in the East* (*Tōyō no fujo*) by Emori Ueki. In the preface, Sasaki expressed her hope that the book would "awaken," "move," and "inspire" Japanese women to immediately start working for their own reform and improvement. The book compared women's subjugation and marriage in Japan, China, and Korea, to the West. Ueki argued that women did not possess equal political and legal rights with men either in the West or the East, and that women were not considered full members of their societies. However, only in the East were women still treated as "slaves," subjugated like "cows and horses," and not treated as human beings. Ueki and Sasaki probably influenced each other in their vision of women's roles in the new society. Like Sasaki, Ueki was critical of the fact that women in the East were not allowed to be active in public and emphasized the need for women's *kōsai* (socialization). According to Ueki, it was important for women to leave the security of their houses to learn to be "members of society" and "subjects of the state," to cultivate their knowledge and virtue, to experience the joy of "social activity," and, together with men, to freely choose their own spouses. To reform society for the good of women, Ueki proposed the following immediate tasks for women: broadening their range of "social activity," forming organizations, founding schools and conducting classes, writing articles and books, delivering speeches, and publishing newspapers and magazines. At the end of the book, Ueki repeatedly referred to women in Europe and America who were still struggling to gain their political rights, and argued that Japanese women should demand their political rights right away as the country was finally in the process of establishing a people's assembly.[91]

Those who contributed to the preface included, in addition to Sasaki, sixteen other women activists. Among them were noted female popular-rights activists such as Toshiko Kishida and Toyoko Shimizu, and members of the Tosa Kōfūkai (Tosa Custom Developing Society). The Tosa Kōfūkai was said to be the first women's society organized in Kochi Prefecture. It was composed mostly of churchwomen who aspired to "develop" new customs, not merely to "correct" old ones, on the basis of Western liberal thought and Protestant moral values.[92] Sasaki wrote a letter praising the Society for its activism and contribution to the preface of Ueki's radical book. She also worked closely with Ueki when he visited Tokyo in late 1888 and moved there for his political campaign in May 1889. When publishers in Tokyo, including Yoshiharu Iwamoto, were reluctant to publish Ueki's book, Sasaki probably used her personal funds to make the publication possible. When the book came into print in September 1889, Ueki acknowledged Sasaki's role in the book's publication. Sasaki was also recorded as its publisher.[93]

While Sasaki was expanding her contacts with the popular-rights movement, her adversary, Saku Asai, came to officially represent the Tokyo WCTU between June 1889 and October 1891. This resulted in the formation of Fujin Hakuhyō Kurabu (Women's White Ribbon Club, WWRC) by Sasaki and her sympathizers. In early 1889, Kajiko Yajima, who had been serving her third term as Tokyo WCTU president, injured herself by falling off a rickshaw. Consequently the Tokyo WCTU scheduled a special election in June 1889 to choose a replacement for Yajima, though at the lower rank of vice president.

During the election campaign, the relationship between Asai and Sasaki deteriorated further. Asai made clear her unconcealed hostility toward Sasaki by promoting herself over Sasaki in the Tokyo WCTU's official magazine. Older than Sasaki by twenty years, Asai wrote an editorial about the merits of having an older member as leader, arguing that seniors were usually more steady and well-versed in social conventions. Furthermore, Asai called on Tokyo WCTU members not to choose a woman who was active, decisive, "social," or skillful in speech, but to choose one who was deeply pious for vice president.[94] Asai garnered the heaviest vote, followed by Yajima's elder sister, Hisako Tokutomi, with Toyojyu Sasaki coming in third.[95]

Sasaki had not intended to create a separate organization but she and her sympathizers simply could not work under Asai. By carrying out their social activist agenda under the aegis of the WWRC, Sasaki's group freed themselves from the control of Asai and other conservatives in the church-women's circle in Tokyo. According to Sasaki, WWRC women were not willing to be confined to their homes. So she gathered her friends together to discuss politics and invited academics to give lectures. Although this is to speculate, they may have been aware that in the United States Willard's attempts to ally herself with the Prohibition Party were opposed by a group called the Non-Partisan WCTU in 1888. Explaining the nature of the WWRC, Sasaki wrote that the WWRC would be neutral between the different political parties but would call the politicians to account for misconduct. She also emphasized the freedom of its members. According to Sasaki, the WWRC had no president or superintendent but only committee members, and it imposed no limits on their activism. The WWRC's goal was to give women who were confined to the house knowledge of the outside world, or "socialization." The WWRC would endeavor to recover the dignity of the nation and its people when they were humiliated by foreigners, would be an envoy for peace, attend to and comfort the injured in times of war, and offer solace when disaster struck. Only when the world and the people were at peace would WWRC members return to women's responsibility, manage their households, educate each other, and devote themselves to creating happy homes. The WWRC wanted to contribute to the work of "civilization" and "social activism."[96]

Between 1889 and 1891, Japan became highly politicized over the promulgation of the Constitution. The opening of the national assembly promised by the government caused local politicians and popular-rights activists such as Emori Ueki to move to Tokyo to advance their political causes and campaigns. Sasaki's WWRC, as well as Asai's Tokyo WCTU, began to work with broader groups of people to promote an ambitious and dynamic political agenda for women. While Sasaki's WWRC members pushed for greater political participation by women, Yajima's group worked for the correction of the sexual double standard under the banner of the Tokyo WCTU's South Branch. Despite the personal conflicts between Asai, Yajima, and Sasaki, members of the Tokyo WCTU and the WWRC collaborated with one another.

Leading the Japanese women's movement for the correction of the sexual double standard was Yajima's niece, Hatsuko Yuasa, whose husband had played a leading role in passing an abolition bill in the Gunma prefectural assembly. While the abolition movement was gaining momentum among Christian and popular-rights activists in Japan through the 1880s, Hatsuko Yuasa drew on her discussions with Emori Ueki to develop an argument in favor of legal monogamy.[97] Borrowing from different theories, values, and concepts to make his point, Ueki's arguments were contradictory as was his conduct. Believing in human rights and freedom, Emori distinguished between political, legal, and social institutions on the one hand and religion on the other.[98] Then he argued that the state should not involve itself in the matter of prostitution, just as the church should steer clear of any involvement in discussions about marriage.[99] Ironically, however, by adding his voice to that of middle-class churchwomen to promote gender equality in Meiji Japan, Ueki provided an ideological basis for the Tokyo WCTU's demand for the criminalization of a husband's extramarital relations. In a speech delivered at the Tokyo WCTU's public meeting in May 1889, Ueki emphasized the injustice of the then current practice of punishing a wife's illicit sexual relationship as adultery but not a husband's. He also criticized the resulting concubinage and polygamous households in which the wife and concubines bore grudges against each other, thereby negatively affecting the household, children, and society. To break this "evil" custom of concubinage, Ueki argued that criminal and civil codes should be created to define the husband's extramarital relationship as adultery and to make it as punishable as the wife's. He also thought it desirable to allow the spouse of the adulterous party, either husband or wife, to initiate divorce and to receive alimony under civil law.[100]

On June 27, 1889 the Tokyo WCTU submitted its first petition for legally privileging monogamy. Its author was Hatsuko Yuasa.[101] Her petition was based on a draft by Ueki,[102] but it also clearly revealed middle-class churchwomen's animosity toward geishas and prostitutes, and would-be concubines who would "steal the property of a household" and "disturb and destroy the legitimate family in order to make her children the household head." Yuasa's petition, elevating the legal status of the legitimate wife and her children over that of concubines and their children, received broad support from middle-class Japanese women who were in favor of a women's movement to correct sexual double standards. The petition gathered more than eight hundred signatures from members of the Tokyo WCTU, the WWRC, and their friends.[103] Women's societies in cities such as Kyoto, Osaka, Kobe, Kochi, Sapporo, Hakodate, and Chiba submitted similar petitions to the Meiji government in 1889.[104]

While generating a women's movement to correct sexual double standards, members of the Tokyo WCTU and the WWRC also participated in the drive to abolish the licensed system of prostitution that was becoming a national movement. Abolitionist politicians such as Ueki and Yuasa's husband started Zenkoku Haishō Dōmeikai (National League to Abolish Licensed Prostitution) in May 1890. Its first meeting, held at the Meiji Women's School in Tokyo, was attended by male and female representatives of various abolitionist groups from all over Japan. Among the founding members and organizations were the Tokyo WCTU, the WWRC, and Japanese male activists, both secular and Christian, such as Emori Ueki, Yoshiharu Iwamoto, Sen Tsuda, Jirō Yuasa, and Shō Nemoto.[105]

Like European activists who campaigned against the state regulation of prostitution, Japanese abolitionists were mindful of the human rights of prostitutes in their argument that the existing system failed to contain the spread of venereal disease and curb immoral conduct.[106] However, the Japanese abolitionists seemed most concerned about the fragile reputation of their country as a "civilized nation." For example, one proposition submitted to the Imperial Diet in 1890 argued that the state licensing of prostitutes was a national "disgrace" and that it would be preferable for Japan to tolerate prostitution without state involvement while tacitly conducting medical inspections of prostitutes.[107] Another letter, written by Tokyo WCTU president Saku Asai to members of the Imperial Diet the same year, argued that the state licensing of prostitution weakened the vigor of the Imperial nation, disgraced the national polity, and violated human rights, and that it should therefore be abolished.[108]

In addition, WWRC members, who included female popular-rights activists, also endeavored to increase women's say and influence in the political arena. For example, Sasaki and Ushioda challenged the male political culture of Meiji Japan in which political and business meetings often took place over *sake* (rice wine) in the presence of female professional entertainers. In September 1889 they sent a letter to a popular political party that was planning to hold a national meeting to discuss the revision of the unequal treaties. In their letter, Sasaki and Ushioda demanded an end to the "evil custom" of serving liquor at political meetings and having female entertainers.[109] Furthermore, Sasaki and Ushioda initiated their own political effort for the treaty revision by sending a letter to Queen Victoria that same month through the Japanese Ministry of Foreign Affairs, requesting the queen to immediately ratify the revision of the treaty.[110]

Nonetheless, because of political developments in the late 1880s, the WWRC's efforts for the political participation of women became less ambitious and more defensive. Women—along with the majority of men, who did not meet the property qualification—were not granted suffrage under the new Constitution. And the Meiji government, identifying the politicization of women that had developed in conjunction with the resurgence of the popular-rights movement as a problem, took measures to suppress political participation by women. When the government issued the Assembly and Political Organization Law (Shūkai oyobi sheishahō) of 1890 to increase its control over popular-rights activists and their political activities, it banned women from attending political gatherings and barred them from becoming members of political associations.[111]

To recover the rights curtailed by this new law, Toyoko Shimizu, a member of the WWRC, initiated an intermittent and long-term struggle by Japanese women against the Japanese government. Historian Sharon Sievers described it as "the Japanese women's equivalent of the suffrage movement."[112] Shimizu was involved in the popular-rights movement in Kyoto in the early 1880s. She came to know Tokyo WCTU members through Emori Ueki and Toyojyu Sasaki and led the petition drive to privilege monogamy in Kyoto in 1889.[113] Shimizu joined the WWRC in late

1889, moved to Tokyo in May 1890 to stay with Sasaki's family for a while, and became a reporter and writer for Iwamoto's *Jogaku zasshi*.[114]

However, by this time the liberal political tide of early Meiji Japan was waning and male popular-rights activists more focused on playing party politics within the political system set by the new Constitution. The meaning of "women's political rights" was diminished and the WWRC's political campaign lost its radical edge. Moreover, Shimizu's argument in demanding gender equality in "political rights" reflected the elitism of urban middle-class women. In an article published in August 1890, Shimizu questioned why—if the government denied women their "political rights" lest they neglect their housekeeping and child-rearing duties—farmers, merchants, and craftsmen, whose chief duties were not to discuss politics, were allowed to attend political meetings. The government should not deny "women's political rights" under the assumption that all women were less able and less knowledgeable than men, she argued. If the government wished to prohibit those who were not capable of participating in political discussion, it should examine each individual, both men and women, using impartial criteria. It was unwise to allow ignorant villagers to qualify but disqualify educated women from engaging in political activity. Furthermore, Shimizu argued, women needed to listen to and participate in political gatherings so as to better assist their husbands and to raise their children to be "loyal subjects."[115] Shimizu's class-specific argument that women should be allowed to participate in and listen to, but not to speak at, political gatherings was supported not only by the WWRC and the Tokyo WCTU but also by middle-class Japanese women more broadly.

By the end of the year, however, another law, the Regulations of the House of Representatives issued in October 1890, prohibited women from sitting in its galleries. Now the debate over women's political rights turned to whether they could listen to male political debates or not. Shimizu again indignantly took up her pen, deploring the fact that women were not only unable to send their representatives to the House but were not even allowed to observe its deliberations. Shimizu argued that the Diet was meant to respect human rights and to discuss matters important to the nation, but in reality it placed one group of people called "women" under the tyranny of another called "men." She demanded that the regulation be repealed, as barring women from sitting in the gallery of the House in session was a clear violation of women's rights to "participate in politics."[116]

In fact, the demand that women be present at and observe male political activities in the public sphere also gained the support of men, who viewed women as facilitators of but not participants in political activity. For example, objecting to the regulation in his magazine, Yoshiharu Iwamoto argued that women should be admitted to the gallery because the presence of women would "purify" the site, make the representatives behave, inspire male representatives' patriotism, humanity, and virtue, and provide welcome relief from "the bleak scene" of all-male political discussions. Iwamoto expected middle-class female activists to influence and facilitate male political debate by their presence in the Diet, much as professional female entertainers did at business and political meetings held at the pleasure quarters.[117] In early October 1890 when Shimizu, Yajima, and Yajima elder sister Hisako Tokutomi visited Count Taisuke Itagaki, who led the political party of the Kochi popular-rights activists, to petition for the repeal of the regulation, Itagaki encouraged them in their efforts—but only so that women could improve the quality of male political participation. Asked for his opinion by Shimizu, Itagaki argued that the House of Representatives was not a government office but a place where people discussed matters of state. Thus, people other than representatives, including women, should be admitted to listen to deliberations over national issues. In his opinion, women were as capable as men and women's awareness of political matters would "increase [the number of male] politicians" among the people and heighten male patriotism. But in Itagaki's view, women's roles were different from men's. He did not encourage women to discuss politics or participate in political activities the way men did.[118]

Thus, although the campaign to regain the right to observe the deliberations of the House of Representatives gained momentum, the women's argument increasingly emphasized their role as men's assistants. The petition submitted to the other popular party for the repeal of the regulation in late October 1890 emphasized the disappointment of women who found time to spare from their household duties but were not allowed to "console" their brothers for their hardships during their deliberations at the House. The petition was signed by twenty-one "representatives of women volunteers," including WWRC members such as Toyoko Shimizu, Toyojyu Sasaki, and Chiseko Ushioda, and Tokyo WCTU members such as Kajiko Yajima, Saku Asai, Hatsuko Yuasa, and Yuasa's mother and Yajima's elder sister, Hisako Tokutomi.[119]

This effort was supported by the newspapers, most of which had been under the editorship of popular-rights activists. Thus the Lower House

Regulation that prohibited women from observing the House in session was successfully repealed in December 1890.[120] After observing the first session, Sasaki did not remain quiet but published a letter to Lower House representatives in March 1891. However, the letter only aimed to influence the representatives, and made no mention of women's right to participate directly in political debates. In her letter, Sasaki asked the House to represent the people and not simply agree with the government, and told them that they should feel ashamed of their "immoral" conduct, refrain from jeering, and faithfully attend the sessions.[121] Jubilant at having regained the right to observe the Lower House in session, WWRC and Tokyo WCTU members no longer questioned the government's prohibition of women participating in political assemblies and joining political organizations. Partial gain of these political rights for women had to await the emergence of another phase of "the Japanese equivalent of the suffrage movement." Thus women did not gain the right to hold and to participate in political assemblies until 1922. They were not officially allowed to join political parties until the postwar Constitution granted female suffrage in 1946.[122]

"How Sublimely Simple!"

While Toyojyu Sasaki, Kajiko Yajima, and Saku Asai agreed with one another over the need for a women's movement at one of the most politicized moments in the Meiji era, progressive Japanese men took on the WCTU's temperance movement in Meiji Japan. This can be partially attributed to World WCTU travelers, especially Mary Leavitt, Jessie A. Ackerman, and Mary West, who modified the "Woman's" and "Christian" nature of the WCTU enterprise in America to promote temperance in early Meiji Japan. Recognizing the Japanese distrust of Christianity, these World WCTU missionaries utilized "scientific" and empirical rather than religious discourse in preaching temperance. For example, during her five-month tour of Japan in 1886 Leavitt quickly realized that Japan was still a "pagan land" despite its "polite culture" and "rapid progress." This realization came to her after she had a surprising experience in a church while closing one of her "well-received" speeches on total abstinence. Leavitt wrote:

> Just at the close, I made a personal appeal to all who had not done so to accept the Christian religion, and the Savior it offers. Though many un-

derstood English, none dissented, but when the interpreter reproduced it, there was a very loud, almost savage "No" from hundreds of throats.[123]

To make her lectures more appealing to the Japanese, Leavitt emphasized the "scientific" aspects of temperance. According to her report, the first Japanese groups she addressed outside the missionary circle in the Tokyo-Yokohama area were the "Medical Society of Japan" and "a society, or club of naval surgeons and their wives."[124] In one of her lectures, translated and published in Japanese, Leavitt emphasized the hereditary nature of drinking habits and the illnesses caused by drinking.[125] Given Japan's nationalistic fervor for modernization and civilization, Leavitt's lectures on temperance were welcomed by progressive Japanese men who believed that temperance "would bring good health, increased production, a higher education, and a purer morality" throughout the nation.[126]

Furthermore, World WCTU missionaries also incorporated the language of Japanese nationalism in their speeches. For example, West emphasized the importance of total abstinence from drinking in order to develop and advance the national interests of Japan.[127] In Tokyo in 1892, West addressed an audience of two thousand Japanese. Using a biblical figure, Nehemiah, as an example of a "model citizen" who rebuilt the walls around his native city to protect it from Sanballat's attack, West urged Japan to build a wall of total abstinence, temperance education, and national prohibition around itself. Condemning Japan's "unequal" treaties with Western nations which prohibited Japan from autonomously setting tariffs, West spoke eloquently:

You citizens of Japan, have also a wall to build, not the wall of seclusion, shutting you out from the world but the new wall of protection against the evils which threaten your nation. . . . I have dwelt upon the danger to your industries from the spread of the drink habit, a danger greater in Japan than elsewhere because your distinctive industries require such exactness of mechanical execution; of its menace to your food supply by destroying annually 4,000,000 *koku*[128] of rice. . . . ; of the burdens of taxation it imposes by increasing crime, pauperism, and insanity. . . . America did not guard against this danger and is now suffering the consequences. The great liquor interest there is almost exclusively in the hands of foreigners. . . . I fear the same will be the case in Japan if you do not now stop the vile stream which has begun to flow into your land. Existing treaties favor this nefarious traffic; while you must pay 40, 50 or even 60 percent duty to export your exquisite workmanship to lands fast learning its value and hence desiring to purchase it, the wine-makers of France or California can bring all the wine they wish into Japan for a maximum duty of 5 percent; . . . Thus you see this temperance question is not one of secondary importance; it touches not only individual life but the well-being of the nation in its industries, its commerce, its moral and social condition, its international relations.[129]

West's lecture was "listened to [with] breathless interest and was often applauded with sounds like thunder that brings rain to make all fruits grow."[130] The temperance cause advocated by teachers from an advanced nation like the United States appealed to broad groups of Japanese, regardless of gender, class, and religion. In Kyoto, the headquarters of several Buddhist sects, Ackerman addressed about six hundred Buddhist students on "What Christianity Has Done to the World." She reported that, despite her concern, "they listened for more than one hour, and frequently applauded."[131] Furthermore, the Japanese nobility also welcomed American World WCTU women's temperance talks. Mary West was invited by aristocratic circles and gave lectures at the Peeress' School, the Educational Association of Noble Ladies, and the Red Cross, "the most aristocratic association in Japan, the Empress being nominal president and one of the imperial princesses presiding."[132]

In fact the perception that the United States was more "civilized" and modern than Japan, as well as the difference in physical size between Japanese and Americans in general, prompted the feminization of Japanese men by American World WCTU travelers and the masculinization of American World WCTU women by the Japanese.[133] WCTU missionaries touring Japan felt empowered by this phenomenon. Leaving Tokyo for a lecture tour in local cities, Ackerman wrote:

Just before the train moved out, one of the young men who had spent some time in America, explained to the crowd that it was a custom in America to send "distinguished persons" on their way with three cheers. He took off his hat, swung it high in [the] air and gave a regular "hip, hip, hurrah," in true American style, and just as the train moved out a perfect volley of cheers filled the air and I left bearing the prayers and good wishes of that enthusiastic gathering. I felt that it was worth while to come all the way to Japan just to hold those meetings in Tokio [Tokyo] and know those little people, among whom I stalked like a "giant great and tall."[134]

Arriving in Numazu where "very few foreigners" lived, Ackerman was similarly greeted at the station by "the pastor of the native church and about a hundred of his members." Ackerman was quite pleased that "the announcement of the arrival of [a] 'foreign lady teacher' brought the people out in such great numbers."[135]

While both Japanese men and women wanted to meet these World WCTU missionary women, Leavitt, Ackerman, and West, who were ambitious about promoting the temperance movement in Japan, associated most closely with Japanese male temperance workers, who were more knowledgeable and resourceful than women. During her stay in Japan from February to April 1890, Jessie A. Ackerman, while meeting with members of both the WWRC and the Tokyo WCTU, concentrated on assisting male temperance workers form a male-led temperance society in Tokyo.[136] As Ackerman had worked as a lecturer and organizer of the Good Templars' Lodge, a male-led temperance organization, before assuming her work in the World WCTU, she had established contacts with male temperance workers in and outside the United States.[137]

Ackerman's efforts resulted in the formation of the Tokyo Kinshukai (Tokyo Temperance Society) in March 1890. Among its leading members were Tarō Andō and Shō Nemoto, who had recently returned to Japan from the United States after forging ties with a transnational network of temperance activists.[138] Tarō Andō, who had once served as Japan's Consul General to the Hawaiian Islands, initiated a temperance movement among Japanese immigrants in the Islands and became acquainted with Ackerman when she visited the Islands. Shō Nemoto had come under the strong influence of M.E. home missionaries and their views on temperance while attending a high school in the California Bay Area in the early 1880s.[139] Attending the University of Vermont with the support of Mr. and Mrs. Frederick Billings, millionaire philanthropists dedicated to the temperance cause, Nemoto became a temperance activist and became friendly with American temperance workers, including Frances Willard and other WCTU members.[140] Upon his return to Japan in 1890, Nemoto had just started promoting the temperance cause in the country, using funds given by the Billings. With the formation of the Tokyo Temperance Society, Tarō Andō assumed the presidency, and Shō Nemoto the vice presidency.[141]

Arriving in Yokohama in September 1892, Mary West worked with male temperance workers who had established temperance societies in Sapporo and Okayama besides Tokyo. West sailed from Yokohama to Sapporo and other parts of Hokkaido with an American Protestant missionary woman, and traveled through the northeast region back to Tokyo accompanied by Sen Tsuda. Returning to Tokyo in October, West conducted a three-week "campaign" carefully planned by "the local committee" led by Shō Nemoto.[142] Her reports to the World WCTU, which were devoted mostly to providing biographical backgrounds of male Christian temperance leaders,[143] described Nemoto as her "good genius in all this Japan work, planning everything, arranging everything, in a wonderful way."[144]

Ironically, observing these World WCTU missionaries who worked closely with Japanese men for temperance, Sasaki realized the significance of the temperance cause to the World WCTU movement and began to engage in male-led temperance work in Japan. Sasaki was a good friend of Shō Nemoto, as they had both attended Dōjinsha in the early 1870s. When Ackerman's efforts resulted in the formation of the Tokyo Temperance Society, Sasaki and Ushioda joined this male-dominated society to lead its women's department.[145] By forging a relationship with male temperance workers, Sasaki's group was trying to strengthen its ties with the World WCTU.

Furthermore, persistent criticism from Asai caused Sasaki's group to redouble its efforts. In an article published in Tokyo WCTU's official magazine in March 1890, Asai said that people who had formed a different organization—a reference to Sasaki and her friends who had formed the WWRC—should no longer retain their membership in the Tokyo WCTU. Asai argued that members who had different opinions would not blend with each other "like water and oil," and that there was no need for her organization to be "united in darkness."[146] This statement further distanced Sasaki and her sympathizers from Asai and her Tokyo WCTU. In April 1891 the women's department of the Tokyo Temperance Society became an independent organization called Tokyo Fujin Kinshukai (Tokyo Women's Temperance Society, Tokyo WTS), and Ushioda became its first president.[147]

Consequently, World WCTU missionaries' efforts resulted in two competing Japanese women's unions in Tokyo, the Tokyo WCTU and the Tokyo WTS. And the disputes between Sasaki and Asai also involved Yajima. In October 1891 Asai resigned the presidency of the Tokyo WCTU because of letters, published in Japanese Protestant newspapers, strongly criticizing the Tokyo WCTU under Asai's leadership for not cooperating with the World WCTU or the male-led temperance organizations.[148] Thus, Kajiko Yajima resumed the presidency of the Tokyo WCTU in February 1892 and also made an effort to work with male temperance activists.[149] The personal antagonism between the three women now culminated in competition between the Tokyo WCTU and the Tokyo WTS for endorsement by the World WCTU as the official branch union representing Japan.

Sasaki's attempt to secure leverage for her group by strengthening its relationship with the World WCTU led to Mary West's intervention and ultimately backfired on Sasaki. Recognizing the power struggle between the leaders of Japanese churchwomen activists, Mary West pushed for the unification of the Tokyo WCTU and the Tokyo WTS under Yajima's leadership. Although Sasaki's Tokyo WTS had established a successful relationship with the male-led Tokyo Temperance Society, the Tokyo WCTU benefited from its long-time affiliation with the World WCTU, Yajima's position as acting principal of a Presbyterian female mission school, and her personal connection with American Protestant missionaries who had been assisting West with her tour and activities in Japan. However, West disapproved of the fact that the Tokyo WCTU had revised its bylaws and pledges by dropping any reference to the temperance cause,[150] and insisted on twelve changes in the Tokyo WCTU's bylaws.[151] West reported:

> Mrs. Yajima, whose name stands in our directory as president of Japan, is a remarkable woman. . . . She is now a widow and the Japanese head of the Presbyterian Girls' School of Tokyo. By Japanese law, all schools must be nominally in the hands of Japanese, so all have Japanese presidents. By virtue of this office, Mrs. Yajima presides over the deliberations of the board of trustees, composed of foreign ladies and gentlemen, and does it with acceptance and dignity. She presided over the majority of my meetings in Tokyo, and in every way proved most efficient. . . . [B]ut she [Yajima] does not speak English, nor do any of the officers of the Tokyo Woman's Society, or the so-called Japan union. This shut them off so completely from knowledge of our work that during the years since Mrs. Leavitt organized them, they had gone off in many directions, modifying their constitution and the pledge itself till they no longer required total abstinence and so could not be considered a W.C.T.U. Then, divisions had arisen among them so that the hardest work I have had to do in Japan had been to reconcile these differences and reunite the factions on a true basis. This is now accomplished and steps are being taken for a real Japan

W.C.T.U. composed of unions I may find, resurrect or form all over Japan.[152]

To realize a national organization, Mary West soon left Tokyo for lecture tours in the western region of Japan, entrusting to Yajima the task of revising the Tokyo WCTU's bylaws and unifying the two factions. At the send-off meeting held in October 1892, Yajima expressed her gratitude to West and declared that Japanese Christian women would be united in the work of temperance.[153] However, Tokyo WTS members refused to be absorbed into the Tokyo WCTU, and only some of West's demands were incorporated into the Japanese version of the Tokyo WCTU's revised bylaws. The new bylaws clearly stated that the Tokyo WCTU was connected to the World WCTU and that one of its purposes was expansion of the work of "prohibiting drinking and smoking." But the Tokyo WCTU never required its members to make a pledge of total abstinence.[154]

Tokyo WTS members finally yielded to West's demand for unification because of Mary West's sudden death on December 1, 1892, during her exhausting trip in the western region. The unexpected tragedy made Mary West an unchallengeable icon to churchwomen in Japan. On December 3, 1892, the Tokyo WCTU held its annual meeting at Yajima's Presbyterian female mission school in Tokyo. Invited by Yajima, Chiseko Ushioda, the president of the Tokyo WTS, who had once studied at her school, was present. Yajima planned to elect officers for the Tokyo WCTU from candidates chosen from both the Tokyo WCTU and the Tokyo WTS so as to unite the two societies. Ushioda attempted to resist Yajima's efforts, but gave in on the grounds that it was the will of the late Miss West. As a result of the election, Yajima maintained her position as president of the Tokyo WCTU and ten other women became vice presidents. They included Toyojyu Sasaki, Chiseko Ushioda, Hisako Tokutomi (Yajima's elder sister), Hatsuko Tsuda (wife of Sen Tsuda), Fumiko Andō (wife of Tarō Andō), and Chika Sakurai, the founder of the Presbyterian Bancho School who had returned to Tokyo from Hokkaido.[155]

In February 1892 a committee was established to form the national organization, and Yajima, Sasaki, Ushioda, and two other members were appointed to it.[156] Then, in April 1893, the Japan WCTU (Nihon Fujin Kyōfūkai) was formed in Tokyo, and was joined by women's societies in Kobe and Okayama.[157] Yajima became the first president of the Japan WCTU, and Sasaki its honorary president. The formation of the Japan WCTU was effected by bringing the active and more outspoken Sasaki and her sympathizers under the authority of the pragmatic and patient but also expedient Yajima.

This move coincided with the departure of key figures from the front-lines of the Tokyo-based WCTU movement, thus causing a setback to the Tokyo churchwomen's feminist movement during the early Meiji era. In January 1892, Emori Ueki died mysteriously at the young age of thirty-three.[158] That same year, Hatsuko Yuasa, Yajima's niece, who had led the petition drive for correction of sexual double standards, left Tokyo for Kyoto to follow her husband.[159] In April 1893, Toyojyu Sasaki, who had lost the power struggle to Yajima, left Tokyo to devote herself to correcting "evil customs" and building a women's school far away in Hokkaido, the land of the Ainu people with whom the Meiji government had started its assimilation policy.[160] Sasaki maintained her contacts with the Japan WCTU and later came back to Tokyo, but withdrew from the frontlines of activism.[161] Toyoko Shimizu, who had led the campaign for women's political rights and once contemplated joining Sasaki in Hokkaido, also distanced herself from the Japan WCTU. In November 1891, she bore an out-of-wedlock child to a fellow popular-rights activist,[162] fell ill, and spent most of early 1892 in hospitals in Tokyo. She was dissuaded from going to Hokkaido by a university professor whom she later married. From then until 1900, Shimizu used her pen to point out the wrongs of gender inequality and the sexual double standard, but her writing increasingly took the form of fiction to protect herself from the rising tide of conservatism and also to protect her husband from association with her "immorality."[163] The loss of key activists from the circle of churchwomen in Tokyo, coupled with the increasingly conservative political current of Japan, pushed Japanese women's feminist consciousness and their movement back by several years.

Furthermore, although West had clarified the relationship between the Japan WCTU and the World WCTU, Japanese male Christian temperance workers did not easily give up their roles in the WCTU's transnational temperance movement, and continued to consider themselves as Japan's representatives to the World WCTU.[164] For example, Shō Nemoto, vice president of the Tokyo Temperance Society, reported to the World WCTU in 1891 that Japanese temperance societies were largely organized by men and that they did the work of the WCTU in America.[165] Upon the death of Mary West, Nemoto, who was then working for the Foreign Ministry, accompanied her corpse, a martyr for the temperance cause, back to San Francisco.[166] In 1893 Sen Tsuda attended the second World WCTU convention in Chicago with Mrs. Chika Sakurai to represent Japan.[167] As late as 1895, Nemoto still referred to the Japan WCTU as "the lady's department of W.C.T.U.," in which "W.C.T.U." meant male-led temperance movements.[168]

Observing this situation, Kate C. Bushnell, who visited Japan in 1894 on a world tour for the special cause of social purity along with Elizabeth W. Andrew,[169] pointed out that "W.C.T.U" work in Japan was "under the management of men." Bushnell wrote:

> Throughout Japan, there is a strong tendency for the work of the W.C.T.U. to pass under the management of men, in consequence of which its very title may, in many instances, become a misnomer. It is exceedingly difficult to make a whole convert to Christianity out of a heathen man. The truth is he would a little rather hold back that part of the coming of the kingdom described as the realm where "there is neither male nor female." A Japanese brother(?) professing to be a most earnest Christian said to us "Why do you spend the time with women, you have only to address the men and when they become temperance men, they go home and tell their households what they must do." How sublimely simple! To his mind, we only need to do half the amount of temperance preaching, and exalt the virtue of obedience and servility in the other half who do not hear![170]

3

Managing WCTU Activism

The Japanese Way in
Late Meiji Japan, 1890–1913

The Japan WCTU's Waning Activism

The Japanese women's movement reached its peak in 1890, the year in which the promulgation of the Meiji Constitution and the opening of the Imperial Diet reversed the liberal political tide of the early Meiji era. The Meiji Constitution, which was promulgated as "a gift" from the Emperor to the people, was based on the Prussian, rather than the American or British, model and was intended to fortify the oligarchy in the name of the Emperor.[1] As such, the limited male franchise allowed only 1 percent of the total population to vote for representatives to the lower house of the bicameral Imperial Diet. Such a development was far from what the popular-rights activists had originally intended, but they, like the majority of Japanese, celebrated the establishment of the constitutional monarchy as a symbol of "civilized" Japan.

As the 1890s unfolded, the popular-rights movement concentrated its remaining energy on the "modern" practice of party politics. The liberal political climate succumbed to a strong backlash against the rapid westernization of previous decades, harshly criticized for destroying "virtuous" Japanese customs and creating "selfish" individuals. The neo-Confucian values of "loyalty" and "filial piety" were reemphasized, and people were redefined as "subjects" of the Emperor, said to be the lineal descendant of the Sun Goddess. As Japan transformed itself from a decentralized feudal state into a centralized modern nation, Japanese women were required to be obedient and loyal not only to their husbands and in-laws but also to the Emperor and the new nation.[2]

Like American women in the late eighteenth century, Japanese women received no assurances regarding their independent political, legal, economic, or civil rights as their country began nation-building. The turn in the political current between the 1880s and 1890s was evident while the Meiji Civil Code was being crafted. The first draft of the code, written in the 1880s by a progressive French adviser to the Japanese government, Gustavo E. Boissonade de Fontarabie, emphasized the conjugal relationship between husband and wife rather than the lineal one between parents and their son as the basis for a family, and spoke of the "rights" and "obligations" of individuals. The majority of Japanese, however, still believed that the will of the superior was absolute, and considered the reference to the "obligation" of superiors (parents and husbands), and the "rights" of inferiors (children and wives) radical.[3] Japanese conservatives thus opposed the draft, arguing that it was a product of Western individualism and that it would destroy the virtuous Japanese *ie* (house) system.[4]

Consequently the draft underwent two major revisions in the 1890s before culminating in the final Meiji Civil Code, enacted in 1898. The final product ensured the continuation of the *ie* through the lineal descendant and stipulated the "rights" of a household head toward other household members and his "obligations" to the state. The rights, obligations, and property of the household head were to be passed on through the principle of male primogeniture and undivided inheritance. Unlike the feudal era, a daughter was to be allowed to become a household head, but only when there was no son, legitimate or illegitimate. Wives as well as minors were defined as "incapable persons," subject to the "household head."[5] Although the new code assumed a monogamous standard for the conjugal relationship and privileged a legitimate son over an illegitimate one, it preserved the sexual double standard despite the numerous petitions submitted by the Tokyo WCTU to the government. The new code continued to criminalize a wife's illicit sexual relations as adultery but not a husband's, and allowed a husband—but not a wife—to file for divorce on the grounds of infidelity.[6]

In the conservative political climate of the 1890s, Japanese women who had been socially and politically active during the early Meiji era were pushed back into domesticity and female education was blamed for creating "selfish" and "disobedient" subjects. The public especially turned against female mission schools under the management of "foreign" and Christian women. Enrollment at female mission schools therefore declined, resulting in the closure of some schools in the 1890s.[7] To adapt to the new situation, leaders of public and private as well as Christian and non-Christian women's schools emphasized female secondary education to create a "good wife and wise mother."[8] Although this concept had successfully replaced the neo-Confucian view of a woman as "borrowed womb" and "obedient daughter" in the liberal early Meiji era, the resurgent conservatism required that the "good wife and wise mother" also be an "obedient" wife and daughter-in-law and a "loyal" subject of imperial Japan.

Japanese women's WCTU activism, which had been carried out mainly by teachers and graduates of female mission schools and churchwomen, was also in deep trouble. Mary West's tragic death had united the two factions of the Tokyo WCTU and created Japan's first national organization, the Japan WCTU, which brought several local churchwomen's societies under its umbrella. Despite these achievements, however, hostility toward Christian women's social activities slowed the growth of feminist consciousness among members of the Japan WCTU. Toyojyu Sasaki, observing this situation from far-away Hokkaido, wrote to her sisters in Tokyo urging them to fight back. Sasaki deplored the fact that women, who "had raised their heads up slightly," had been "beaten" down by conservatism and had withdrawn underground. She called on Japanese WCTU women to "rouse" themselves and to continue to use their knowledge and education in society.[9] A few leaders did keep their spirit of protest alive despite the mounting conservatism, but their statements and activism were suppressed by the Meiji oligarchy which was successfully tightening its grip on the nation. The government began to sensor the Japan WCTU's magazines and banned the publication of several issues in the 1890s, further reinforcing the negative image of Christian women's organizations as being undesirable and harmful to the public and the nation.[10]

Given the situation, Kajiko Yajima could not rally Japan's first women's national organization to effectively fight back and launch a nationwide women's movement. Although Yajima continually petitioned the government for the correction of sexual double standards in the civil and criminal codes and for the abolition of the licensed prostitution system,[11] her efforts no longer evoked the enthusiasm among urban Japanese women as they had between 1889 and 1891. Thus, when the third annual Japan WCTU convention was held in April 1896, members from only two local unions, one in Tokyo and the other in Chiba,[12] attended, although there were about ten local women's societies affiliated with the Japan WCTU then.[13]

American Protestant and
World WCTU Missionary Women in Japan

The impetus to counteract Japanese women's dwindling WCTU activism came from the cooperative relationship between the World WCTU, the Japan WCTU, and American Protestant missionary women, itself a result of the World WCTU's initiative in the late 1890s. After returning to the United States in 1891 from her "around-the-world" organizing tour, Mary Leavitt advised the World WCTU to secure the services of Anglo-American Protestant churchwomen resident overseas.[14] Unlike the Tokyo WCTU, the World WCTU branches that she formed in other parts of the world were usually led by Anglo-American Protestant missionary women. Thus it seemed most appropriate for the World WCTU to enlist Anglo-American missionary women working overseas, some of whom were members of the WCTU in their homelands, for its expansion in the world.

At the third World WCTU Convention held in London in 1895, "a new plan was favorably reported to establish resident white-ribboners in China, Straits Settlements, Bahamas and wherever thought best" with the World WCTU contributing $600 a year to each resident worker. At the convention, a decision was also made to urge Protestant churchwomen, mostly Anglo-American missionaries, in the world to appoint "one or more members of the different denominations and associations" in order to "draw their fellow-members into" the World WCTU.[15]

In Japan, in 1895 the World WCTU successfully recruited Mary F. Denton, a resident missionary sent to Kyoto from the ABCFM.[16] During the 1880s, before she became an ABCFM missionary, Denton had been a public school teacher and an active member of the WCTU in Southern California. While there she became acquainted with Frances E. Willard when Willard visited the area in 1883.[17] Having arrived in Kyoto in 1888 to work as a missionary teacher at an ABCFM-supported female school, Denton began assisting American World WCTU women organize unions and give lectures. At the request of the World WCTU, Denton agreed to "act as their correspondent and secretary for the organization" of a national Western missionary women's union in Japan. Denton soon secured pages for the World WCTU in the *Japan Evangelist,* an interdenominational Christian newspaper published in English in Yokohama. She also began to work for the formation of a national organization for Western female residents in Japan to carry out "aggressive work in the Japanese churches" for WCTU causes and to prepare "for the reception of Miss Willard and Lady Henry Somerset" who were planning a world tour.[18]

These events coincided with interdenominational American missionary women's efforts to build a home for "rescued" Japanese women in cooperation with the Japan WCTU. As the commodification of Japanese women accelerated with the capitalistic development of Japan's economy, American churchwomen, who had been engaging in "rescue" work as well as "purity crusades" in various parts of the world, made an urgent appeal on the need to build a home for rescued Japanese women in Japan. In 1891, concerned about the future of several Japanese women who had been rescued and converted to Christianity in San Francisco but "were obliged to be sent back to Japan," Flora B. Harris, an M.E. missionary wife working in San Francisco, urged her fellow missionary workers in Tokyo to keep the rescued women under Christian influence upon their return to Japan.[19]

Also in 1892, Kate Youngman, a Presbyterian missionary woman in Tokyo, saved nine girls from being sold into prostitution in Gifu, an area recently hit by an earthquake. With funds from Miss E. Merritt, a philanthropist in New York, Youngman started "rescue" work in Tokyo by using her own residence. Furthermore, in 1893 Youngman's initiative received the official support of the Ladies Conference in Tokyo-Yokohama, an interdenominational meeting of foreign missionary women. In 1894 the Ladies Conference appointed a committee composed of American missionary women, including Kate Youngman, Maria True, and Matilda Spencer, to start the rescue home project. The project was also assisted by Japan WCTU officers such as Kajiko Yajima and Chiseko Ushioda. Through the joint efforts and contributions of American missionary women and Japanese WCTU officers, a plot of land with an old house in the suburbs of Tokyo was purchased in 1894. The rescue home project, however, required more funding and work to get it off the ground.[20]

American missionary women working for this rescue home project in the Tokyo-Yokohama area saw Denton's call to form a national WCTU for Western missionary women working in Japan as a golden opportunity. By organizing the national WCTU which required members to pay dues, the deadlocked rescue home project would be able to secure interdenominational missionary support and funds from all over Japan. While attending a missionary conference in Kobe in September 1895, Maria True indicated her strong support for Denton's effort. Denton therefore delegated the matter to True, who worked in the region where the largest number of

Protestant missionaries resided. As a result, the World WCTU branch of foreign women in Japan was organized at the Ladies' Christian Conference of Tokyo-Yokohama in 1895. Matilda Spencer of the M.E. Church became its first president.[21]

The new union was called "the Auxiliary WCTU of Japan" since its members intended to be an "auxiliary" to the World WCTU. Although the constitution of the Auxiliary stipulated that it would "assist and encourage the workers" of the Japan WCTU for "the promotion of Temperance, Social Purity, Sabbath Observation, etc.," Western missionary women still experienced language and cultural barriers between them and their Japanese sisters and thus felt that "more could be done, and in much less time" if their organization was kept separate from the Japan WCTU. The Auxiliary's constitution also stated that it would form departments similar to those currently existing in the WCTU in America, thus encouraging Auxiliary members to take up WCTU causes in addition to their rescue efforts. Nonetheless, Protestant missionary women subordinated temperance to their Christian and benevolence work, and thus the bylaws of the Auxiliary, like those of the Japan WCTU, did not require each member to make a pledge of abstinence from drinking and smoking.[22]

The Auxiliary was based in the Tokyo-Yokohama area, but it intended to become a national organization and had the clear means to do so. In accordance with its constitution, eight committees were formed to take charge of the eight departments. The three most important of these were located in the Tokyo-Yokohama area, while the remaining five were set up in other local cities with relatively large missionary populations. The constitution also required the formation of a "membership committee" made up of representatives of each of the participating denominations in the Tokyo-Yokohama area, and of representatives of other areas where ten or more missionaries, regardless of denomination, resided.[23] The Auxiliary thus used both the city-based interdenominational networks, which connected missionaries of different denominations working in the same city, and the denomination-based intercity network, which linked missionaries of the same denomination in different areas.

These networks of American missionary women, now strengthened by the formation of the Auxiliary, were successfully utilized by a new class of World WCTU missionaries sent to live and work as residents in a specific country for a substantial period of time to strengthen the organizational basis of the WCTU union in that country. Between 1896 and 1913, the World WCTU sent four additional World WCTU "around-the-world" missionaries, who fell in this category, to Japan. They were Clara Parrish (who worked in Japan from 1896 to 1898), Kara G. Smart (1902–1906), Flora E. Strout (1908–1910), and Ruth F. Davis (1909–1913). The World WCTU also hired Eliza Spencer-Large, a former Canadian Methodist missionary working in Japan who had been discharged from her mission, between 1898 and 1901.[24] Unlike earlier World WCTU travelers who visited Japan between 1886 and 1894, Parrish, Spencer-Large, Smart, Strout, and Davis lived in Tokyo for several years while guiding, coordinating, and promoting WCTU activism in Japan. As a result, between 1896 and 1913 Japan WCTU and Auxiliary members worked closely together under the guidance of the World WCTU workers, and also cooperated with male temperance workers who established a national organization in 1898.

Founding the Organizational Basis for WCTU Activism in Japan

Arriving in Japan in October 1896, the World WCTU's seventh "around-the-world" missionary, Clara Parrish, soon realized the troubled condition of the fledgling Japanese women's national organization under Yajima's leadership. With WCTU expertise in generating a mass movement, Parrish decided that the upcoming Japan WCTU's annual meeting would be "the largest temperance meeting ever held" in the country. She reported in January 1897:

> The printed directory of the native women gives the names of the officers of ten local unions, but a correspondence with them reveals the fact that nearly all are greatly discouraged. What wonder! Mrs. Yajima is busy with her school work, and cannot go to give the needed instruction and inspiration, and there has been no one else. Under similar conditions, enthusiasm would wane anywhere. Their annual meeting comes in April. Mrs. Yajima has given us "the right of way," and we shall endeavor to have all things bend to make this the largest temperance meeting ever held in Japan, using western methods as much as possible, and asking all other societies to contribute something to the program.[25]

In an ambitious endeavor to promote the WCTU's philosophy and methods advocated by Frances Willard to the Japan WCTU and the Auxiliary, Parrish translated Willard's *Do Everything: A Handbook for World White Ribboners* into the Japanese language.[26] In the book, Willard argued that "everything [was] not in Temperance Reform but Temperance Reform should be in everything," and that "agitate, educate, and organize . . . [were] the deathless watchwords of success." Willard's book also emphasized the importance of using "systematically united efforts" to generate a women's mass movement and provided pragmatic and detailed guidelines on how to organize and manage WCTU unions and activities.[27]

Recognizing that the Japanese women's union had never been organized along the lines of the WCTU despite its affiliation with the World WCTU, Parrish attempted to enforce the application of WCTU methods on it, while also introducing Western parliamentary procedure and a democratic system of representation. In keeping with the temperance cause and the "Do Everything" policy, Parrish successfully persuaded the Japan WCTU at its 1897 convention to broaden the scope of its work. As a result, fifteen Japanese superintendents were appointed to take charge of fifteen departments, including "Work among Soldiers" and "Scientific Temperance Instruction in the Public Schools."[28] At the 1898 convention, the Japan WCTU, following Parrish's suggestions, made changes to its constitution and determined that a local union's representation at the national convention should be in the ratio of one delegate for every twenty-five members.[29]

To strengthen WCTU activism in Japan, Parrish also assisted in the work of the Auxiliary. When the Auxiliary held its first annual conference in November 1896, Parrish became recording secretary and took charge of the World WCTU pages in the *Japan Evangelist*. She also promoted the translation of WCTU leaflets and tracts into Japanese for use by missionary women in their regular gospel activities.[30] At the same time, Parrish tried to obtain funds for their deadlocked rescue home project to take care of debt and secure a new building. By the end of 1897, she received a favorable response from Mr. Charles N. Crittenton, the American millionaire philanthropist who had been assisting the WCTU with its "rescue" work.[31] Parrish secured the services of Eliza Spencer-Large to take charge of the rescue home project in 1898, which led the World WCTU to hire Spencer-Large as its resident worker in Japan until 1901.[32] In 1903 the rescue home finally gained a new building with contributions from the Crittenton Mission and Miss E. Merritt in New York as well as funds raised by Japan WCTU and Auxiliary members.[33]

Her good relations with Auxiliary members allowed Parrish to use their intracity interdenominational and intercity denominational networks to transform the Japan WCTU into a national organization. As a former national organizer for the WCTU's Young Women's Unions (Ys) in America, Parrish traveled throughout Japan to persuade Japanese students at local city female mission schools, which were under the management of Auxiliary members, to become Japan WCTU members. Parrish's organizing efforts quadrupled the paid membership of the Japan WCTU to almost 1,100. As a result, at the fourth World WCTU Annual Convention in Toronto in 1897 the Japan WCTU was awarded the banner for the largest percentage increase in membership.[34]

Furthermore, Parrish was able to reconcile the two distinct national unions of Japanese women and foreign resident women in Japan by persuading Auxiliary members to assist the Japanese women's national organization. At the second annual meeting of the Auxiliary in 1897, Parrish called on female foreign residents in Japan "wherever possible, to identify themselves with the Japanese unions, thereby strengthening the hands of their sisters and fellow workers."[35] She succeeded in making the foreign residents' union an auxiliary to the Japan WCTU rather than to the World WCTU. Consequently, the female foreign residents' national union became "the Foreign Auxiliary" to the Japan WCTU, and commenced paying a portion of its members' annual fees to the Japan WCTU's treasury instead of the World WCTU's. This entitled it to send representatives to the Japan WCTU's annual conventions and to have its members assume any office connected with the Japan WCTU.[36]

While she successfully strengthened the organizational infrastructure of WCTU activism in Japan and "raised" its standards to those of the World WCTU, Parrish was nonetheless naive about Japanese cultural and social conditions as well as the individual agency of Japanese churchwomen and American missionary women. For example, Parrish believed that she was reinstating the word "Christian" in the Japan WCTU's Japanese name by persuading Japanese members to change their organization's name to Nihon Kirisutokyō Fujin Kyōfūkai (Japan Christian Women's Reform Society) at the 1897 Japan WCTU convention.[37] However, unlike Parrish, both Japan WCTU and Auxiliary members were well aware of the strong anti-Christian sentiment of the Japanese public and thought that "the society could not and would not thrive if it was known to be a Christian organization."[38] Thus, contrary to Parrish's expectations, Japanese WCTU women did not use the new name in public until 1905.[39] In addition, both American missionary women and Japanese churchwomen interpreted Willard's emphasis on temperance as introduced by Parrish in their own way. Foreign Auxiliary members, who were initially "not in sympathy with

W.C.T.U. methods"[40] and regarded them as being too secular, soon realized the efficacy of temperance for their gospel work. One American missionary woman wrote that the WCTU's temperance work was "not only . . . combined, but that the latter [was] a distinct help to evangelistic work in general, by opening up many doors for direct Christian teaching."[41] Some Japanese WCTU officers on the other hand thought Parrish was advocating nondrinking for its own sake over and above other causes and resisted it by arguing that advancing women's status was a much more urgent task than temperance work. Thus Taneko Yamaji, editor of the Japan WCTU's official magazine, argued that unless Japanese women's virtues and independence were developed first it would be virtually impossible to promote nondrinking. For many members of the Japan WCTU, temperance continuously took a backseat to other causes.[42]

In light of these misunderstandings and disagreements with members of the Japan WCTU, Parrish turned to Japanese male Christians, who had been the main promoters of the temperance cause and who had more status, resources, and freedom to support her endeavors. On lecture tours for WCTU causes in Japan, Parrish was often accompanied by Rev. Kanichi Miyama, a male temperance evangelist appointed by the M.E. Conference in Tokyo who had successfully promoted the temperance cause with Tarō Andō in Hawaii in the late 1880s.[43] Parrish also cooperated with other Japanese male temperance workers and an M.E. missionary doctor, Julius Soper, in forming a national organization of male-led temperance societies. Parrish's efforts resulted in the inauguration of Nihon Kinshu Dōmei (Japanese Temperance Union) in late 1898, uniting twenty Japanese male temperance societies from all over the nation and one foreign male society.[44] Leading the union were Christian male temperance workers such as Tarō Andō, Shō Nemoto, and Sen Tsuda who had been cooperating closely with American World WCTU women since the late 1880s. "Cordially invited" to become "associate members of the Board of Control" of the league were five women of the Japan WCTU who had been assisting Parrish and male temperance workers.[45] Once again, male temperance workers continued to play important roles in the World WCTU's temperance movement in Japan.

In the conservative Japanese climate of the 1890s, nineteenth-century American churchwomen's strategy of stretching women's sphere by emphasizing women's special capacity without confronting male authority was a practical means of sustaining and expanding the Japan WCTU's social activism. Collaborating with men, Parrish successfully invigorated the

WCTU movement in Japan and secured a niche for the Japan WCTU in late Meiji Japan. As Parrish had originally declared in January, the 1897 WCTU national convention became the largest temperance meeting ever held in the country, in distinct contrast to the 1896 Japan WCTU convention held before her arrival. Even so Parrish remained unsatisfied, speculating that "the largest audience that assembled at any time did not exceed 800" because of "the heaviest rains of the season."[46] The following year, she made the Japan WCTU national convention an even larger event by bringing together Japanese WCTU women, Foreign Auxiliary members, male temperance workers, churchpeople, and "the most distinguished 'honorables' of the land—members of Parliament, foreign ministers, judges, and even former members of the Emperor's cabinet itself."[47]

Parrish's achievement in promoting temperance work, however, fell short of strengthening the Japan WCTU in its fight against the conservative political forces in the country; instead it encouraged its members to assist male temperance workers by using women's special ability and nonpolitical influence. Although the 1897 and 1898 conferences were presided over by Yajima and other Japan WCTU officers, and Japan WCTU and Foreign Auxiliary members presented reports and participated in business discussions, the greatest fanfare was reserved for male speakers, especially those of high social standing who were committed to the temperance cause. Although these men emphasized women's special ability they nevertheless assigned women to secondary roles and restricted them to the women's sphere. Parrish reported that the 1897 convention opened with speeches by Dr. Soper and two "Japanese gentlemen discussed woman's place in reform." According to her report, "the central thought" of their speeches was that "we must have the *help* of our mothers, wives, and daughters, if we are to overcome the evils of the past," and their arguments were "to the great satisfaction of the writer."[48]

Reporting on the 1898 convention, Parrish wrote enthusiastically about the attendance of "the real nobility of the country," including "the political aristocracy which [was] usually so difficult to secure." Among these men were "Hon. Tarō Andō, Ex-minister at foreign court; Hon. Shō Nemoto, a member of the new Parliament; and Hon. Mr. [Keigo] Kiyoura, a member of the former Matsukata Cabinet."[49] While Andō emphasized the primacy of temperance as a cause for reform,[50] Kiyoura, in Parrish's words, argued that "everything depended upon the home," and that "as woman was the centre of the home influence, she must be educated, or the community, and the larger home—the government—would suffer [a] loss."[51] According to a transcript of Kiyoura's speech published in the Japan WCTU's official magazine, he asserted further that civilization would promote the division of professional labor and women should execute their duties at home. In his opinion, women's societies should work to purify society through women's innate capacity for benevolence and morality rather than through political activity.[52]

At the same time, Parrish supported Kajiko Yajima, who was patient and skillful in her capacity as president of the Japan WCTU. Parrish wrote that although Yajima was "so far from the center of operations, and unable to read English," she often surprised her "by her foresightedness and knowledge" of WCTU ways. Parrish described Yajima as "a superior woman, wise in her discussions with her countrymen concerning woman's place in the world, not embittering them, yet often carrying her point and convincing by her own womanliness."[53] In fact, at the fifth World WCTU Convention held in Edinburgh in 1900, Parrish went so far as to say that Yajima was "the Frances Willard of the East!" She praised Yajima as "a priceless jewel to our organization, the emancipator of the women of her land, and . . . the Greatest, these days, of our international band."[54] Outliving the founding members of WCTU activism in Japan, Yajima eventually acquired the charisma that Willard had enjoyed in the organization. Yajima's pragmatism was crucial for the Japan WCTU in not only surviving the conservative era but also in establishing itself as a respectable organization with social influence. However, Yajima may not have been as willing or as capable of manipulating the hegemonic ideology of womanhood for the advancement of women's status as Willard.

Overall, Parrish provided vital assistance to the troubled Tokyo churchwomen's organization to enable it to survive and grow in the increasingly conservative political climate of the late Meiji era. The WCTU methods she propagated did a great deal to transform the structure and appearance of the Japan WCTU on the model of the WCTU in America. At the fifth World WCTU convention in 1900, Parrish reported her achievements in Japan as follows:

> We saw the National W.C.T.U. Convention of Japan grow from a purely local meeting of half a dozen women, with no delegated powers, [which] therefore could not be called a convention at all, to a meeting of four or five hundred members, some of them coming a distance of fully five hundred miles. We saw these bodies organized as conventions are in the West, with secretaries, press reporters, committees on credentials, courtesies,

publications, telegrams, and even a stenographer. We saw our banners and mottoes displayed; our flags intertwined. We saw native women preside, with the grace and dignity of queens, during the whole of a three days' session, and we saw them introduce to immense audiences at night some of the most distinguished "honorables" of the land.[55]

Ushioda and Socialist Consciousness

While Yajima collaborated with Parrish in promoting the growth of the Japan WCTU in the 1890s, Chiseko Ushioda, along with a few other Japan WCTU members, maintained the spirit of protest and reform after Sasaki's departure. The WCTU structure promoted by Yajima and Parrish, often described as a "department store of women's activism" due to its involvement in a variety of causes in the United States, allowed Japan WCTU members with different interests to work for causes that they felt were important. One such cause was antipollution. Ushioda and her sympathizers came to play an important role in Japan's first antipollution movement by demanding that a mining company discontinue its operations. This group of Japan WCTU activists was critical of Japan's capitalistic development at the expense of the poor.

The mining company operated a mine in Ashio, north of Tokyo in Tochigi prefecture. It had originally been developed by the Meiji government in an effort to promote Japanese industries in the late 1870s. Ten years later, the Meiji government sold the Ashio mine to the Furukawa family, one of the emerging *zaibatsu* (financial cliques). Under the new owners, production of copper in the mine soared, ultimately polluting a nearby river with poisonous waste. By the 1890s, the devastating effects on farming, fishing, and people's lives in the area were so grave that the pollution problem became a political issue. Although the Meiji government ordered the Furukawa family to take preventive measures in 1897 in response to victimized farmers' demands that the Ashio mine be shut down, the situation did not improve. When the farmers protested once again, the government ruthlessly suppressed them.[56] Subsequently, in the early 1900s women from the pollution victims' group, whose husbands and brothers had been arrested by the police, became activists themselves, presenting petitions to members of the Imperial Diet and conducting sit-ins in front of the House of Peers.[57]

At this time, Shōzō Tanaka, a former Diet member who had led the victims' protest movements, began to organize a volunteer group in Tokyo to investigate the pollution problem. Joining him was a group of Japanese Christian activists who had been supporting pollution victims since the late 1890s.[58] At Tanaka's suggestion, Ushioda, Yajima, and other Japan WCTU members joined the volunteer group on a one-day investigative trip to the pollution site. Shocked by the devastation in the area, Ushioda called for the formation of a women's relief group backed by the Japan WCTU. As a result, Kōgaichi Kyōsai Fujinkai (Mine-Pollution-Site Relief Women's Society, MRWS) was organized in late 1901, electing Ushioda as its president.[59]

Ushioda had acquired political clout through her work as a WCTU activist since the days of the Tokyo WCTU. Her MRWS aroused the compassion of women and students for the victims, and they started a movement to stop the pollution and to safeguard the welfare of the victims. Ushioda wrote to the owner of the Ashio copper mine, repeating the farmers' demand that the mine be shut down, and published and distributed a leaflet calling for support to end the pollution and to aid the victims. Although the Ministry of Education ordered public school principals to prohibit students from visiting the pollution site, more than one thousand students participated in a field trip organized by the MRWS. In order to raise funds and public support, Ushioda traveled extensively with male Christian activists to speak about the devastation of the pollution victims, and the MRWS collected 7,101 yen by June 1902. MRWS members repeatedly visited the victims along the polluted river to provide medical care and to distribute relief. Twelve orphans and daughters of impoverished farmers were sheltered in 1901 at the "rescue" home in Tokyo, managed by the Foreign Auxiliary with the assistance of the Japan WCTU. The MRWS also provided vocational classes for the female pollution victims.[60] Ushioda's leadership in the MRWS received broad support from Japan WCTU members, and she was elected president of the Japan WCTU in April 1903. However, after a few months Ushioda died of stomach cancer, thus returning the presidency to Kajiko Yajima.[61]

Protest and political activism in the Japan WCTU resumed its downward slide with Ushioda's death. The rise of antipollution activism had coincided with the emerging labor and socialist movements of the late 1890s, in which women and Christian activists played important roles. But this led to the reinstatement of the ban on women joining political organizations and attending political meetings as per Article 5 of the Police Security Law (Chian keisatsuhō) issued by the government in 1900 to repress the labor and socialist movements. Although female members of a short-lived socialist group, Heiminsha (Commoners' Association), led a movement to reverse Article 5, only a few Japan WCTU members joined. By then the antipollution movement had lost momentum due to the government's suppression and appeasement measures, and the public's attention shifted to the looming international problems leading to the Russo-Japanese War. Although Heiminsha women successfully introduced a petition for revision of Article 5 in the Imperial Diet in January 1905, the government forced the organization to dissolve in October after it voiced its opposition to Japan's imperialistic war. Assisted by liberal members of the Lower House, petitions continued to be introduced in the Diet until 1909 but fruitlessly so, and the socialist women's political movement waned.[62]

Eventually the Japan WCTU realized the importance of women's political rights through their work in antiprostitution campaigns and the influence of the International Woman Suffrage Alliance (IWSA), but this did not happen until the more liberal Taisho era (1912–1925). The Japan WCTU cooperated with young bourgeois women in reversing Article 5 in the early 1920s and in demanding woman suffrage through the 1920s and the 1930s. Led by a younger generation of officers with a good command of English, the Japan WCTU established Nihon Fujin Sanseiken Kyōkai (Japan Women's Suffrage Association) in 1921 in order to represent Japan in the international woman suffrage movement led by the IWSA.[63]

Propagating Temperance in Late Meiji Japan

American WCTU methods and strategies, advocated by American World WCTU missionaries to save the dwindling Tokyo churchwomen's organization, Americanized the Japan WCTU. But on the other hand, the sociohistorical context of late Meiji Japan also Japanized the temperance movement led by the American World WCTU missionaries, who had ambitious plans for social change. For example, curbs on drinking, the cause that Willard believed to be at the heart of WCTU activism in non-Christian societies, were hampered by the deeply rooted Japanese custom of sake drinking. In Japanese society, offering sake is a symbolic gesture of hospitality, appreciation, or generosity, and drinking the offered sake in turn signifies acceptance and respect. Moreover, the high tax on liquor, attributed to the growing protemperance sentiments of the Japanese middle class, became a good source of national revenue—an ironical result of the American WCTU missionaries' efforts. In frustration, Parrish wrote in 1898:

> The laws and customs which control the sale and use of liquor in this land, are so entirely different from those of western countries that a foreigner feels powerless at times, especially in public speech, to say what would tend to decrease the evil, or even to be understood by Japanese friends.[64]

Smoking, on the other hand, was so widespread among both Japanese men and women that it was a less formidable target of WCTU campaigns in Japan. Parrish believed that the Japanese per capita consumption of tobacco was one of the highest in the world, and that the Japanese were "most willing to listen and [be] open to conviction" as long as it was on the issue of tobacco.[65] Foreign Auxiliary members were especially willing to participate in an antitobacco crusade because they were bothered by the fact that smoking was so prevalent among Japanese women as well as men.[66]

Unable to initiate a mass movement among Japanese adults for temperance on drinking and smoking, American WCTU workers turned to impressionable children and youngsters. Across the Pacific in the United States, where the immigrant population was increasing, the WCTU had recognized the importance of influencing children and youth, and established the Young Woman's Branch (Ys) in 1894 to enlist young women of college-going age as members. It also started the Loyal Temperance Legion (LTL) in 1896 to recruit boys and girls of primary and high school age.[67] Parrish had introduced the WCTU's new efforts to Japan by establishing two departments promoting the work of the Ys and the LTL, respectively, by 1897.[68]

Collaborating with male Temperance Union workers, Foreign Auxiliary members, and younger generation Japan WCTU members, Parrish successfully led the antismoking movement for Japanese youth by appealing to the ardent nationalism of late Meiji Japan. She suspected that "the ashen hue of the flesh, the dull eye and sunken cheeks of so many of the half grown boys" she met in Japan, were caused by the widespread habit of smoking. Parrish promoted the "fact" that in America during the time of the Spanish-American War, "of the young men who had volunteered, in the states, 90 percent of those who used cigarettes were rejected as unfit to serve their country, while only 10 percent of nonusers failed to pass their medical examinations."[69] Nonsmoking among Japanese youth became an important cause to secure fit soldiers for Japan's imperialistic ambitions in Asia. In 1900, concerned about the health of future soldiers, the Imperial Diet passed an antismoking bill introduced by Shō Nemoto, prohibiting minors from smoking.[70]

At the same time, WCTU's "work among children" came to take on special meaning in Japan. While Christians never exceeded 1 percent of its population, Japanese parents seemed to pay the utmost "attention" and be willing to "sacrifice" for their children. When Jessie Ackerman, an extensive traveler for the World WCTU, made her second visit to Japan in 1901, she reported on the importance of work among children in Japan as follows:

> The very fact of the great interest in the well-being of children, would make it an easy matter to establish a temperance movement that would soon include thousands in its ranks. . . . The young women are coming slowly into active service, and to-day the battle cry is, "Capture the children!" . . . Japan needs a special worker for children. There is but one L.T.L. and I am convinced that one could be formed in every city, village, and hamlet, regardless of religious belief, for even among non-Christians there is a great desire to promote those things that pertain to the welfare of the children.[71]

While Japan WCTU old-timers were more committed to their own movement to correct sexual double standards and to abolish the licensed prostitution system, American World WCTU resident missionaries emphasized juvenile work to realize their vision of WCTU work in Japan. By emphasizing to women the "sacredness and value" of "the vocation of motherhood," without allowing themselves to be a "toy of men," Smart introduced new methods and vocabularies that would also help Japanese women's efforts. At her welcoming reception in 1902, Kara Smart declared:

> As an organization, we firmly believe that the hope of Temperance Reform is in the pre-emption of childhood and youth by the slow, but sure processes of education to total abstinence for the individual, and prohibition for the state. . . . Can we choose a work which shall bring about greater and more beneficent results for the future of your nation, than to reach and to teach these young people that "there is but ONE standard of

purity for men and women, and that they are *equally* capable of living up to it? Can we present to them a purpose more beautiful in thought and in reality than that of attaining the "White Life for Two?"[72]

To spread the temperance movement among Japanese children and young students, the WCTU in America infused personnel, expertise, and money into its work in Japan. To aid Clara Parrish, the Ys in America established the Missionary Fund in 1898. And to support a Japanese LTL worker assisting Kara Smart, the LTL in America began raising money in 1905, an effort later called the Anna Gordon Japan Fund. To raise money, the members of local Ys and LTLs in the United States held bazaars and Japanese entertainment nights and sold WCTU booklets and postcards.[73] Their efforts enabled Parrish, Smart, Strout, and Davis to hire younger Japanese women as assistants and to introduce WCTU methods of juvenile work to Japan.[74] Parrish and Smart translated the WCTU's English materials into Japanese.

Smart, Strout, and Davis toured Japanese schools with their young Japanese assistants to provide "scientific temperance instructions" by using physiological charts and materials, and they were welcomed not only at mission schools but also at private and public schools and even at Peeress School.[75] Smart introduced the strategy of recitation and essay contests on "prohibition, total abstinence, narcotics, purity and kindred topics" among pupils and students of public and private schools.[76] She believed the medal contests were "faster and surer than any other known force" in overcoming "indifference and opposition" to WCTU causes, because the children of saloon keepers, wine drinkers, and white ribboners as well as their parents, siblings, and relatives would turn out to hear the young people speak.[77]

World WCTU missionaries also approached Japanese pupils and students directly through the departments of LTL, Ys, and Sunday school work which organized boys, girls, young men, and young women "into armies against [the] three-fold enemy" of "smoking, alcohol drinking, and foul thinking."[78] They taught Japanese children "temperance truth" from the "religious," "moral," and "scientific" standpoint.[79] To spread WCTU juvenile work nationwide, Ruth Davis and Azuma Moriya, a Japanese LTL organizer, in 1909 started giving classes once a month "to train young Japanese women who wish to do temperance work among children, either through" an LTL or Sunday school.[80]

By effectively utilizing the WCTU's pragmatic methods, organizational skills, and American money, and by modifying the tools to suit the socio-cultural context of late Meiji Japan, the temperance movement led by American World WCTU missionary women came to have a substantial influence on some social issues. By 1922, WCTU activism among children and youth had generated enough support to pass the "antidrinking bill," another bill introduced by Shō Nemoto in the Diet to prohibit minors from drinking intoxicating liquors.[81] Transplanted into anti-Christian and prodrinking late Meiji Japan, the movement focused its temperance re-form work on minors.

Nationalism, Imperialism, and the WCTU Movement in Japan

While the pragmatism of American WCTU missionary women was re-sponsible for the success of their temperance among Japanese minors, Japan's two imperialistic wars, the Sino-Japanese War (1894–1895) and the Russo-Japanese War (1904–1905), greatly affected the course of the Japan WCTU. As the Emperor established himself as the divine symbol of the nation and the father of the people during the late Meiji era, the Japanese churchwomen's organization could not continue to exist without proving that its members were "loyal" subjects of the Emperor and the state. In-deed, many Japanese churchwomen were as eager as the Japanese public in their support for and collaboration with the Japanese government in ad-vancing Japan's status as an imperialist power in the Western-dominated world hierarchy. As the Japan WCTU cooperated with the Japanese gov-ernment in fighting the two wars, it is hard to tell whether the Japan WCTU used the opportunity to improve its public image and expand its influence or whether the Japanese government took advantage of the or-ganized power of churchwomen to assure itself of the people's allegiance to the state. In this process, the Japan WCTU transformed its purpose from that conceived of by American WCTU workers, namely, to reform Japanese society in light of the American WCTU's vision, to one that aimed to expand Japanese churchwomen's influence in Japan and Japan's control over its neighbors.

Japanese Christians easily combined the Christian emphasis on selfless service in God's cause with patriotic devotion to the Emperor and the nation. Barring a small group of Christian socialists, Japanese Christians enthusiastically accepted Japan's imperialistic expansion in Korea, Taiwan, and Manchuria. At the same time, despite anti-Christian accusations that followers of the "one and only God" were potential traitors to Imperial Japan, the majority of Japanese Christians were as patriotic and loyal to the Emperor as were non-Christians and anti-Christians. Umeko Tsuda was a good illustration of this.[82] Even though she left Japan at age six and converted to Christianity while growing up in pious Protestant communities in America, for her Christianity and the Emperor system were not only compatible but mutually reinforcing. Excited about the Japanese victory in the Sino-Japanese War in 1895, Umeko Tsuda wrote that she attributed the victory to "the intense patriotism" of the people rather than Western methods or clever military tactics. She proudly stated that in her country "men and women, educated and uneducated, even down to the lowest ranks of society, [had] shown themselves capable of understanding the highest ideals of self-sacrifice for a cause which they [had] been taught to regard as sacred." Drawing an analogy between Japanese obeisance to the Emperor and Christian devotion to God's cause, Umeko Tsuda asserted that Christianity would only strengthen the willingness of the Japanese to sacrifice themselves for their nation:

> Patriotism . . . is in itself a religion. The same feeling of joy experienced by the Christian martyrs when being tortured for a righteous cause, is felt in the sufferings experienced in this war for the country's honor. The same feelings which we can imagine the friends would experience on hearing of the suffering and death of a martyr—feelings of grief, mingled with a holy joy—are felt when the news of a death on the battle-field is received. The Emperor is the being for whom all this is done. He is the personification of the country. He is the one for whom all fight and endure. He is, in truth, a god who receives the services of his worshippers, and at the same time, guides and protects them. . . . Christianity will only tend to strengthen the feeling of devotion to the country and to a cause. Without in any way lessening the zeal, it will make it run into broader channels, and the result will be a purer and higher type of patriotism than has ever been known in any country in the world.[83]

American Protestant and World WCTU missionaries successfully introduced their wartime practices to the Japan WCTU through Japan's two imperialistic wars. During the Sino-Japanese War, the Japan WCTU published and distributed a booklet that praised soldiers for dying gloriously for their nation and preached the gospel as a way the bereaved regain their strength and sense of peace through faith in God.[84] In 1897, when Clara Parrish broadened Japan WCTU activism by establishing fifteen departments along the lines of the WCTU in the United States; one of these was the Department of Work among Soldiers, created in the Japan WCTU. In America this department aimed to raise soldiers' morality to the level of Protestant middle-class women by reaching out to "the Army and Navy with Gospel and Temperance work." The soldiers' department in the Japan WCTU, however, undertook "little or no work" because there was "no definite plan to follow" until the Russo-Japanese War. At this time Kara Smart decided to make the department fully operational by promoting WCTU practices in Japan.

In 1904, Smart and the superintendent of the Japan WCTU's soldiers' department published their recommendations for work among soldiers both in the Foreign Auxiliary's pages of the *Japan Evangelist* and in the Japan WCTU's official publication. They called on local members of the Japan WCTU and the Foreign Auxiliary to establish a soldiers' department and to raise funds so that they could conduct evangelical temperance work among Japanese soldiers while providing them "comfort," "cheer," and "encouragement."[85] Soon members of the two organizations began visiting hospitals with gospel and temperance literature. Some of them met soldiers on station platforms and "busied themselves in sewing on missing buttons, mending rips, and in many other ways making [soldiers] as comfortable and pleasant as possible," while others visited battleships to show their welcome and gratitude to foreign and Japanese crews.[86]

Of all the work the WCTU did for soldiers in Japan, the comfort bag campaign was a particular success. The comfort bags can be traced at least as far back as the U.S. Civil War when churchwomen, many of whom later became leaders of the WCTU, played leading roles in the U.S. Sanitary Commission and other soldiers' aid societies. For example, Mary A. Livermore recorded that every box of supplies sent by local women's aid societies contained handwritten notes to soldiers and a good supply of "comfort bags," which "usually contained a small needle-book, with a dozen stout needles in it, a well-filled pin-ball, black and white thread, buttons, etc."[87] Later, the WCTU used "comfort bags" to distribute temperance and gospel literature along with practical amenities to servicemen.[88] In the

United States, the WCTU's comfort bag campaign reflected American churchwomen's commitment to the cause of temperance as well as their desire to make a motherly, selfless contribution to their nation and its boys.

However, when Japanese WCTU women carried out the comfort bag campaign during the Russo-Japanese War, it quickly turned into an outlet for Japanese women's patriotic zeal and was welcomed both by the Japanese government and the public. In 1904, the Japan WCTU's *Fujin Shinpō* started to carry a picture of the "comfort bag" used in America, directions for making one, and an explanation of its features. As an experiment, Japan WCTU members sewed and filled six hundred bags. These were accepted solely by the Navy, as the Army had rejected them. Soon, sailors who received the bags responded with letters and postcards of gratitude, and the War Department of the Japanese government, initially reluctant to accept bags from the churchwomen's organization, asked the Japan WCTU to procure more bags—for the Army as well as the Navy. Eventually, members of the Imperial household and aristocracy joined the Japan WCTU's comfort bag campaign as it was embraced by people from all walks of life.[89]

Under Yajima's leadership the Japan WCTU enthusiastically responded to the War Department's request. Designated by the Department as the organization in charge of the comfort bag campaign, the Japan WCTU gave sewing instructions for the bag, sold machine-made bags, collected them after they were filled by people, and inspected each one to remove items that were objectionable to the WCTU cause and the Japanese government. Since the state no longer objected to the Bible, Japanese WCTU women took out the cigarettes as well as antiwar and antigovernment literature, and replaced them with temperance and religious leaflets, gospels, or Testaments. The War Department provided free transportation for the bags collected and checked by the Japan WCTU, and asked for no less than ten thousand bags at one time, and as many as ten thousand lots. According to Smart, Kajiko Yajima, whom the government made individually responsible for every bag, bore "the burden joyously and fearlessly" and announced that the Japan WCTU "would not only reach that high mark, but would surpass it."[90] After the massive success of the campaign, the Japan WCTU became a respectable organization in Imperial Japan. Henceforth it began publicly carrying the word "Christian" in its Japanese name, and became known as Nihon Kirisutokyō Fujin Kyōfūkai.[91]

Kajiko Yajima, Kara G. Smart, and Tsuneko Gauntlett, (Smart's interpreter) from "Union Signal," December 29, 1904. *Courtesy of the Chicago Historical Society Prints and Photographs Department.*

"Instigators of Their Own Illusions"

At the turn of the century, Japan's imperialistic expansion into neighboring countries was not antithetical to the interests of American churchwomen on the transnational network of Anglo-American missionaries and the WCTU in Asia. In China, antiforeign sentiment culminated in attacks against foreign consulates, Protestant missions, and Chinese converts during the Boxer Rebellion of 1900. Thus American Protestant missionaries welcomed Japan's role in suppressing the rebellion with American and European troops and Japan's expeditionary forces remaining in China. American missionary women, who fled the danger and confusion in China for the security and tranquility of Japan, praised Japan's military action as an effort to bring about "justice."[92] Japan's war against Russia was also in accord with the national interests of the United States, which wanted to check the expansion of Russian and European power in China. Although the Foreign Auxiliary created the Department of Peace and Arbitration in 1904 to "counteract the tendency for militarism" in the world, its members supported the participation of Japanese WCTU women in Japan's war efforts and their use of female mission schools as centers for comfort bag campaigns during the war.[93]

While promoting the WCTU movement in Japan during the Russo-Japanese War, Kara Smart recognized the war's positive effect on expanding the scope of the WCTU's work in Japan. She reported:

> Today the ears of high and low are opening to hear the message we bring. . . . The war, instead of hindering our work, as we once feared it would, has magnified a thousand fold our opportunities, and has opened avenues for our entrance we had thought could not be reached perhaps for years. . . . The hospitals are full of sick and wounded soldiers, over fifty thousand being in Japan already, and many more on the way. . . . Many of the authorities in the hospitals have earnestly invited Christian workers to hold weekly meetings and to do personal work therein.[94]

After the war, Smart renewed her efforts to raise American money by emphasizing the need for the WCTU movement in Japan. She argued that temperance work among Japanese soldiers should be promoted because "800 out of 1,000 of the cases of illness in the camps and barracks [were] due to the drinking of alcoholic liquors." Furthermore, there was a special need for purity work because "two-thirds of the soldiers who [were] returned as 'sick'" had contracted sexually transmitted diseases like syphilis, which Smart described as "the result of immorality." Smart asked her comrades in the United States to send money to secure temperance, purity, and gospel leaflets for free distribution in Japan.[95]

As the Japanese public became less hostile to Christianity and more receptive to WCTU movements promoted by American and Japanese churchwomen, American World WCTU missionaries and Auxiliary members poured their motherly affection on Japan, to which they had committed themselves. Like American missionaries and scholars who found more similarities than differences between the Japanese and Christian Anglo-Saxon races after Japan's victory over Russia,[96] American WCTU workers now viewed Japan as a progressive nation that embodied the WCTU movement's principles better than Russia. According to them, Japan owed its victory to its success in keeping its armies "sober" despite its "inferior warships and guns."[97] Nevertheless, Japan was described as a "young" country which had progressed largely through "its imitative and ambitious spirit" and was still in need of "moral uplift" and America's "superior experience and training."[98] This young Asian nation's need for American guidance was further emphasized on account of its growing impact over its neighbors in Asia. As Japan's imperialistic presence in Asia increased, it would become "the keystone" of WCTU influence in the East, largely determining "the character" of the people in "China, Korea, and Manchuria."[99] This appeal compelled American churchwomen to raise funds to support American World WCTU resident missionaries, the Foreign Auxiliary, and the Japan WCTU for their work in Japan.[100]

The positive image of young Japan that World WCTU missionaries were partially responsible for creating, together with the Japanese government's control of the press, which concealed Japanese atrocities and injustices in neighboring countries, blinded both Japanese and American WCTU workers to the reality of Japanese imperialism. Shedding a positive light on Japan's colonization of its neighbors, Japanese and American WCTU workers collaborated with each other to increase the role of Christians and the WCTU specifically in the "uplift" of the lands newly placed under Japan's rule.

As early as 1906, the Japan WCTU's *Fujin Shinpō* carried an article calling for the need to send Japanese WCTU organizers to "cultivate the spiritual fields" in Korea by organizing Korean Christians for their cause.[101] For five months from 1907 to 1908, Tsuneko Watanabe, a graduate and teacher of a Congregational female mission school in Kobe who served as president of both the Japan WCTU Kobe Union and the Japanese Congregational women's missionary society, visited Korea to assist in Japanese evangelization efforts started by Japanese Congregationalists.[102] Concurrently but separately, Anglo-American residents in Korea also endeavored to increase their influence by establishing a WCTU branch. Although it was not until 1923 that a Korean women's union was established,[103] their efforts resulted in the creation in November 1911 of a WCTU branch among Anglo-American residents in Seoul, which Ruth Davis called "the Foreign Branch in Korea."

Miss Pindar, who had worked for the WCTU in England but at the time resided in Seoul, became the first president of this union. Through the invitation of Dr. Mary M. Cutler of the American Methodist Mission in Seoul, who served as treasurer of this WCTU branch, Ruth Davis and Tsuneko Watanabe visited Korea in 1912. Davis and Watanabe's efforts to promote the WCTU movement in Korea were welcomed and facilitated not only by American and Japanese churchwomen but also by the Japanese colonial government's officers and their wives. Davis and Watanabe visited the cities of Seoul, Chemulpo (present-day Inchon), Pyongyang, Chinnampo, Taegu, and Pusan, giving temperance lectures at churches, YMCAs, female mission schools, hospitals, and Japanese "Ladies' Patriotic Society." This resulted in the formation of a Japanese women's union in Seoul and another Western women's union in Chinnampo in 1912.[104] Their collaboration inadvertently supported the Japanese colonial government, whose ultimate purpose was the subjugation of Korean Christians as well as American Protestant missionaries and the enforcement of Japanese rule in Korea.[105]

While advocating WCTU methods and philosophies as envisioned by American middle-class Protestant women in Japan, American World WCTU missionary women became agents of the "Americanization" of Japan. As participants in the transnational network of the World WCTU, Japanese WCTU women also played a part in this Americanization process. Concurrently, however, by collaborating with Japanese women to expand the WCTU's influence in Japan and in Japan's colonies, American World WCTU missionaries stationed in Japan came to accept Japan's imperialistic expansion in East Asia and ultimately assisted in the "Japanization" of the region, which later put Japan and the United States on a collision path. This uneasy relationship between American World WCTU missionary women and their Japanese clients is best described in the words of historian Ian Tyrrell:

Collaboration and solicitation always played their parts as the WCTU confronted the non-Anglo-Saxon world. Often it was the non-American, even the non-Western clients who sought to extend the [World] WCTU's domain, and the leaders of the movement in America were as much the victims of misleading assessments of power and potential at the periphery as they were the instigators of their own illusions.[106]

4

Beyond Japan to California

Issei Christian Activism in
Northern California, 1870s–1920

Japanese and American Churchpeople in the California Bay Area and the Moral Uplift of the Japanese Immigrant Community

By the time the first World WCTU around-the-world missionary Mary Leavitt visited Japan in 1886, a transnational network between American churchpeople and Japanese immigrants had emerged on the American Pacific Coast. Japan's encounter with the technologically advanced West in the 1850s triggered the immigration of Japanese students to the United States in the 1860s. After the Meiji Restoration in 1867, increasing numbers of Japanese students, many of whom were from the former samurai class which had lost its means of livelihood with the fall of Tokugawa feudalism, began to cross the Pacific. They did so in order to advance their career opportunities in the new Meiji Japan and to assist their fledgling nation by learning about modern civilization from the United States. Those who were sponsored by the government went to the East Coast, but many who were self-funded landed in the California Bay Area and attended school while struggling to earn a living doing housework for a family as a "schoolboy."[1]

Arriving in San Francisco in the 1870s, these self-supporting Japanese pioneers found the necessary assistance from American clergy and churchwomen activists who had been working among Chinese immigrants since the mid-nineteenth century. Thus Christianity had a strong grip over the Issei pioneers in San Francisco. The first Issei organization in California was Fukuinkai (Gospel Society), an interdenominational organization of Japanese students who associated themselves with American Methodists, Presbyterians, and Congregationalists in San Francisco.[2] In

1877, using funds from the women's society of the First Congregational Church in San Francisco, the Gospel Society rented a room in the basement of the Methodist Episcopal (M.E.) Chinese Mission House, which was under the management of Rev. Otis Gibson, and began to hold regular gatherings. As the first Japanese immigrant organization, the Gospel Society also endeavored to meet the needs of their compatriots in the area by providing accommodations, conducting English classes, and finding jobs for them as "schoolboys" or "schoolgirls" at the M.E. Chinese Mission House with the assistance of American churchwomen from different denominations.

Although denominational differences among Gospel Society members, coupled with Japanese racism against the Chinese, led to the formation of several offshoots, it continued its activities until the San Francisco earthquake in 1906. It worked in close association with the Home Missionary Society of the M.E. Church which formed a separate mission for the Japanese (M.E. Japanese Mission) in 1886.[3] The Gospel Society came under the influence of Rev. Merriman C. Harris, who had returned from thirteen years of missionary work in Japan and had become the superintendent of the M.E. Japanese Mission. Among the early members of the Gospel Society were Shō Nemoto and Kanichi Miyama, who were later involved with the WCTU's transnational temperance movement. Shō Nemoto, who played a major role in establishing antidrinking and anti-smoking laws for minors in Japan, gave up drinking and pledged abstinence when he was a member of the Gospel Society in San Francisco. Kanichi Miyama, who later promoted gospel and temperance work in California, Hawaii, and Japan often collaborating with American and Japanese WCTU workers, was ordained by Rev. Otis Gibson at the M.E. Chinese Mission House. Miyama played a leading role in establishing and managing the Gospel Society in its early days, and became vice superintendent when the M.E. Japanese Mission was established in San Francisco.[4]

Japanese women, although very small in number, were also active in the Gospel Society in its early days and endeavored to form a separate women's society. Among them were self-supporting students and wives of Japanese government officials and businessmen. The fact that the Japanese immigrant community at its inception owed a great deal to American churchwomen allowed female members to participate in the management and activities of the Society on a more egalitarian basis than in later years. For example, female members were granted the right to elect and to be elected to the board in 1883, and a few of them were in fact elected as board members of the Society.[5] While enjoying equal status in managing the Society, female members also wanted to form a separate women's society. In 1883, "seven to eight" female members of the Gospel Society invited "four to five" nonmembers and formed Fujin Jizenkai (Female Charitable Society) to conduct charity and evangelical work.

Although the mobile and transient nature of the Japanese immigrant community in the early 1880s kept the Female Charitable Society from taking off, the arrival of leading Japanese women in the course of the decade enabled it to become active in the late 1880s. These women included Mrs. Miyama, Rev. Miyama's American-educated, newly wedded wife from Japan, and Mrs. Fujii, the wife of the newly appointed Japanese consul-general in San Francisco. Also influential was Mrs. Flora B. Harris, who had worked as a missionary in Japan. As the influence of Rev. and Mrs. Harris over the members of the Gospel Society grew and as the wives of the elite Japanese took over the leadership of the Female Charitable Society, however, female members of the Gospel Society came to focus on the separate organization. This put an end to the joint management of the Gospel Society by men and women.[6]

During this period, Tel Sono joined the Female Charitable Society.[7] Unlike many members of the Society who were financially dependent on their elite Issei husbands, Tel Sono was a self-supporting student who was also working as a "schoolgirl" for American families. Thus, she interacted more closely with American women than other members of the society. According to her autobiography (published in English by her American benefactress), Sono left her husband, a former samurai who could not adjust to the rapid changes that followed the Meiji Restoration, and came to the United States on her own in an attempt to learn "the custom[s] of people where women stood on the [same level] with men." Arriving in San Francisco in her late thirties in 1886, Sono soon learned that the bank where she had deposited her savings had gone bankrupt. Through the help of the Gospel Society and a public employment office, she was able to support herself by doing housework for American families. When she was out of work, she stayed in a room in the basement of the M.E. Chinese Mission House studying English and attending church services. When a public school rejected her because of her advanced age, her employer made it possible for her to attend a private school. Under an arrangement made by her "kind teacher," her school fees were waived in exchange for her teaching art to kindergarten children. Sono graduated from the school and was baptized at the M.E. Japanese Mission in 1889.[8]

As a working woman, Sono was much more sympathetic to Japanese prostitutes than other members of the Female Charitable Society. While Sono was active in the society, she approached Japanese men and women engaged in the prostitution business, whom "everybody [had] been afraid to speak against." When one Japanese prostitute died, Sono and male members of the Gospel Society made it possible for the woman to be buried in the Japanese Mission burial grounds. Attending her funeral and the Buddhist ceremony that followed (the expenses of which were covered by the brothel manager and the woman's coworkers), Sono spoke in her sermon about the grief of the woman's parents when they would learn about their daughter's life in America.[9]

However, as the pioneer Issei community faced the strong anti-Asian sentiments of the American public, the Gospel Society and Female Charitable Society, composed mainly of elite Isseis in San Francisco, increasingly emphasized the moral reform of their community so as to avoid the misfortunes that had befallen the Chinese immigrant community. In the late nineteenth century, when China's last dynasty was on the wane and unable to fend off the military encroachments of the Western powers, the center of world civilization in Japan's view shifted from China to the West. Having started on the path of westernization before China, Japan now considered China a backward country.

Japanese prejudice against China was further reinforced by American racism, which targeted Chinese immigrants in California during the late nineteenth century. West Coast American labor organizations directed their animosity against Chinese immigrants because they were willing to provide "cheap labor," while the American middle class criticized Chinese prostitutes, who traded their sexuality in a semifeudal manner. By 1870, American racism against the Chinese halted Reconstruction-era reform efforts to extend naturalization rights to nonwhite persons other than those of "African nativity or descent." Foreign-born Asians were categorized as "aliens ineligible for citizenship" until the mid-twentieth century. In 1875 Congress passed the Page Law forbidding the entry of Chinese, Japanese, and Mongolian contract laborers, as well as women of any nationality who would engage in prostitution. In 1882 the Chinese Exclusion Law stopped the entry of all Chinese laborers into the United States.[10]

To prevent American racism from targeting Japanese immigrants, the Issei elites wanted to demonstrate that the Japanese were different from the Chinese, being more "civilized" and more like Americans. Thus they became increasingly concerned about the existence of Japanese prostitutes and other less-educated "indigent" Japanese in the United States who could not easily be taught American middle-class moral and cultural values. Despite the Page Law, Japanese prostitutes spearheaded the migration of Japanese laborers and found work in mining camps in the interior in the early 1880s. In the late 1880s, they appeared in cities on the Pacific Coast to meet the demand of growing Japanese immigrant communities. Concurrently, Japanese laborers, who had just ended their three-year contract terms in Hawaii, started to immigrate to the U.S. mainland.[11] As the Japanese community in San Francisco multiplied and diversified in the 1890s, American newspaper articles picked up on the existence of Japanese prostitutes in San Francisco and spread the image of San Francisco's "immoral" male-dominated Japanese immigrant community.[12]

This development negatively affected the Issei community in the city. The American middle class came to fear the influence that adult Japanese bachelors studying at American public schools would have over innocent American children. In 1893 the San Francisco School Board decided to force Japanese students out of public schools for whites into the segregated schools for Chinese children. However, adult Japanese male students were self-supporting students of the Issei elite, many under the strong influence of American churchpeople. The collaborative efforts of the American clergy and schoolteachers together with the Japanese government and immigrant leaders successfully reversed the decision. Even so, elite Japanese immigrants felt a strong need to eliminate undesirable elements from their community.[13]

In an attempt to keep the American public from targeting on their community, Japanese immigrant leaders began to try to stop the migration of indigent persons. Believing that the high visibility of Chinese prostitutes was one of the main reasons why anti-Chinese sentiment was so strong in America, in the late 1880s and early 1890s elite Japanese immigrants appealed to the Japanese government to take measures against the overseas migration of Japanese prostitutes.[14] In 1894 Rev. and Mrs. Harris reported that young Japanese men in San Francisco had organized an "Anti Vice Society" to "destroy a social blight which they keenly [felt] to be a national disgrace."[15] Internalizing Protestant American middle-class values and standards, the pioneer Issei elites believed that they could avoid becoming the target of the public's anti-Asian hostility by promoting the moral uplift of their community and by eliminating undesirable elements.

Japanese churchwomen in the Bay Area also participated in this effort by calling upon their trans-Pacific network of Japanese WCTU women.

Like the elite males, they believed that moral suasion was ineffective in preventing newly arriving Japanese women from engaging in prostitution in America, and sought the legal intervention of the Japanese government. Mrs. Masue Kawaguchi, of Sausalito, California, who had been an active member of the Female Charitable Society in the Bay Area but also retained her Tokyo WCTU membership, mailed the following letter to her fellow WCTU members in Tokyo in 1890:

> Three years ago when I came to this land, Japanese women in this area counted only ten or so. I met seven to eight of them at such occasions as church meetings. Then I heard the number of Japanese women was grad-ually increasing and I wondered where those women had gone. Asking around, I learned that many of them were engaging in the business, which I hesitate to mention. So, with the efforts of like-minded sisters such as Mrs. Miyama and Mrs. Fujii, we founded the [Female] Charitable Society to work for the newly arriving women and to prevent them from falling into the evil paths. The two sisters, however, had left for Hawaii and New York, and those of us who were left behind with limited power had been concerned about the issue that was too difficult to tackle. In collaboration with Miss Tel Sono and male members, we had been active to meet every steamer and to ask every arriving woman about their future means of liv-ing. Six to seven out of ten responded ambiguously and promised to see us at the church or the Charitable Society. By the following day, however, these women hid themselves somewhere and many fell into the business that appears and disappears mysteriously. . . . I ask the sisters of your Union to make efforts for the prevention. . . . I request you to petition the appropriate authorities for [its] control and to make further efforts for some good means.[16]

After receiving similar letters from abroad, the Japanese Foreign Ministry and Tokyo WCTU women recognized the urgent need to stop the overseas migration of Japanese prostitutes. As early as 1891, the Japanese Ministry of Foreign Affairs presented a Japanese Woman Protection Bill to the Im-perial Diet, which proposed to punish not only those who solicited or as-sisted in the migration of Japanese women for prostitution but also the prostitutes themselves.[17] Tokyo WCTU women petitioned the Imperial Diet for the passage of this bill despite the fact that it would criminalize Japanese prostitutes.[18]

However, the bill never became law because the large foreign currency remittance by Japanese prostitutes working overseas were vital to Japan's economic development.[19] Nevertheless, the Foreign Ministry issued an ordinance in 1893 to prefectural governments in charge of issuing passports, instructing them to make an extra effort to prevent Japanese women from being kidnapped or lured into prostitution for export.[20] For Japanese WCTU women, the Foreign Ministry's ordinance was necessary but not sufficient, and the demand for the prohibition of the overseas migration of Japanese prostitutes became the third pillar of the Japan WCTU movement, following the revision of the civil and criminal law to correct the sexual double standard and the abolition of the licensed prostitution system.[21]

Reflecting middle-class Japanese women's animosity toward geishas, concubines, and prostitutes during the Meiji era, discussed in chapter 2, Japanese churchwomen both in Japan and the Bay Area were more concerned about the reputation of their nation than with the plight of Japanese prostitutes. They were chagrined at the image that these "unenlightened" women created of "Japanese" women overseas, and viewed their overseas existence as a national "disgrace."[22] Despite the collaborative efforts of the Japanese government, elite Japanese immigrants, and Japanese churchwomen activists on both sides of the Pacific, however, Japanese prostitution in San Francisco did not suffer a setback. Rather the business was driven into the back alleys of Chinatown. At the same time, bars and restaurants replaced brothels in the Japanese immigrant community so that Japanese barmaids and waitresses could work for tips rather than wages.[23]

American and Japanese Churchwomen and Prostitutes

Japanese churchwomen who sought to improve their community's morality and image in collaboration with male community leaders in the Bay Area, worked with American churchwomen who had been engaged in missionary work in California since the mid-nineteenth century. Their work was based on the same evangelical impulse as the American Protestant churchpeople who dispatched missionaries overseas. After the Civil War, while churchwomen in the East were eagerly organizing to "save" their "heathen" sisters in foreign lands, the attention of churchwomen in

California was directed to Chinese women on American shores. In the 1860s, American churchwomen in San Francisco started an interdenominational evangelical effort for Chinese women in the city, culminating in the establishment of the Woman's Union Mission to Chinese Women and Children, San Francisco, in 1869.[24] In the 1870s, these interdenominational American churchwomen's efforts were divided and consolidated along denominational lines by denominational women's missionary societies. Presbyterian women formed the California Branch of the Woman's Foreign Missionary Society of the Presbyterian Church, Philadelphia, in 1873, which developed into the Woman's Occidental Board of Foreign Missions (WOBFM). They secured a room to shelter "rescued" Chinese women and girls, which evolved into the Presbyterian Chinese Mission Home in San Francisco, better known as Cameron House because of its brave matron, Miss. Donaldina M. Cameron.[25] As for the Methodists, Rev. and Mrs. Otis Gibson initiated work among Chinese women[26] to raise funds and to work on behalf of "rescued" women within the M.E. Chinese Mission House in San Francisco. Their efforts resulted in the organization of the Woman's Missionary Society of the Pacific Coast (WMSPC) in 1870. The "rescued" women were accommodated in the rooms of the Chinese Mission House. In 1901 they were transferred to a separate building, which later became the WHMS's Oriental Home.[27] When Frances Willard visited San Francisco in 1883, it was Rev. Gibson who escorted her through Chinatown. This inspired Willard to expand WCTU activism across the Pacific and around the world, thereby internationalizing the WCTU network.

Although American churchwomen were willing to extend their rescue efforts to Japanese women in the city, their monolithic view of Asian and "Japanese" women were resented by middle-class Japanese churchwomen who wanted to differentiate themselves from "Chinese" women and to eliminate Japanese prostitutes from the U.S. Pacific Coast. Instead of "rescuing" Japanese prostitutes, Japanese churchwomen's activism in San Francisco focused on the "protection" of virtuous Japanese women. Thus American churchwomen had to modify their approach to make it acceptable to middle-class churchwomen activists. Some American missionary women, such as Flora Best Harris, who had worked with the Japanese for two decades and was well-versed in their language and customs, spoke up for Issei churchwomen and assisted them in their efforts. To obtain support for the "home" established in San Francisco by a minister of the (Japanese) Pine Methodist Church and his wife to provide safe housing for female students and working women from Japan in 1893,[28] Flora Best

Harris appealed to the Oriental Bureau of the Woman's Home Missionary Society (WHMS) of the M.E. Church which had taken over WMSPC's work for Asian women. While the M.E. Chinese Mission House was capable of providing shelter for Chinese as well as Japanese women, Harris insisted on the need for a separate home for Japanese women in San Francisco. She wrote:

> Some of your readers may wonder why a Japanese and Chinese home cannot be combined. The experiment has been tried, and good has been accomplished; but such a plan could never by any possibility become permanent in its character, any more than a home filled with English women and the daughters of southern Europe could hope for lasting success. Rescued girls of Japan could be placed under the same restrictions as those required for the Chinese girl under like circumstances; but the Japanese working woman accustomed to considerable freedom in her native land, expects to come and go as freely as in Japan. A little home of the Christian Association type is the only practicable way of helping her in right living.[29]

Persuaded by this argument, the WHMS's Oriental Bureau became the primary provider for the Japanese Woman's Home and appointed Miss Ella J. Hewitt, a missionary who had recently returned from Japan, as its director.[30] With the increased number of Japanese women in California, work among Japanese women came to be administered independently by the WHMS's Japanese Committee in 1903, and by the Bureau of Japanese and Korean Work in 1905 when Japan made Korea its "protectorate."[31] With $4,000 contributed by a WHMS auxiliary in Wyoming, the Home was furnished with a new building in 1904 and became the Ellen Stark Ford Home (ESF Home) for Japanese and Korean women and children.[32]

Unlike the "rescue" homes in Chinatown, the ESF Home in the Issei community in San Francisco was closed to Japanese prostitutes. Although American missionary women, who worked closely with elite Issei, felt a strong impulse to save "heathen" women, whether they were respectable or not, they remained faithful to middle-class Issei churchwomen's desire to raise the image of "Japanese" women among the American public. Flora B. Harris herself often engaged in the "rescue" of Japanese prostitutes and requested her fellow American missionary women working in Japan to build a home in Japan for "rescued" Japanese women awaiting deportation, as discussed in chapter 3. However, Harris wrote in 1894 in the WHMS's official magazine that the Japanese Woman's Home in San Francisco was a place for "the innocent or simple hearted, ensnared through ignorance" and not for those "hardened offenders."[33]

In the early 1900s, with growing numbers of Japanese women arriving in the Bay Area, "the tiny rooms" called the Japanese Woman's Home were "overflowing" with Japanese students and workers.[34] The brothel dens in Chinatown, meanwhile, were occupied by Japanese prostitutes. Reporting on her "rescue" work in 1905, Miss Margarita Lake, the director of the ESF Home at the time, pleaded for "a friend, home, and refuge" for Japanese prostitutes, but still insisted that "we could not invite any of these girls to our Home, for it [was] filled with the pure and innocent."[35] The ESF Home remained a place where Christian influence was provided to virtuous Japanese women who had crossed the Pacific to study, to work as domestics, or to be married, and to unfortunate Japanese children in need of parental protection. According to Rev. Herbert B. Johnson who became superintendent of the M.E. Japanese Mission in 1904,[36] the mission of the ESF Home was to conduct "preventive" but not "rescue" work.[37]

Since the ESF Home was only open to the "pure and innocent," some Japanese prostitutes found shelter at "rescue" homes in San Francisco's Chinatown. According to records from the WOBFM of the Presbyterian Church that managed Cameron House, the House had Japanese inmates between 1890 and 1907. Mrs. Annie Sturge, the wife of Dr. Ernest Sturge who supervised the Presbyterian Japanese churches and missions on the Pacific Coast, took charge of the Japanese work. The number of Japanese women living there reached its peak in 1905 when twenty-two previous residents were joined by eighteen new ones. According to Annie Sturge, among the eighteen new arrivals, "six were rescued from a life of shame, six others came from their own free will and sought shelter under our roof and six more were entrusted to our care by the Immigration Bureau for deportation."[38]

It was easier for American matrons to get Japanese prostitutes in than to hold them, and their stories were "less thrilling" than those of Chinese prostitutes.[39] Started in the mid-nineteenth century, the traffic in Chinese women soon came under the control of Chinese secret societies. Tighter U.S. measures to exclude Chinese prostitutes and the soaring cost of procuring women in the 1870s and 1880s created systematic corruption and increased the incidence of kidnapping.[40] On the other hand, many Japanese prostitutes came to the United States, lured by male and female procurers who portrayed America as a land where people could get rich quickly. By the time they learned the truth, however, they were in debt for their trans-Pacific journey and thus unable to escape the "shameful" business for fear of even worse conditions for themselves or their families in Japan.[41]

Moreover, the prospects for the rescued Japanese women staying at the House were somber, unlike those of rescued Chinese women. In the Chinese community, the practice of foot binding hampered middle- and upper-class Chinese wives from emigrating to the United States, while U.S. exclusion laws kept working-class wives out. Thus, some rescued Chinese women, who subscribed to American moral and cultural values under the influence of American missionary women, married Chinese Christian men selected by American missionary matrons. Constituting an important part of the middle-class Chinese immigrant community in San Francisco, these Chinese Christian women collaborated with American missionary women in their rescue efforts.[42] In contrast, the middle-class Japanese community had a strong drive to exclude prostitutes. According to Annie Sturge, the rescued Japanese women in the Home were either deported to Japan or escaped repatriation by returning to their business.[43]

Some Japanese women trapped in the business of prostitution, however, were able to use their stay at Cameron House as a stepping-stone to a better life and to assist American churchwomen in their rescue efforts in return. One such woman was Waka (Asaba) Yamada, a once-married woman who had sailed to the United States in an attempt to reverse her own parents' declining fortunes. Waka spent the late 1890s in a brothel in Seattle but managed to flee to San Francisco with her suitor, an Issei newspaper reporter. But their funds ran out while they were on the run, and so Waka was sent to a brothel in San Francisco. From there she escaped to Cameron House in the early 1900s. Her suitor pursued her to Cameron House, but Donaldina Cameron, who monitored visitors to the House very strictly, denied him access to her. He subsequently poisoned himself to death in despair.

Waka was baptized and remained in Cameron House for a few years, assisting in American churchwomen's rescue work as a Japanese interpreter and taking classes in English and sewing given by American and Japanese teachers. She also attended a nearby private school owned and run by her future husband Kakichi Yamada, the son of a farmer who had come to the United States at age twenty to work and receive an education.[44] Donaldina Cameron described Waka as a "clever, interesting girl, who after sad and bitter experiences in her own life [knew] how to sympathize with, help and guide her unfortunate sisters who [sought] shelter in our Home."[45] Waka had also become indispensable to Annie Sturge in her Japanese work in the House. With the assistance of Waka and Japanese pastors of the First Japanese Presbyterian Church in San Francisco, the number of Japanese residents at Cameron House increased in the early 1900s.[46] When Waka married Kakichi Yamada and returned to Japan after the 1906 earthquake destroyed his school,[47] Annie Sturge was in "crying need . . . for a consecrated Christian Japanese woman who [would] devote her whole time to their country women in this institution."[48] But although Japanese women continually arrived at Cameron House, none of them were able to replace Waka Yamada. Thus, they remained "transients" and gradually disappeared from the House after 1907. In 1912 Annie Sturge wrote, "for the past two years very little has been done in the Rescue Work of Japanese women and girls for the lack of a suitable Matron who understood their language."[49]

The Sound Development of the Japanese Immigrant Community and the Practice of "Picture Brides"

Neither Issei churchwomen's work to protect virtuous Japanese women nor American missionary women's efforts to rescue and transform Japanese prostitutes into Christian ladies could prevent the American public from targeting the Japanese community in San Francisco. In their attempt to safeguard Japanese communities on the American Pacific Coast from American racism toward Asians, Issei community leaders intensified their collaboration with the Japanese government as well as American authorities. In August 1900, rising anti-Asian sentiment among American workers who demanded the reenactment of the soon-to-expire Chinese Exclusion Law and the adoption of similar measures against Japanese laborers, pressured the Japanese government to stop issuing passports to Japanese laborers bound for the continental United States. Nonetheless, this measure was ineffective as Japanese workers continued to arrive in California via the Hawaiian Islands.

Furthermore, opposition to adult male Japanese students studying at public schools in San Francisco surfaced once again, resulting in the San Francisco School Board's decision to segregate Japanese students in 1906. This decision was revoked after the intervention of President Theodore Roosevelt. But he also issued an executive order to prohibit the entry of aliens whose passports had been issued for destinations other than the

U.S. mainland, thus closing the door to Japanese immigration via the Hawaiian Islands. At the same time, the two governments reached a so-called "gentlemen's agreement" when the U.S. ambassador to Japan and the Japanese foreign minister agreed that the Japanese government would cease to issue passports to Japanese laborers in exchange for the U.S. government admitting Japanese students, businessmen, as well as the family members of bona fide Japanese residents into America.[50]

Concurrently, Issei leaders endeavored to unite and help the Japanese consulates control the flow of Japanese immigrants to the Pacific Coast. In 1900, when the San Francisco Board of Health enforced the inoculation of the entire Chinese and Japanese population in the city against bubonic plague, Issei leaders, indignant at this discriminatory treatment, developed a network connecting Japanese immigrant communities along the entire Pacific Coast. The same year Japanese residents in San Francisco formed the Japanese Deliberative Council of America to "expand the rights of Imperial subjects in America and to maintain the Japanese national image." The founding members of the Council included Issei Christian leaders of various denominations, a Buddhist leader, and a Japanese government representative. Similar organizations were soon formed in other cities such as Oakland and San Jose, and in 1906 the local councils coalesced into a statewide organization, the United Japanese Deliberative Council of America. The United Council became the Japanese Association of America in 1908, linking Japanese communities on the Pacific Coast under the auspices of the Japanese government through its consulates.[51]

Issei leaders and organizations, in collaboration with the Japanese government, tried to secure the sound development of Japanese communities in America. Their efforts resulted in the spread of the picture bride practice. As the new century unfolded, the measures taken by the U.S. and Japanese governments slowed the arrival of the Japanese working class. Those who were already in America had improved their status from self-supporting students and laborers to small businessmen and farmers, and now wanted to establish families in the new land. Some sent for wives they had married before crossing the Pacific. Others returned to Japan to marry and brought their brides back with them. The majority, however, could not afford the time or money to go back to Japan to get married. According to a Japanese community newspaper, the practice of the picture bride began in 1905 or 1906 when two Issei men in San Francisco married women in Japan after exchanging pictures. Although one of the marriages was successful while the other ended in failure, the practice of the picture bride, whereby a marriage procedure was completed under Japanese law after an exchange of letters and pictures without the bride and groom ever meeting each other, soon spread among Issei bachelors in California.[52] The picture brides of Japanese residents in the United States crossed the Pacific with passports issued by the Japanese government. Japanese immigration to the United States was partially regulated by the branch of the Japanese government that controlled the issuance of passports, unlike Chinese immigration, which was completely in the hands of American authorities executing U.S. laws.[53]

Although Issei leaders admitted that it was clearly undesirable for a man and a woman to get married before meeting each other, they viewed the picture bride practice as an "appropriate," "efficient," and "essential" means for the "sound development" of the Japanese "race" and "colonies" in America.[54] Japanese churchwomen as well as American missionaries working among the Japanese, such as Dr. E. A. Sturge, supported the practice and Issei efforts to turn their community from one of sojourners to one of permanent settlers.[55] As increasing numbers of Japanese picture brides arrived in San Francisco in the late 1900s, the WHMS's ESF Home provided temporary accommodations and care for newly arrived Japanese brides waiting to meet their grooms.[56] A Japanese Young Women's Christian Association started by an interdenominational group of Japanese churchwomen in the Bay Area in 1912, also provided safe accommodations and classes in English, sewing, and music for virtuous girls and wives of their community.[57] Furthermore, to protect the practice from the growing suspicion of the American public, the Japanese government imposed strict requirements on the parties. Thus the husband had to have a minimum amount of money in savings, determined by occupation, the age difference between the couple could not be more than thirteen years, and brides had to pass both a physical and a reading examination before their departures.[58]

Mary M. Bowen, Unhappy Picture Brides, and Issei Communities

While Japan's ambitions for an empire that equalled those of Western powers forced Japanese women to be "good wives and wise mothers" dedicated to the prosperity of their husbands' households and their nation, Issei community efforts to transform their society from one of sojourners to one of permanent settlers meant that picture brides had to play the same role in America. Although a picture bride was liberated from the control of in-laws to whom she was required to be always filial, she came under the surveillance of tightly-knit community networks controlled by male Issei elites who demanded her subjugation to her husband.

The practice of marrying picture brides was not so different from traditional Japanese marriage customs, in which a couple's family network and their parents' opinion played an important role. But it was an adventure for a bride to start her married life with a stranger in a foreign land. Deprived of the protection and assistance of her own family and relatives, a wife's fortune depended entirely on her unknown husband, and the experiences of picture brides in the United States were often rather disappointing. Living in America, far away from his family and future bride, a prospective husband often gave a false impression of himself by sending old touched-up pictures, exaggerating his occupational status, and mailing sophisticated love letters written by a well-educated friend. A picture bride who crossed the Pacific dreaming of her fairy-tale married life with a rich gentleman was often shocked by the gap between her expectations and the reality of her husband and life in America. Thrown into a strange land, however, she had no alternative but to marry as required by U.S. law[59] and to join her husband in his work in a store, farm, or labor camp while keeping house. Most couples who began their married lives this way cooperated with one another to overcome hardship and eventually came to share common interests and much-loved children, just like their counterparts in Japan.[60]

However, some disappointed picture brides tried to liberate themselves from the bonds of marriage by resorting to *kakeochi* (elopement). In Japan *kakeochi* normally referred to the elopement of a couple whose parents were opposed to their marriage, but in Issei communities it meant that a wife had left her husband to be with another man. This indicates that the behavior of an Issei wife was controlled by her husband rather than by her parents or parents-in-law. During the late 1900s and early 1910s, Issei community newspapers carried numerous elopement stories about desperate picture brides fleeing from their husbands. Side by side with these articles were ads placed by the husbands offering a reward for their wives' return. The eloping couples were eventually found by the tightly knit Issei community networks. The Japanese Association cooperated with husbands in their search for "unfaithful" wives and numerous prefectural associations also assisted in the wife hunts. Because of the language barrier, eloping couples could only hide in Issei communities in different cities or in labor camps, which were under the umbrella of interconnected Japanese community networks.[61] Once a couple was found, "unfaithful" wives could be deported to Japan in disgrace, as the Japanese civil code granted a husband the right to decide the site of his wife's residency and Issei men closely followed the Japanese practice. Upon the request of Issei community leaders, Cameron House and the M.E. WHMS's Oriental Home in San Francisco sometimes provided temporary housing for women awaiting deportation.[62]

A majority of American missionaries did not question the power structure or cohesiveness of the Issei community. But there was at least one missionary woman in California who challenged the gender hierarchy of both American and Issei societies in the pursuit of her calling. She was Rev. Mary M. Bowen, a former missionary of the M.E. WHMS and founder of the Independent Japanese Mission in Sacramento. Her attempts to rescue unhappy Japanese picture brides, whom she viewed as "victims of the 'photograph marriage,'"[63] created great controversy in Issei communities in northern California at the turn of the century.

Mary Bowen was born into the Southern gentry class,[64] married young of her own will and had one daughter, but was forced by her father to get a divorce at age nineteen.[65] Perhaps her bitter experience with the divorce caused her to obstinately resist male authority. Bowen never remarried. Instead she taught at women's educational institutions in Ohio and Pennsylvania,[66] and worked as a missionary of the M.E. WHMS in Georgia and Ohio[67] while contributing articles to various magazines. In 1893, she came to California and associated herself with the Methodist First Church in Oakland, which was then assisting in Issei church work. The M.E. Church's newspaper, the *California Christian Advocate*, sometimes carried reports about the church's parish work written by Mary Bowen, who was described as an "assistant and visitor."[68] She also became a member of the California WCTU.[69]

In the late 1890s, Bowen began working actively among Japanese immigrants and joined Japanese pastors in their evangelical efforts for the growing Japanese immigrant communities in California. Like American World WCTU missionaries in Japan, she bypassed the gender hierarchy of Japanese society and interacted freely with Japanese men. Nor was she subject to the supervision of male clergy, as American churchwomen conventionally were. In 1898, while teaching at an English-Japanese school attached to the (Japanese) Pine Methodist Church in San Francisco,[70] she often traveled to the Sacramento Valley and promoted temperance and the

Christian gospel among the increasing number of Japanese farm laborers in the area. In 1899, she wrote as an "evangelist":

> If the accusation be true that every mother has her favorite child, though she herself is unconscious of it, then it is possible that the farm-side of the work has been mine. Up and down the valley, among camps and tents and out through sun-parched vineyards, I have driven at all hours, from four in the morning to long after dark. The loneliness and isolation of these farmers touches the deepest feelings of a Christian heart.[71]

Bowen's unstinting efforts on behalf of Japanese men, however, met with the disapproval of Rev. Merriman C. Harris, who supervised M.E. missionary work for the Japanese in California. Under his supervision, only ordained Japanese male preachers were allowed to do evangelical work among their countrymen. While American Methodist women were active in church and missionary work, they were discouraged from seeking ordination and preaching the gospel among men.[72]

Bowen therefore decided to pursue her calling by herself. She commenced her work in March 1899 in Sacramento, independently of the M.E. Japanese Mission. Flora B. Harris, the able but faithful wife of Rev. Harris, took up her pen to speak on behalf of Bowen in a Methodist newspaper:

> Mrs. Bowen, for some time associated with the Sacramento work, is now busily engaged in a large school for Japanese students of English, a service for which she is especially well qualified. Although, as the *Advocate* recently noted, no longer officially connected with the Japanese church, she is in a position to help our people very effectively in an independent way, and we bid her God-speed in the good work. They remember with gratitude her skillful care of the sick and suffering in the past, and regard her as a type of what the Christian nurse should be, albeit called "evangelist and teacher."[73]

Despite Flora B. Harris's goodwill, however, Mary Bowen did not intend to limit herself to being a nurse, an evangelist, and a teacher. What Bowen wanted to create in Sacramento was not simply an English school for the Japanese, but an "Independent Japanese Mission" consisting of a church, school, and boarding house for the Japanese, similar to other M.E. Japanese missions on the West Coast. The only difference was that a woman, not a man, would be at the helm. For this purpose, Bowen sought ordination.

As early as 1908, an article in the *Sacramento Bee* referred to her as "Rev. Mary Bowen."[74] In 1916 the Church of the United Brethren in Christ first listed her as an ordained minister in its *Year Book*.[75] In 1924, Bowen was ordained in the M.E. Church by Local Elder's orders.[76] Thus, Bowen managed to run her own mission outside the male-controlled M.E. home missionary enterprise.

Since Bowen was not familiar with the Japanese language or customs and many Japanese immigrants were not yet accustomed to English or American practices in the early 1900s, their interactions at Bowen's Independent Japanese Mission in Sacramento were fraught with misunderstanding. During the pioneering days of the Sacramento Issei community, Bowen extended her assistance to self-supporting Japanese students and laborers in various ways: by providing accommodations, English instruction, financial aid, and so on. In return, some of her beneficiaries showed their deep appreciation.[77] However, Bowen also imposed her moral and cultural values on the Japanese immigrants, and some of them fought back. When dealing with Japanese immigrant men, Bowen sometimes called in the police when she felt she couldn't handle them. For example, in 1900 she got into an argument with one of the residents of her Mission, Mr. Uichirō Urabe, called in the police, and had him detained on charges of insanity. Urabe was released through the efforts of three doctors, one Japanese and two American, but Bowen later accused the Japanese doctor and a Japanese teacher working at her mission of assault. This misunderstanding was straightened out in court, but it soured relations between Bowen and those she had accused.[78]

When Bowen began to engage in "rescuing" unhappy Japanese picture brides caught up in unfortunate marriages, the disputes between her and some Issei men grew more heated. Once a Japanese woman had taken shelter in Bowen's Independent Japanese Mission, she was under Bowen's protection. Bowen exercised her authority by monitoring the woman's visitors, thus putting the woman beyond her husband's reach, although he was being assisted by Issei community authorities and their networks. In 1908, a Japanese wife named Yoshi Tsunoda ended her unhappy marriage while staying at Bowen's Mission. Yoshi had come to the United States in 1907 as a picture bride, but her husband, Seishichi Tsunoda, abused her because she refused to contribute financially to their household by working as a prostitute. By the time Yoshi arrived at Bowen's Mission, she had been so badly beaten that she had difficulty walking. Tsunoda visited Bowen's Mission several times to see Yoshi but Bowen refused his requests.

Rev. Mary Bowen and members of her Independent Japanese Mission in
Sacramento. *Courtesy of the Sacramento Archives and Museum Collection Center.*

In February 1908, Tsunoda shot himself to death in front of the Mission.
His suicide was a message to Bowen that his authority as Yoshi's husband
overrode Bowen's. Another woman under Bowen's care filed the first divorce suit brought by a Japanese woman in Sacramento Superior Court.
She was Kie Urabe, picture bride of the very same man, Uichirō Urabe,
whom Bowen had earlier reported to the police. When Kie arrived at
Sacramento to start a new life, however, Urabe left Kie at Bowen's Mission
and never returned. While staying at the Mission, Kie filed for divorce in
Sacramento Superior Court in February 1908. The summons was published but Urabe did not respond and Kie won the case when her husband
was found guilty of desertion in August 1908.[79]

These two cases led the male-run Issei press to scrutinize Bowen and
her mission closely. Although male Issei opinion was divided about her assisting the two Japanese women, her conduct was regarded as unwomanly.
Her critics included the author of a series of articles in the San Francisco
Issei newspaper, *Shin sekai* (New World), who blamed Bowen for encouraging "obedient" Japanese women to flee from their husbands. The author

argued that it was improper for the Japanese Independent Mission, which was a gathering place for immigrant Japanese men, to provide accommodations to women with disreputable pasts under the guise of "rescuing" them. He insisted that a woman should only be "rescued" by "admonishing a daughter to be obedient to her father," by "persuading a younger sister to respect her elder brother," or by "encouraging a wife to reconcile the relationship with her husband," but not by taking a wife away from her husband.[80] Defending Bowen, on the other hand, was another series of articles published in *Shin sekai*. These articles denied that Bowen, a minister serving Christ, had encouraged a Japanese woman to separate from her husband. According to this author, Bowen had endeavored to reunite Yoshi and Seishichi Tsunoda, but when she failed, she recommended that they end the marriage by mutual agreement. Instead of blaming Bowen, this author accused Uichirō Urabe and Seishichi Tsunoda of improper conduct as husbands, and expressed his appreciation for Bowen's contributions to the Issei community in Sacramento. Both authors, however, agreed that Rev. Mary Bowen often lacked "common decency" as a woman.[81]

Male Issei resentment of Bowen intensified as her efforts to protect Issei women involved her mission in Issei marital problems in the late 1900s and the early 1910s. Kie's divorce was followed by that of Shino Fujiwara who, while staying at Bowen's mission, also successfully negotiated a divorce from her husband through her own efforts in 1908. Shino and her husband had got married in Japan and both were well educated; she had once worked as a schoolteacher and he was a college graduate. In Sacramento, while her husband had difficulty finding a job, Shino contributed to their household income by sewing and tailoring. Yet their relationship soon turned sour. Shino suffered from migraine headaches and when she refused her husband's sexual advances, he accused her of being in an extramarital relationship. When Shino sought shelter at Bowen's Mission, her husband asked the secretary of the Sacramento Japanese Association to mediate between them. Learning that they were contemplating deporting her to Japan, Shino hired a *tsūben*, a bilingual Issei who made his living by doing legal and clerical work for the Issei, and filed a divorce suit in 1908. This seemed to be the second divorce case ever filed by a Japanese woman in Sacramento Superior Court. After reaching an agreement that the two could live separately in the United States, Shino withdrew her divorce petition.[82]

Although it was not Bowen's intention to encourage divorce among Issei women, the practice of unhappy Issei wives filing for divorce in local courts with the aid of bilingual *tsūbens* quickly spread. Because there were fewer Japanese women than men in the immigrant community of the 1900s and 1910s, it was not so difficult for a Japanese woman to be self-supporting by engaging in work such as cooking, cleaning, and serving. It was particularly easy for Japanese women living in urban Issei communities, which had numerous bars and restaurants, to find work as waitresses and barmaids. When they had saved enough money, they hired Japanese *tsūbens* and filed for divorce. In the city of Sacramento, which had 82 Japanese wives in 1905 and 481 in June 1915,[83] the records of the Sacramento Superior Court show that there were at least 29 divorce cases filed by Japanese by the end of 1915. Twenty-four of them were initiated by the wives and most ended in the wife's victory and a judgment against the husband on the grounds of willful neglect, desertion, or cruelty.[84] In these cases, the wives often worked as barmaids or waitresses at Japanese bars and restaurants in order to become economically independent.[85] The number of divorce cases in Sacramento increased in the late 1910s.[86]

Issei leaders in northern California became alarmed by the growing elopement and divorce rate in their communities. Issei wives getting a divorce in pursuit of personal happiness ran counter to the Issei community's efforts to transform itself from a community of sojourners to one of permanent settlers. What bothered male Issei leaders the most was the fact that Issei wives were initiating most of the cases.[87] The number of divorces in Issei communities was less than 10 percent of all Issei marriages, and divorce itself was not new to Japanese immigrants, as Japan was said to have the highest divorce rate in the world, followed by the United States.[88] However, in Japan divorce was still a male decision usually negotiated out of court between the household heads of the two families—the husband and the wife's father or brother.[89] Uprooted from their families and encouraged by changes in American values surrounding Issei communities in California, Japanese women came to act on their own in search of true love and freedom from unfulfilling marriages.

The male-managed Issei press described the phenomenon as a "degradation of female morality" and the "Americanization" of Issei women. According to Issei men, American society afforded people a good living but treated "women with excessive respect," thus making them "vain" and "arrogant." They also felt that Japanese women living in the United States were adopting the "weaknesses of American women" and were quickly "losing the supreme virtue of Japanese women," namely, "obedience" and "chastity." Issei men in the press appealed to their women to preserve the "virtue of Japanese women" and to be "obedient" while assisting their husbands.[90]

In 1911, when Yoshi, the abused picture bride whose husband had committed suicide in front of Bowen's mission in 1908, complained about Bowen to the Issei press, a Sacramento Issei newspaper responded by criticizing Bowen extensively. Yoshi was upset with Bowen because Bowen, suspecting her of having had an abortion, pressured Yoshi's boyfriend to marry her. The author of a number of Bowen-bashing articles portrayed Yoshi as an *inpu* (lewd woman), and Bowen as a *kaiō* (suspicious old woman) who came to Sacramento after being reprimanded by M. C. Harris of the M.E. Japanese Mission, "tricked" Japanese immigrants, and "lined her pockets" by pretending to be a Christian worker.[91] Aware of the disputes between Bowen and M. C. Harris, a father figure for Japanese immigrants in northern California, the male-run Issei press harshly criticized Bowen for challenging the gender hierarchy in both the M.E. home missionary enterprise and the Issei community. This time, there were no articles defending Bowen and her mission for providing accommodations to Japanese women of questionable virtue and sometimes enabling them to flee from unwanted marriages. While Bowen's rescue of "Japanese" women met the individual needs of unhappy picture brides trapped in unfortunate marriages, it conflicted with the Issei community's efforts to develop on a sound footing.

Issei WCTU Activism

Following the lead of Protestant missionaries, American WCTU women in California began to work among foreign immigrants in the 1880s. After Willard's visit to the opium dens of San Francisco with Rev. Gibson of the M.E. Mission in 1883, the California WCTU formed a department to work among foreigners in 1885.[92] The temperance cause spread to Issei communities through contacts between elite Issei and American churchpeople, some of whom had links with the WCTU. Under Methodist influence, members of the Gospel Society, the first Issei organization in California, became strict teetotalers and nonsmokers.[93] When Rev. and Mrs. Harris took charge of the newly separated M.E. Japanese Mission in 1886, they further promoted temperance among Japanese Methodists in San Francisco, which resulted in the formation of the Gospel Society's subsidiary temperance society in 1887.[94]

American WCTU women came close to organizing an Issei church-women's union in the late 1880s presumably with the help of Flora B. Harris, a friend of Frances E. Willard,[95] and Mary Bowen, an active member of the California WCTU. Both women worked among Japanese Methodists in San Francisco at the time. As a result, Tel Sono, the self-supporting female student under their influence whose story was related at the beginning of this chapter, decided to work with American WCTU women. She affiliated herself directly with the North San Francisco WCTU for a few months in 1889.[96] However, other Issei churchwomen, mostly wives of elite Issei, preferred to stay within their community assisting male Issei community leaders. Thus, when Tel Sono left California there was no other Issei woman to join the American women's union.[97] American WCTU women had tried without success to organize an Issei union among Japanese immigrant women in California in the 1880s and 1890s.[98]

Japanese churchwomen's reluctance aside, work among the Chinese was a greater priority for California WCTU women in the 1890s. In 1894, the California WCTU organized the Chinese Department to assist Mrs. M. S. Carey in San Jose who had been working among the Chinese for the National WCTU.[99] In 1895, the department changed its name to the Oriental Work Department and Mrs. L. P. Williams, an officer of the M.E. WHMS, became its superintendent.[100] Campaigning fiercely for such causes as woman suffrage, prohibition, and Sabbath observation, California WCTU women attempted to mobilize as many votes as possible on their side. Since first-generation Chinese or Japanese immigrants were barred from American citizenship and American-born Japanese sons were still very young, they turned to American-born Chinese sons who were reaching voting age. Expecting the Chinese native sons of Christian mothers to be strong allies of WCTU activism in California, L. P. Williams wrote:

> It was publicly announced before the 1896 election that hundreds of native born Chinamen would vote. I took pains to go to the Registrar's office in San Francisco, and found that twenty registered, and in Oakland two. Nearly all the men in the Chinese churches are in favor of woman suffrage, even favoring women going to General Conference in the M.E. Church. I know of but one who was opposed—and he died last winter.[101]

Although she soon realized that first-generation Chinese immigrant men in general were not easily persuaded to become Christians or to support WCTU causes and that they objected to their native sons voting for female suffrage, she did not agree with the anti-Asian exclusionists who charged that Asian immigrants could never be assimilated into American society.[102] At the same time, WCTU officers were often wives of eminent Protestant ministers and businessmen and also opposed the exclusion of Asian laborers who provided "cheap labor" in the United States.[103] They described Chinese immigrants as nondrinking people, as opposed to Irish or German immigrants, and felt "a burning shame" about the way Chinese immigrants had been treated in their "professedly Christian land."[104] L. P. Williams wrote that Chinese adults would "not take kindly to the gospel of universal brotherhood, which we preach but do not practice," and thus "we [might] not be able to do a very great work amongst the Asiatic people of mature age."[105]

Nonetheless, facing strong resistance to the gospel from Chinese immigrants of mature age, American WCTU women in California, like Protestant and World WCTU missionary women working in Japan, came to devote themselves to the placement of American-born Asian children, mainly Chinese and Japanese, under their influence. When the Supreme Court case of *Wong Kim Ark v. the U.S.* made it clear in 1898 that American-born Asians could not be stripped of their citizenship,[106] American WCTU women renewed their commitment to working among Asian children, recognizing that they would grow up to be American citizens. As public schools in California increasingly segregated Asian children, Williams saw a special mission for American churchwomen in conducting Sunday schools for them and in providing their ethnic schools with teachers and materials.[107] She wrote in 1898:

> Fifteen years ago there was hardly to be seen a Chinese or Japanese child in America. Today there are 2,000 of the former in San Francisco—little urchins in yellow blouses, born under the Stars and Stripes laugh at Congressional legislation and close-barred gates, as the Supreme Court of the United States has recently declared that all boys born in the United States are citizens and voters, when of age. Shall these have a pagan or Christian citizenship? The former might imperil our institutions. India, China, and Japan must have their schools, but is it no less important that we in America push our educational work among these people on our own shores?[108]

Through her missionary connections Williams started to distribute WCTU tracts and leaflets among Japanese immigrants.[109]

Issei churchwomen did not object to the California WCTU advocating American middle-class Protestant values to their children, as this would promote the acceptance of their children by the American host society. They assisted in the distribution of WCTU leaflets in their community. However, Issei churchwomen's activism in the 1890s was primarily focused on eliminating prostitution and increasing the number of respectable women in their community, so as to improve its image and ensure its sound development. From their perspective, the Japanese WCTU women, who shared their language and cultural background and who were equally concerned about the reputation of "Japanese" women, seemed to be more workable allies than American WCTU women. As previously mentioned in this chapter, Masue Kawaguchi, a resident of Sausalito but still a member of the Tokyo WCTU, had requested her fellow Tokyo WCTU members in 1890 to petition the Japanese government to stop the overseas migration of Japanese prostitutes. A trans-Pacific network between Japanese WCTU women in Japan and on the American Pacific Coast had been in operation since then.

It was in response to the Japan WCTU's call that WCTU unions were formed among Issei churchwomen on the American Pacific Coast. Between 1905 and 1906, three Japan WCTU officers, all former or incumbent teachers of female mission schools in Tokyo, visited the United States. In 1905, two of the three, Chiyoko Kozaki and Utako Hayashi, landed in Vancouver within a two-month interval of each other. Each toured the south, visiting Issei churches of various denominations on the American Pacific Coast and calling on Issei churchwomen, many of whom they had known at school, at church, or through WCTU activism in Japan, to organize Japan WCTU branches.[110] Sharing the nationalism and urban middle-class elitism of Issei churchwomen, Kozaki, who was also concerned about the presence of uneducated Japanese laborers in the United States, argued that respectable Japanese women had to organize in order to demonstrate the "dignity of the Japanese." She said:

> Depending on what we saw and heard during our tour, the reason why Japanese are excluded by white people is that many of those arriving in this land are not educated Japanese who know manners but country people who have never even seen Tokyo. They are indifferent to socialization or courtesy and do not care about maintaining their dignity. Their behavior is often disgraceful in the eyes of white people, and thus Japanese tend to be criticized. So I hope people who are sensitive to these matters will

come in large numbers. I think it is most meaningful that branch unions of the Japan WCTU are being formed—as many as five or six on the [Pacific] Coast—in order to show the dignity of Japanese people overseas.[111]

As a result, Issei branches of the Japan WCTU were formed in Seattle, Portland, Oakland, Los Angeles, and Riverside in 1905.[112]

The collaboration between Japanese WCTU women and Issei churchwomen to promote a favorable image of the Japanese in the United States, however, was rather uneasy. In San Francisco, middle-class Issei churchwomen must have agreed with Kozaki's argument, but they refused to form a Japan WCTU branch because they were offended by Kozaki's negative perception of multicultural and multiracial American society and her monolithic description of the Issei community in San Francisco. Traveling with her husband, who was a Congregational minister well known both in Japan and among Japanese communities in America, Kozaki was generously received by well-established Issei families. But her report on San Francisco published in the Japan WCTU's official publication presented a negative image of San Francisco and the Issei community in the city.

Never having experienced the multiethnic crowds of San Francisco before, Kozaki felt that "moral sanctions" were nonexistent in the city. She also wrote about bars and air-gun shops[113] in San Francisco's Japan Town where "Japanese women of a dubious sort" conducted their business and "a surprisingly large number of Japanese pimps" were economically dependent on them. Kozaki argued that the Japanese in San Francisco were "the worst" in the country, which explained why anti-Japanese sentiment among Americans was most evident there.[114] Like the American public, Kozaki's image of the Issei community in San Francisco was based on the existence of prostitution, which she regarded as "immoral' and unacceptable. Her report enraged Issei churchwomen in the city. One Issei woman protested:

> For two years, ladies in San Francisco have been holding receptions to welcome noble ladies from Japan and listening to their talks. However, why do these noble ladies from Japan denounce women in San Francisco to an extreme, and make cold remarks as if among Japanese women living on the American West Coast there were none who were of good conduct or who were not shameful?[115]

Kozaki talked to women from the Japanese Methodist and Congregational churches in San Francisco and Oakland in an attempt to establish a few Japan WCTU branches in the Bay Area, and successfully established the Oakland Japanese WCTU in November 1905. But she was unable to do so in San Francisco, which had the largest population of Japanese immigrants in America.[116]

When Kajiko Yajima, the third Japan WCTU officer to visit the American Pacific Coast between 1905 and 1906, came to the Bay Area on her way to the seventh World WCTU Convention in Boston in 1906, Issei churchwomen in San Francisco were still "very offended."[117] But Yajima used her family networks to strengthen Issei WCTU activism in the Bay Area. Yajima's niece, Otowa Okubo, one of the founding members of the Oakland Japanese WCTU, was living in Oakland with her husband at the time. Her husband was the main contributor to and a minister at the Oakland Japanese Independent Congregational Church. Since American World WCTU missionaries had helped Yajima consolidate the organizational basis of the Japan WCTU in Japan, she tried to bring American WCTU women in California and Oakland Japanese WCTU members together. Assisted by Otowa's daughter, Ochimi Okubo, who served as her interpreter, Yajima spoke at the Oakland WCTU and Alameda County WCTU conventions.[118] In 1907, the Oakland Japanese WCTU acted on Yajima's advice and affiliated itself with the California WCTU.[119] It also started publication of a bimonthly newsletter in 1907 with money given by Yajima in appreciation of Ochimi's services.[120]

The membership and influence of the Oakland Japanese WCTU steadily grew. In 1907, Oakland Japanese WCTU members numbered eighteen, seven of whom had been Japan WCTU members in Japan.[121] By 1916, its membership had increased to fifty-five.[122] The readership for its newsletter was no longer limited to California, and circulation reached eight hundred in 1913.[123] By the end of 1920, four additional unions, including one in San Francisco, had been established among Issei churchwomen in California, affiliated with the WCTU of California.[124] These unions dispatched delegates to their city, county, and state WCTU conventions.[125] Of all the Issei WCTU unions established on the American Pacific Coast,[126] however, only the Oakland Japanese WCTU continued to be active and to publish its newsletter until 1941.[127]

Responding to the affiliation of Issei women with the California WCTU, the latter created an independent department for Japanese work in 1907 and appointed an American woman experienced in working with the Japanese as its superintendent.[128] So emerged a loose network of American, Japanese, and Issei churchwomen who shared the vocabulary and methods of WCTU activism in the early twentieth century. While each superintendent of the WCTU's Japanese Work Department drew upon personal connections to promote American WCTU causes and activism, Issei unions functioned in the Japanese language, pursuing their own activist agenda under a WCTU structure that granted each union local autonomy.

Kara Smart became the first superintendent of the Japanese Work Department after working for four years as a World WCTU resident missionary in Tokyo.[129] She obtained WCTU materials translated into the Japanese language from the Japan WCTU, and distributed them among Japanese immigrants with the help of clergymen and missionaries working with the immigrants.[130] Rev. Mary Bowen, who took over as superintendent in 1909 while running her Independent Japanese Mission in Sacramento, conducted evangelical and rescue efforts through her mission.[131] Clara Johnson, the wife of Rev. Herbert B. Johnson who was then in charge of the M.E. Japanese Mission, replaced Bowen in 1913. She promoted WCTU activism at M.E. Japanese churches with the assistance of Japanese ministers under her husband's supervision. Clara Johnson created a Little Temperance Legion (LTL) among Japanese children in Berkeley, and encouraged American churchwomen to participate in the California WCTU's "Americanization" efforts by conducting Sunday school, evening classes, and Bible studies for the Japanese and their American-born children.[132]

While cooperating with projects initiated by the superintendent of the California WCTU's Work among Japanese Department, Issei WCTU members also had activist goals of their own, which were determined in coordination with Issei churches and Issei community organizations such as the Japanese Association in America. The few remaining records of the Oakland Japanese WCTU indicate that the union was focused on providing mutual support and improvement initially for a small group of middle-class Issei churchwomen in the Bay Area. Gradually, it became influential among Issei women in the United States through its bimonthly newsletter, one of a very small number of publications about and for Issei women at the time. Ochimi Okubo, Yajima's grandniece who was involved in Oakland Japanese WCTU activism in its early days, later wrote that the union aimed to "bring back and heighten *kyōyō* (culture/education)" among its members, who were immersed in daily chores in their new land, by exhorting them to live up to the standard of "Japanese" women.[133] In an article in the newsletter, reprinted in an Issei newspaper in Sacramento in 1912, another member argued that it was especially necessary for Issei women in America, who had "total freedom" from their parents, relatives, and seniors, to read books and increase their knowledge for the sake of improving the *Yamato minzoku* (Yamato nation).[134]

Oakland Japanese WCTU women, who subscribed to middle-class Protestant American moral values, also participated in Issei community efforts to eliminate prostitution from their society. The first notable project of the Oakland Japanese WCTU was to provide shelter to Japanese refugees escaping from the 1906 San Francisco earthquake. But when some of the Japanese refugees attempted to resume their "shameful" business in Oakland, Oakland Japanese WCTU members tried to close them down. Ochimi Okubo later wrote that she worked as an interpreter for the Oakland city police and an American minister at the Oakland First Congregational Church. Encountering Japanese prostitutes in America and hearing them say that they were engaging in the business of their own free will stunned her and caused her to feel deep "disgrace."[135] The Oakland Japanese WCTU collaborated with American and Issei churchpeople, the Japanese Society in America, Issei youth organizations, and the city of Oakland to close down the houses of "ill repute" in the Oakland Issei community.[136] Ochimi Okubo later returned to Japan, ultimately becoming a leading officer of the Japan WCTU and one of the prime leaders in Japan WCTU's campaign to abolish the licensed prostitution system in Japan in the 1920s and 1930s.

As the wives and daughters of Issei community leaders, Oakland Japanese WCTU members also worked for the sound development of their community. To transform their society from one of sojourners to one of permanent settlers, they believed, like their husbands, that more Japanese women should emigrate to America as picture brides and fulfill their duty by bearing and raising children and assisting their husbands. Otowa Okubo, Yajima's niece and an active member of the Oakland Japanese WCTU, warned in 1912 that "degraded families" were responsible for the anti-Japanese sentiments of the American public. Although she demanded marital faithfulness from husbands in order to establish sound families in America, she echoed male Issei leaders in promoting the "Japanese female virtues" of "chastity" and "self-sacrifice" among Issei women.[137] Living on the front lines of American racism and American cultural dominance,

Issei churchwomen attempted to combat anti-Japanese prejudice by upholding the dignity of "Japanese" women and their community in America.

These efforts by elite Issei swiftly corrected the gender imbalance and successfully increased the number of families in their communities.[138] Ironically, however, the growth of the Japanese communities—fed by the immigration of picture brides, the birth of their children in California, and the expansion of the Japanese farming business—actually ignited the anti-Japanese sentiments of the American public. American-born Japanese children were American citizens by virtue of the Fourteenth Amendment. Their presence allowed the Japanese to circumvent the 1913 California Alien Land Law, which prohibited ownership of land by "aliens ineligible for citizenship" and restricted leases by them to three years.[139]

The practice of the picture bride, portrayed as an uncivilized "Asiatic" custom that ignored love and morality, became the target of exclusionist forces during the late 1910s. To avoid anti-Japanese sentiment from growing any further, the Japanese government decided to stop issuing passports to picture brides after March 1920. But eight months later, in November, California passed a much more restrictive land law forbidding Japanese immigrants from entering into leasing and sharecropping arrangements in an attempt to limit them to being agricultural laborers. While the trans-Pacific network of Japanese, Issei, and American churchpeople effectively promoted the values and vocabularies of the Anglo-American, Protestant, and capitalist systems in Japan and the Issei communities in California, it was unable to mediate between Japan and the United States in the competition and, ultimately, the collision between them during the very nationalistic early twentieth century.[140]

Epilogue

The middle-class American Protestant gender ideology and activist methods advocated by American Protestant and WCTU missionaries were interpreted and assimilated into Japanese society at historically specific moments and localities by middle-class Japanese men and women who had intentions and expectations of their own. This process of translation highlights the hidden contradictions, subthemes, and subtlety of American foreign missionary and WCTU enterprises. If American Protestant and World WCTU missionary women were culturally imperialistic in seeking to impose their own cultural values on the Japanese and attempting to reformulate Japanese society in light of their vision, Japanese men and women, whose activism was animated by their own expectations in Japan and California, were nationalistic and imperialistic as well. They contemplated borrowing the missionaries' methods and vocabularies in order to advance not only their own status in their communities but also that of their nation and society in the world. This uneasy collaboration between American Protestant missionaries, World WCTU workers, and middle-class Japanese men and women in Japan and California made the trans-Pacific expansion of the WCTU movement possible.

American Protestant and WCTU missionary women, who worked for specific causes in Japan, consciously or unconsciously promoted their belief in the supremacy of the Anglo-American capitalist system, political liberalism, and Protestant moral values. Being free agents of American capitalism, however, they were able to function as a third power intervening between the power structures of the world and Japanese societies. In fact, their social activism was often benevolent and humanitarian, seeking to reach out to the class marginalized by the Japanese power structure. They were willing to train their clients and students to become better players of capitalism in the Anglo-American Protestant cultural mode, and assisted them in advancing their status in the expanding Anglo-American capitalist system. The projects run by American churchwomen, in whose eyes all non-Christian women were "heathens," were more egalitarian and inclusive than their class-conscious Japanese protégés, many of whom came from the former ruling class of Tokugawa Japan.

American Protestant and WCTU missionaries did not intend to confront the capitalist expansion that often involved coercion backed by military power and created new marginalized groups, but wanted only to influence its course and process. They aimed for an amelioration but not a suspension of the expansion. At the same time, while working for salvation and social reform, American middle-class Protestant and WCTU missionaries also expanded their own personal and organizational influence and advanced their status in their own communities and the world. However, to increase their influence among the Japanese, they often accommodated their activism to the political and social currents of Japanese society and forged alliances with Japanese elites and authorities. Meiji Japan not only avoided being colonized but became a colonizer itself by adapting what it had learned from the modern civilized West to its own purposes. As a consequence, American Protestant and WCTU missionary women, who collaborated with Japanese elites and middle-class churchwomen to expand their influence in Japan, came to facilitate not only the expansion of the modern capitalist system and Anglo-American cultural values but also Japanese colonial rule in neighboring Asian nations.[1]

In the same vein, the transnational network of American and Japanese churchwomen did not contemplate destroying the ideology that supported the male-dominated gender structures of American and Japanese societies but only aimed to stretch them. They "manipulated" the religious, moral, and scientific discourse which was accepted at the turn of the century, and successfully stretched women's sphere by emphasizing women's special abilities that were different from men's. Given the rigid gender hierarchy that subjugated both American as well as Japanese women, however, women's work in the stretched but separate women's sphere was subordinated to men's work. Because World WCTU missionary women not only stood outside the Japanese gender hierarchy but also liberated themselves from the control of American male clergy, they were able to carry on their work on an equal footing with Japanese men. But they might not have taken full advantage of their position to challenge the male-dominated gender hierarchy either among the Japanese or in the United States. Although the transnational movement of American and Japanese missionaries endeavored to reform society for the sake of women, their endeavor involved factors other than gender and thus their achievements did not benefit women as a whole. Overall, they upheld rather than undermined the fundamentals of the social order.

The expansion of transnational women's activism connecting American and Japanese churchwomen on both sides of the Pacific was not a one-way process in which American women dominated Japanese women. Instead, it was a two-way process in which they worked out mutually beneficial relationships. Being tactfully pragmatic, American Protestant and WCTU missionary women, while promoting their values and systems, were sensitive to conditions in the society in which they worked. Working among men and women of a different culture through trial and error, liberal American missionary women reconstructed their monotheistic and universalist worldview and often spoke for the Japanese, sometimes even for Japanese imperialism. The transnational network of American and Japanese churchwomen expanded through negotiation and collaboration, each side bringing to the process its own expectations.

The relationship between the American missionary women and the Japanese who worked with them was remarkably amicable. In my research, I often came across evidence of friendship between American missionary women and their Japanese clients and students on both sides of the Pacific. Along with Mary A. West, martyr of the temperance cause who "worked for the benefit of Japan," I encountered favorable and often laudatory accounts of the life and work of American Protestant and WCTU missionaries such as Mary Kidder, Maria True, Mary Denton, and Flora B. Harris written by institutions, communities, or individuals who had benefited from their work. Although Mary M. Bowen's rescue efforts may have conflicted with Issei leaders' emphasis on community survival, and may be forgotten in Sacramento's Japanese American community (partially on account of its internment experience during World War II), I discovered that her grave in a multiracial seminary in Sacramento had been paid for by her "Japanese friends" and that her gravestone is surrounded by others bearing Japanese family names.[2]

This is not to say that the transnational relationship between American and Japanese churchwomen did not encounter any friction, yet I cannot help but reconsider the meaning of the American Protestant and WCTU missionary enterprises that pioneered contact and communication between women of different races, cultures, and nations in the late nineteenth century—especially given the events of 9/11, the violence on the Palestinian-Israeli borders and in Iraq, and the increasingly negative image of "Americans." Although the transnational churchwomen's activism was middle-class in nature and sought to secure their future and increase their influence, their commitment to working "selflessly" to uplift their "heathen" sisters reversed the strong anti-Christian and antiforeign sentiments of the Japanese and encouraged a variety of Christian and non-Christian Japanese groups to get involved. While originally assimilationist and universalist with an intent of evangelizing the world, American churchwomen's evangelism created educational opportunities for both American and Japanese women, allowing them to interact with and affect each other. Their experiences enabled them to work out mutually beneficial relationships and expanded WCTU activism across the Pacific to Japan and to Issei communities in northern California. Although their transnational network was not able to prevent the two nations from engaging in World War II, friendships formed by its members at the individual level endured both during and after the war. I wonder if the transnational networks sustained by the financial contributions, energy, and sometimes lifelong service of individual American and Japanese churchwomen, actually had a greater impact than we thought on the late-nineteenth and early-twentieth-century world scene.

Appendix

List of Organizations

World Woman's Christian Temperance Union (World WCTU) [1884]
American Board of Commissioners for Foreign Missions (ABCFM) [1810]
Board of Foreign Missions of the Presbyterian Church, U.S.A. [1837]
Board of Foreign Missions, Reformed Church in America [1832]
Ladies' Board of Missions of the Presbyterian Church, New York [1870]
Woman's Board of Foreign Missions, Reformed Church in America [1875]
Woman's Christian Temperance Union (WCTU) [1874]
Woman's Home Missionary Society, Methodist Episcopal Church
     (WHMS) [1880]
Woman's Foreign Missionary Society of the Presbyterian Church,
     Philadelphia [1870]
Woman's Union Missionary Society of America for Heathen Lands
     (WUMS) [1860]

IN JAPAN

Auxiliary WCTU of Japan (later renamed Foreign Auxiliary) [1895]
Commoners' Association (Heiminsha) [1903]
Japan WCTU (Nihon Fujin Kyōfūkai, later renamed Nihon Kirisutokyō
     Fujin Kyōfūkai) [1893]
Japanese Temperance Union (Nihon Kinshu Dōmei) [1898]
Japan Women's Suffrage Association (Nihon Fujin Sanseiken Kyōkai)
     [1921]
Mine-Pollution-Site Relief Women's Society (Kōgaichi Kyōsai Fujinkai)
     [1901]
National League to Abolish Licensed Prostitution (Zenkoku Haishō
     Dōmeikai) [1890]

Tosa Custom Developing Soceity (Tosa Kōfūkai) [ca. 1889]
Tokyo Temperance Society (Tokyo Kinshukai) [1890]
Tokyo WCTU (Tokyo Fujin Kyōfūkai) [1886]
Tokyo Women's Temperance Society (Tokyo Fujin Kinshukai) [1891]
Women's White Ribbon Club (Fujin Hakuhyō Kurabu) [1889]

IN CALIFORNIA

Alameda County WCTU
California Branch of the Woman's Foreign Missionary Society of the
    Presbyterian Church, Philadelphia [1873], precursor of the Woman's
    Occidental Board of Foreign Missions
California WCTU [1879]
North San Francisco WCTU
Oakland WCTU
Woman's Missionary Society of the Pacific Coast (WMSPC), Methodist
    Episcopal Church [1870], precursor of the Oriental Bureau of the
    Woman's Home Missionary Society
Woman's Occidental Board of Foreign Missions, Presbyterian Church
    [1878]
Woman's Union Mission to Chinese Women and Children, San Francisco
    [1869]

IN JAPANESE IMMIGRANT COMMUNITIES IN CALIFORNIA

Female Charitable Society (Fujin Jizenkai) [1883]
Gospel Society (Fukuinkai) [1877]
Japanese Association of America [1908]
Japanese Deliberative Council of America [1900], a precursor of Japanese
    Association in America
Japanese Young Women's Christian Association in San Francisco [1912]
Oakland Japanese WCTU [1905]
United Japanese Deliberative Council of America [1906], a precursor of
    Japanese Association in America

IN EUROPE (BERLIN)

International Woman Suffrage Alliance (IWSA) [1904]

Notes

NOTES TO THE INTRODUCTION

1. Helen E. Tyler, *Where Prayer and Purpose Meet: The WCTU Story, 1874–1949* (Evanston: Signal Press, 1949), 118.

2. See, For example, Ellen C. DuBois, *Woman Suffrage and Women's Rights* (New York: NYU Press, 1998), 30–42; Mary D. Earhart, *Frances Willard: From Prayers to Politics* (Chicago: University of Chicago Press, 1944); Ruth Bordin, *Woman and Temperance: The Quest for Power and Liberty, 1873–1900* (Philadelphia: Temple University Press, 1981; reprint, New Brunswick: Rutgers University Press, 1990); Anne Firor Scott, *Natural Allies: Women's Associations in American History* (Urbana: University of Illinois Press, 1993); Carolyn DeSwarte Gifford, "Frances Willard and the Woman's Christian Temperance Union's Conversion to Woman Suffrage," in *One Woman, One Vote: Rediscovering the Woman Suffrage Movement,* ed. Marjorie Spruill Wheeler (Troutdale, Oreg.: New Sage Press, 1995), 117–134; Kenneth D. Rose, *American Women and the Repeal of Prohibition* (New York: NYU Press, 1996).

3. Ian Tyrrell, *Woman's World/Woman's Empire: The Woman's Christian Temperance Union in International Perspective, 1880–1930* (Chapel Hill: University of North Carolina Press, 1992), 27–28; Patricia Grimshaw, "Settler Anxieties, Indigenous Peoples, and Women's Suffrage in the Colonies of Australia, New Zealand, and Hawai'i, 1888 to 1902," *Pacific Historical Review* 69, no. 4 (November 2000), 553–572; Rose, *American Women and the Repeal of Prohibition,* 25–26.

4. Scott, *Natural Allies,* 85–110; Peggy Pascoe, *Relations of Rescue: The Search for Female Moral Authority in the American West, 1874–1939* (New York: Oxford University Press, 1990), 32–69; Barbara L. Epstein, *The Politics of Domesticity: Women, Evangelism, and Temperance in Nineteenth Century America* (Middletown, Conn.: Wesleyan University Press, 1981).

5. Max Weber, *The Protestant Ethic and the Spirit of Capitalism,* trans. Talcott Persons (London: HarperCollins Academic, 1991).

NOTES TO CHAPTER 1

1. J. C. Hepburn to J. C. Lowrie, 21 August 1872, Presbyterian Church (U.S.A.) Board of Foreign Missions Correspondence and Reports, Japan (hereafter PMJ).

2. Nao Aoyama, *Meiji jogakkō no kenkyū* (Tokyo: Keiō tsūshin, 1970), 3–47; Nobuhiro Miyoshi, *Nihon kyōiku no kaikoku* (Tokyo: Fukumura shuppan, 1986), 116–121; Tokutarō Shigehisa, *Oyatoi gaikokujin; kyōiku, shūkyo* (Tokyo: Kashima shuppankai, 1968), 21–24.

3. Masanao Nakamura, "Creating Good Mothers," in *Meiroku Zasshi: Journal of Japanese Enlightenment*, trans. William R. Braisted (Cambridge: Harvard University Press, 1976), 401–404. Masanao Nakamura (1832–1901) was a Confucian scholar who went to England with Tokugawa government funding from 1866 to 1868. Impressed by Western values and civilization, on his return Nakamura translated a number of English books such as Samuel Smile's *Self Help* and John S. Mill's *On Liberty* into Japanese. Nakamura was baptized in 1874, but later became a freethinker. Masao Takahashi, *Nakamura Keiu* (Tokyo: Yoshikawa kōbunkan, 1966).

4. Aoyama, *Meiji jogakkō no kenkyū*, 3–47; Miyoshi, *Nihon kyōiku no kaikoku*, 144–149.

5. Tokutarō Shigehisa, *Oyatoi gaikokujin*, 56–65; Akio Dohi, *Nihon purotesutanto kirisutokyōshi* (Tokyo: Shinkyō shuppan, 1980), 77–80.

6. Dana L. Robert, *American Women in Mission: A Social History of Their Thought and Practice* (Macon, Ga.: Mercer University Press, 1997), 1–124; Barbara Welter, "She Hath Done What She Could," in *Women in American Religion*, ed. Janet Wilson James (Philadelphia: University of Pennsylvania Press, 1976), 111–125; R. Pierce Beaver, *All Loves Excelling: American Protestant Women in World Mission* (Grand Rapids, Mich.: William B. Eerdmans Publishing Co., 1968).

7. Robert, *American Women in Mission*; Susan Hill Lindley, *"You Have Stept Out of Your Place": A History of Women and Religion in America* (Louisville, Ky.: Westminster John Knox Press, 1996), 70–89; Patricia R. Hill, *The World Their Household: The American Woman's Foreign Mission Movement and Cultural Transformation, 1870–1920* (Ann Arbor: University of Michigan Press, 1985); Beaver, *All Loves Excelling*; Mrs. W. I. Chamberlain, *Fifty Years in Foreign Fields: China, Japan, India, Arabia* (New York: Woman's Board of Foreign Missions, Reformed Church in America, 1925), 7–8.

8. The ratio of female missionaries in American foreign missionary enterprises increased to 67 percent in 1925. See Beaver, *All Loves Excelling*, 109.

9. Scott, *Natural Allies*, 213, note 35; Hill, *The World Their Household*, 195, note 1.

10. Yasuko Utsu, *Saisō yori yori fukaki tamashiini; Sōma Kokkō, wakaki hino henreki* (Tokyo: YMCA shuppan, 1983), 40–42.

11. Ochimi Kubushiro, *Yajima Kajiko den* (Tokyo: Ōzorasha, 1988), 2.

12. S. R. Brown to J. M. Ferris, 28 February 1869, Reformed Church in America, Board of Foreign Missions, Japan Mission Correspondence (hereafter RCJ); "Mrs. Mary Eddy Miller," *Japan Evangelist* 17, no. 7 (July 1910): 242–249; Chamberlain, *Fifty Years in Foreign Fields*, 8–10; Rui Kohiyama, *Amerika fujin senkyōshi: Rainichi*

no haikei to sono eikyō (Tokyo: Tokyo daigaku shuppankai, 1992), 159–177; Mary Kidder, *Kidā shokanshū,* trans. and ed. Ferris Jogakuin (Tokyo: Kyōbunkan, 1976), 1–6; S. R. Brown, *S. R. Buraun shokanshū,* trans. and ed. Michio Takaya (Tokyo: Shinkyō shuppan, 1978), 365–366.

13. M. Kidder to J. M. Ferris, 22 September 1870, RCJ; S.R. Brown to J. M. Ferris, 5 March 1870, RCJ.

14. S. R. Brown to J. M. Ferris, 5 March 1870, RCJ; Mary E. Miller, "Reminiscences of Early Missionary Life in Japan," *Japan Evangelist* 2, no. 6 (August 1895): 321–326; "Mrs. Mary Eddy Miller," *Japan Evangelist* 17, no. 7 (July, 1910): 242–249; William E. Griffis, *A Maker of the New Orient; Samuel Robbins Brown* (New York: Flemming H. Revell Co., 1902), 127–130; Kohiyama, *Amerika Fujin Senkyōshi,* 159–177; Kidder, *Kidā shokanshū,* 1–6; Brown, *S. R. Buraun Shokanshū,* 1–4.

15. M. Kidder to J. M. Ferris, 22 September 1870, 21 October 1871, 22 January 1872, 26 February 1872, RCJ; S. R. Brown to J. M. Ferris, 23 September 1870, 24 June 1872, 4 September 1872, RCJ.

16. M. Kidder to J. M. Ferris, 30 September 1872, 7 December 1872, 22 February 1873, RCJ; M. Miller to J. M. Ferris, 4 December 1873, 22 January 1874, 7 March 1874, 26 September 1874, 8 November 1874, 3 December 1874, 8 January 1875, RCJ; M. Miller to a Sunday school, 11 February 1874, RCJ; Kidder, *Kidā Shokanshū,* 43–79; G. F. Verbeck, ed., *History of Protestant Missions in Japan* (Yokohama: R. Meiklejohn and Co., 1883), 20, 46; Chamberlain, *Fifty Years in Foreign Fields,* 14, 30–31; Ferisu Jogakuin, ed., *Ferisu jogakuin hyakunenshi* (Yokohama: Ferisu jogakuin, 1970), 32–36.

17. M. Miller to J. M. Ferris, 19 April 1873; 22 August 1873, 4 December 1873, RCJ; E. Rothesay Miller to J. C. Lowrie, 17 December 1873, PMJ; Kohiyama, *Amerika fujin senkyōshi,* 252–262; M. Miller to J. M. Ferris, 4 December 1873, RCJ.

18. M. Miller to J. M. Ferris, 26 September 1874, 3 December 1874, 8 January 1875, 10 February 1875, RCJ; Ferisu Jogakuin, ed., *Ferisu jogakuin hyakunenshi,* 36–39; Verbeck, *History of Protestant Missions in Japan,* 50.

19. J. C. Hepburn to J. C. Lowrie, 21 August 1872, PMJ.

20. M. Miller to J. M. Ferris, 8 January 1875, RCJ.

21. Ibid.

22. Ferris Jogakuin, ed., *Ferisu jogakuin hyakunenshi,* 40–42, 47–50.

23. J. C. Hepburn to J. C. Lowrie, 12 October 1878, PMJ.

24. J. C. Hepburn to J. C. Lowrie, 7 May 1880, PMJ.

25. Toshiko Kishida (1863–1901) was born into a wealthy merchant family in Kyoto. Delivering her speech entitled "*hakoiri musume*" in October 1883, Kishida stated that a daughter confined to a box would resort to *kakeochi* (elopement), and her parents would have to send "unnecessary servants" to catch her. Because of the speech, she was arrested on charges of violating the *Shūkai jorei* (Public Meeting Regulation) and of contempt for government officials. At the trial, prosecutors asserted that her speech was political since the "box" referred metaphorically to the

Public Meeting Regulation, and that she had insulted government officials by calling them "unnecessary servants." Kishida was fined five yen for the former charge. See Toshiko Kishida, "Hakoiri musume," in *Kishida Toshiko hyōronshū*, ed. Yuko Suzuki (Tokyo: Fuji shuppan, 1985); Sharon L. Sievers, *Flowers in Salt: The Beginnings of Feminist Consciousness in Modern Japan* (Stanford: Stanford University Press, 1983), 26–53; Toshio Konya, *Josei kaihō no senkusha: Nakajima Toshiko to Fukuda Hideko* (Tokyo: Shimizu shoten, 1984), 16–98.

26. Masamichi Asukai, *Rokumeikan* (Tokyo: Iwanami shoten, 1992).

27. Foreigners were not allowed to live in the interior without government permission until 1899. Thus, some missionaries taught English at native schools in the interior so that they could obtain government permission to live outside the foreign concessions and to engage in evangelical work.

28. These women's foreign mission boards realized the need to coordinate foreign missionary work. In 1884 they organized the Central Committee of Presbyterian Women, which was composed of representatives from each of the boards. See Lois A. Boyd and R. Douglas Brackenridge, *Presbyterian Women in America: Two Centuries of a Quest for Status* (Westport, Conn.: Greenwood Press, 1983), 36–37, 54–57; Kohiyama, *Amerika fujin senkyōshi*, 70–76.

29. Susan M. Yohn, "'Let Christian Women Set the Example in Their Own Gifts': The 'Business' of Protestant Women's Organizations," in *Women and Twentieth Century Protestantism*, eds. Margaret L. Bendroth and Virginia L. Brereton (Urbana: University of Illinois Press, 2002), 213–235. Kohiyama, *Amerika Fujin Senkyōshi*, 61–113.

30. Hill, *The World Their Household*, 116–117.

31. Virginia L. Brereton and Christa R. Klein, "American Women in Ministry: A History of Protestant Beginning Points," in *Women in American Religion*, ed. Janet W. James (Philadelphia: University of Pennsylvania Press, 1976), 171–190.

32. "Organized Missionary Work and Statistics: Foreign Mission Work of Women's Societies," *Missionary Review of the World* (January 1890): 73–75.

33. Kohiyama, *Amerika fujin senkyōshi*, 189–238.

34. A. K. Davis, "Mrs. Maria True," *Japan Evangelist* 3, no. 6 (August 1896): 317–320; Michiko Kameyama, *Onnatachi no yakusoku: M. T. Tsurū to nihon saishono kango gakkō* (Tokyo: Jinbun shoin, 1990), 7–36.

35. M. True to Mrs. Perkins, 29 May 1879, PMJ; M. True to J. C. Lowrie, 3 September 1880, PMJ; Testuya Ōhama, *Joshigakuin no rekishi* (Tokyo: Joshi Gakuin, 1985), 69–120.

36. M. True to J. C. Lowrie, 17 November 1884, PMJ.

37. M. True to J. C. Lowrie, 3 December 1884, PMJ.

38. Ōhama, *Joshigakuin no rekishi*, 168–178; "The First Decade of the Bancho School," *Woman's Work for Woman* (September 17 (1887): 233–234.

39. M. True to J. C. Gillespie, 5 February, 10 June 1887, 28 November 1887, PMJ; Ōhama, *Joshigakuin no rekishi*, 178–188.

40. J. C. Gillespie to M. True, 22 April 1887.

41. Dohi, *Nihon purotesutanto kirisutokyōshi,* 77–80.

42. J. C. Hepburn to J. C. Gillespie, 12 April 1888, PMJ.

43. M. True to J. C. Gillespie, 28 November 1887, PMJ; Ōhama, *Joshigakuin no rekishi,* 185.

44. W. Imbrie to J. C. Gillespie, 14 June 1887, PMJ.

45. D. Thompson to J. C. Gillespie, 27 October 1887, PMJ.

46. M. True to J. C. Gillespie, 14 August 1888, PMJ.

47. M. True to J. C. Gillespie, 5 February 1887, PMJ.

48. M. True to J. C. Gillespie, 10 June 1997, 28 November 1887, 21 March 1888, PMJ; J. C. Gillespie to Tokyo, 6 June 1888, PMJ.

49. Ōhama, *Joshigakuin no rekishi,* 217–230.

50. W. Imbrie to J. C. Gillespie, 9 March 1889, PMJ; Anna K. Davis to J. C. Gillespie, 17 January 1893, PMJ.

51. For the Methodists' case, see William T. Noll, "Laity Rights and Leadership," in *Women in New Worlds: Historical Perspectives on the Wesleyan Tradition,* eds. Hilah F. Thomas and Rosemary Skinner Keller (Nashville: Abingdon, 1981), 219–232. For Congregational foreign missionary women, see Sandra C. Taylor, "The Sisterhood of Salvation and the Sunrise Kingdom," *Pacific Historical Review* (February 1979): 45.

52. Presbyterian Church (U.S.A.) Board of Foreign Missions Japan Letters Index; Kohiyama, *Amerika fujin senkyōshi,* 315–316, n. 31.

53. M. True to J. C. Gillespie, 10 June 1887, PMJ.

54. *Manual of the Board of Foreign Missions of the Presbyterian Church in the U.S.A. for the Use of Missionaries and Missionary Candidates* (revised and adopted 16 December 1889): 14, Presbyterian Church (U.S.A.) Department of History and Records Management Services, Philadelphia, Pa.; Boyd and Brackenridge, *Presbyterian Women in America,* 166.

55. M. True to J. C. Gillespie, 1 March 1890, PMJ. Anna K. Davis, who had been working with True, wrote to the General Board to express her "satisfaction with the New Manual" which provided "perfect justice." Anna K. Davis to J. C. Gillespie, 23 October 1890, PMJ.

56. G. W. Knox to J. C. Gillespie, 18 March 1890, PMJ. American Congregational missionary women won a "vote" on all mission matters in 1893.

57. Mrs. Hepburn to J. C. Gillespie, 11 April 1890, PMJ.

58. Mrs. Hepburn to J. C. Gillespie, 8 May 1890, PMJ.

59. *The Presbyterian Church USA Board of Foreign Missions, Minutes* (1890–1891), 8, 37, 42, 47–48, 58.

60. R. Pierce Beaver sees missionary women as feminists, while scholars such as Jane Hunter and Marjorie King disagree. See Beaver, *All Loves Excelling;* Hunter, *The Gospel of Gentility: American Women Missionaries in Turn-of-Century China* (New Haven: Yale University Press, 1984); Marjorie King, "Exporting Femininity,

Not Feminism: Nineteenth Century U.S. Missionary Women's Efforts to Emancipate Chinese Women," in *Women's Work for Women,* ed. Leslie A. Flemming (Boulder: Westview Press, 1989), 117–135.

61. Yukichi Fukuzawa, "Nippon fujin ron, kōhen," in *Fukuzawa Yukichi on Japanese Women; Selected Works,* trans. and ed. Eiichi Kiyooka (Tokyo: Tokyo daigaku shuppankai, 1988), 39.

62. Ekken Kaibara, "Onna daigaku," in *Ekken zenshū* (Tokyo: Ekken zenshū kankōbu, 1910).

63. Ekken Kaibara, *Onna daigaku hyōron; shin onna daigaku* (Tokyo: Jiji shuppan, 1899); Shizuko Koyama, *Ryōsai kenbo to iu kihan* (Tokyo: Keiso shobō, 1991), 13–24; Raymond R. Moser, "The Disappearing Daughter-in-Law: The Victorian Woman, the Japanese Enlightenment and the Roots of Ryōsai Kenbo," unpublished paper for UCLA History Department.

64. Itsue Takamure, *Nihon koninshi* (Tokyo: Rironsha, 1953), 98–149.

65. Kazuo Kasahara, ed., *Nihon joseishi,* vol. 4 (Tokyo: Hyōronsha, 1973), 202.

66. Hidemasa Maki, *Jinshin baibai* (Tokyo: Iwanami shoten, 1971), 145–149.

67. In the Tokugawa caste system, the samurai occupied the highest strata, followed by farmers, artisans, and merchants. After the Meiji Restoration, in 1871, former nobles and lords became *kazoku* (peers); but former samurai, who came to be labeled *shizoku,* and the rest, who composed *heimin* (commoners), stood on the same ground.

68. Hideo Ōtake, *"Ie" to josei no rekishi* (Tokyo: Kōbundō, 1977), 247–248.

69. Arinori Mori, "On Wives and Concubines, part 1," in *Meiroku Zasshi,* 104–105; Yukichi Fukuzawa, "The Equal Numbers of Men and Women," in *Meiroku Zasshi,* 385–386.

70. Ōtake, *"Ie" to josei no rekishi,* 247–252.

71. Kikue Yamakawa, *Onna nidai no ki* (Tokyo: Heibonsha, 1972), 18; Ōhama, *Joshigakuin no rekishi,* 178.

72. Julia D. Carrothers, *The Sunrise Kingdom: Life and Scenes in Japan, and Woman's Work for Woman There* (Philadelphia: Presbyterian Board of Publication: 1879), 72–73.

73. Mrs. E. R. Miller, "Education of Women," in *Proceedings of the General Conference of the Protestant Missionaries of Japan Held at Osaka, Japan, April 1883,* ed. G. F. Verbeck (Yokohama: R. Meiklejohn and Co., 1883), 220.

74. Peggy Pascoe examines Presbyterian missionary women's attempts to empower "rescued" Chinese prostitutes in San Francisco's Chinatown by propagating the ideology of the "Christian home" and Victorian womanhood. See Pascoe, *Relations of Rescue.*

75. Miller, "Education of Women," 220.

76. M. Kidder to J. M. Ferris, 22 August 1873, RCJ.

77. Miller, "Education of Women," 226.

78. Susan A. Searle, "Schools and Colleges for Girls: Their Aim, Scope and Re-

sults," in *Proceedings of the General Conference of Protestant Missions in Japan Held in Tokyo October 24–21, 1900* (Tokyo: Methodist Publishing House, 1901), 256–270.

79. Carrothers, *The Sunrise Kingdom,* 190–191, 219–226, 234–245.

80. The membership was extended to men in 1891 to assist in Youngman's efforts to build a sanitarium for lepers. Kōzensha, *Aru gunzō: Kōzensha hyakunen no ayumi* (Tokyo: Nihon kirisutokyō shppankyoku, 1987), 40–66.

81. M. Miller to J. M. Ferris, 19 January 1882, RCJ.

82. Ferisu Jogakuin, ed., *Ferisu jogakuin hyakunenshi,* 61–62; Ōhama, *Joshigakuin no rekishi,* 269–273.

NOTES TO CHAPTER 2

1. Scott, *Natural Allies,* 85. Earhart, *Frances Willard,* 145–148, 155–157; Bordin, *Woman and Temperance,* 34–51; Frances E. Willard, *Glimpses of Fifty Years: The Autobiography of an American Woman* (Chicago: Woman's Temperance Publication Association, 1889), 368.

2. Carolyn DeSwarte Gifford, "'The Woman's Cause Is Man's'? Frances Willard and the Social Gospel," in *Gender and the Social Gospel,* eds. W. J. Deichann Edwards and C. DeSwarte Gifford (Urbana: University of Illinois Press, 2003), 21–34; Suzanne M. Marilley, "Frances Willard and the Feminism of Fear," *Feminist Studies* 19, no. 1 (Spring 1993): 123–146.

3. DuBois, *Woman Suffrage and Women's Rights,* 30–42; Bordin, *Woman and Temperance,* 52–71; Rose, *American Women and the Repeal of Prohibition,* 9–33; Gifford, "Frances Willard and the Woman's Christian Temperance Union's Conversion to Woman Suffrage," 117–133.

4. Frances E. Willard, *Do Everything: A Handbook for the World's White Ribboners* (Chicago: Woman's Temperance Publishing Association, 1895; reprint, New York: Garland Publishing, 1987), 35.

5. Willard, *Glimpses of Fifty Years,* 368–371.

6. Tyrrell, *Woman's World/Woman's Empire,* 19–23.

7. Willard, *Do Everything,* 7–18.

8. Willard, *Glimpses of Fifty Years,* 430–436; Frances E. Willard, "Mrs. Mary Clement Leavitt," *Union Signal,* 27 January 1887. Until the "Leavitt Fund," which later changed its name to the "World Fund," was established in 1885, Leavitt's travel was supported by donations from "friends" at each destination around the world.

9. Willard, *Do Everything,* 11–13.

10. Ibid., 15.

11. "Lady Henry Somerset's Address at the Recent World's First Conference in London," *Union Signal,* 15 September 1892.

12. At the end of her article, Ryder used the title, "World's W.C.T.U. Organizer and Lecturer for India," *Union Signal,* 11 April 1889.

13. "Our Round-the-World Missionary," *Union Signal,* 5 August 1886.

14. "Our Round-the-World Missionary," *Union Signal,* 18 November 1886, 30 December 1886.

15. Leavitt reported the formation of missionaries' unions in Yokohama and Tokyo as well as Japanese women's temperance unions in Kyoto and Kobe for which missionary women were "ready to help and advise." In addition, Iwamoto's *Jogaku zasshi* wrote that a few more local Japanese female unions were organized with assistance from male Japanese Christians and/or Western Protestant missionary women. Unlike many other countries where the World WCTU's unions were led by Anglo-American missionary women, many of these unions in Japan were headed by Japanese women or men. "Our Round-the-World Missionary," *Union Signal,* 26 August 1886; 2 September 1886; 18 November 1886; 4 October 1888; *Jogaku zasshi,* no. 37 (5 October 1886): 140; no. 41 (15 November 1886): 19; no. 44 (15 December 1886): 75–76; no. 46 (5 January 1887): 119–120.

16. "Our Round-the-World Missionary," *Union Signal,* 5 August 1886.

17. "Our Round-the-World Missionary," *Union Signal,* 2 September 1886; *Jogaku zasshi,* no. 30 (25 July 1886): 305–306; Nihon Kirisutokyō Fujin Kyōfūkai, ed., *Nihon kirisutokyō fujin kyōfūkai hyakunenshi* (Tokyo: Domesu shuppan, 1986), 36.

18. *Nihon kirisutokyō fujin kyōfūkai hyakunenshi,* 40; Azuma Moriya, "Yajima Kajiko," *Fujin shinpō,* 10 December 1922, 24–25.

19. "Our Round-the-World Missionary," *Union Signal,* 18 November 1886.

20. Irwin Scheiner, "Christian Samurai and Samurai Values," in *Modern Japanese Leadership: Transition and Change,* eds. Bernard S. Silberman and H. D. Harootounian (Tucson: University of Arizona Press, 1966), 171–194; Irwin Scheiner, *Christian Converts and Social Protest in Meiji Japan* (Berkeley: University of California Press, 1970); Aizan Yamaji, "Historical Theory of Modern Japanese Churches," in *Essays on the Modern Japanese Church: Christianity in Meiji Japan,* trans. and ed. Graham Squires and A. Hamish (Ann Arbor: University of Michigan Press, 1999), 67–69.

21. Yoshimi Fujita, *Meiji Jogakkō no sekai* (Tokyo: Seieisha, 1984), 7–28; Aoyama, *Meiji Jogakkō no kenkyū,* 137–400.

22. Takahashi, *Nakamura Keiu,* 155–172.

23. Kiyoe Nobechi, *Josei kaihō shisō no genryū: Iwamoto Yoshiharu to Jogaku zasshi* (Tokyo: Azekura shobō, 1984), 163–202; Fujita, *Meiji Jogakkō no sekai,* 28–78; Aoyama, *Meiji Jogakkō no kenkyū,* 663–766.

24. *Jogaku zasshi,* no. 29 (15 July 1886): 278; no. 30 (25 July 1886): 305–306; no. 31 (5 August 1886): 1–3; no. 32 (15 August 1886): 21–22, 40; *Union Signal,* 2 September 1886; *Nihon kirisutokyō fujin kyōfūkai hyakunenshi,* 35.

25. *Jogaku zasshi,* no. 37 (5 October 1886): 140(3).

26. *Jogaku zasshi,* no. 41 (15 November 1886): 1–3.

27. *Fukuin Shinpō,* 21 May 1884, 2.

28. *Fukuin Shinpō* 26 March 1884; 4 March 1885. Indicative of the radicalism of the WCTU from the perspective of American missionary women, the attendees

included one American missionary woman named Kate Youngman. Youngman initiated Graham Seminary but was opposed to male control over women's work in the Presbyterian mission in Tokyo and left the school to engage in independent work. Kate M. Youngman to Gentlemen, 3 November 1877, PMJ; Kōzensha, ed., *Aru gunzō*, 35–80; Ōhama, *Joshigakuin no rekishi*, 121–132.

29. *Jogaku zasshi*, no. 40 (5 November 1886): 196–197; no. 41 (15 November 1886): 16–176.

30. *Jogaku zasshi*, no. 44 (15 December 1886): 75–76; Kajiko Yajima, "Nihon Kirisutokyō fujin Kyōfūkai ryakushi," in *Bankoku kirisutokyō fujin kyōfūkai annai*, trans. and ed. Takeshi Ukai (Tokyo: Kyōbunkan, 1898), 48–62; Azuma Moriya, "Waga kai no rekishi," *Fujin shinpō*, no. 237 (28 March 1917): 20–21.

31. Jessie A. Ackerman, "Our Second Round-the-World Missionary in Japan," *Union Signal*, 24 July 1890.

32. Emma Brainerd Ryder, "Stray Notes from Japan," *Union Signal*, 11 April 1889; Mary A. West, "Work in Japan," *Union Signal*, 29 December 1892. As of January 2004, the so-called Japan WCTU officially calls itself in English Japan's Christian Women's Organization.

33. *Jogaku zasshi*, no. 55 (12 March 1887): 98–99.

34. *Jogaku zasshi*, no. 55 (12 March 1887): 83–85; no. 56 (19 March 1887): 103–106; no. 58 (2 April 1887): 147–149; no. 59 (9 April 1887): 165–166; no. 60 (16 April 1887): 185–186.

35. Mary C. Leavitt, "Nihon no shimai ni tsugu," parts 1–3, *Jogaku zasshi*, no. 36 (25 September 1886): 111–112; no. 37 (5 October 1886): 131–132; no. 39 (25 October 1886): 171–172.

36. The popular-rights movement was led by former samurais from the two powerful anti-Tokugawa domains: Kochi (Tosa) and Saga (Hizen). While the Saga group looked upon the English parliamentary government as a suitable model, the Kochi group was more liberal and insisted on greater popular sovereignty.

37. The government expelled Nobuyuki Nakajima from Tokyo in its attempt to suppress the popular-rights movement in 1887. Moving to Yokohama with her husband, Toshiko (Kishida) Nakajima taught at the Ferris Seminary in the late 1880s and the early 1890s. Both Kishida and her husband died of tuberculosis at a young age. See Itoya, *Josei kaihō no senkusha*, 16–98; Yūko Nishikawa, *Hana no imōto* (Tokyo: Shinchōsha, 1986), 179–180.

38. Toyojyu Sasaki, "Sekinen no shūkan o yaburubeshi," parts 1–3, *Jogaku zasshi*, no. 48 (22 January 1887): 154–155; no. 52 (19 February 1887): 34–35; no. 54 (5 March 1887): 75–77.

39. Toyojyu Sasaki, "Tokyo fujin kyōfūkai no kaiin aishi ni tsugu," *Jogaku zasshi*, no. 56 (19 March 1887): 114–116.

40. The other two speakers were an American female physician, Dr. Kelse, and Mrs. Miya Ebina, a Tokyo WCTU officer and niece of Kajiko Yajima. *Jogaku zasshi*, no. 62 (30 April 1887): 38.

41. "Joshi no enzetsu," *Jogaku zasshi*, no. 63 (7 May 1887): 41–43.

42. Maria True, "Zenryō naru mohan no kachi," part 1, *Jogaku zasshi*, no. 72 (20 August 1887): 23–25.

43. One of the other female speakers was Miss Shige Kushida, and the two male speakers were Sen Tsuda and Rev. G. Verbeck. *Jogaku zasshi*, no. 84 (12 November 1887): appendix 80(3). Shige Kushida later went to the United States and remained socially active in the Japanese immigrant community in the Bay Area. Married, Shige (Kushida) Togasaki was a longtime member of the Oakland Japanese WCTU. See Mei T. Nakano, *Japanese American Women: Three Generations, 1890–1990* (Berkeley: Nina Press, 1990), 24; "Ko Togasaki fujin o omoute" *Zaibei Fujin Shinpō* (Japanese Women's Herald in America) 28, no. 5 (November 1929): 1–2.

44. *Jogaku zasshi*, no. 98 (25 February 1888): 23.

45. Toyojyu Sasaki, "Onore no omoi," *Tokyo fujin kyōfū zasshi*, no. 1 (14 April 1888): 4–5; "Jiko no omoi sunawachi fujin no omoi wa danshi to kotonaru setsu," *Tokyo fujin kyōfū zasshi*, no. 3 (16 June 1888): 3–6.

46. "Let Your Women Keep Silence in the Churches," *Union Signal*, 1 July 1886, 7–8.

47. Toyojyu Sasaki, trans., *Fujin genron no jiyū* (Tokyo: Shūeisha, 1888).

48. Kokkō Sōma, *Mokui* (Tokyo, 1936; reprint Matsumoto: Kyōdo shuppansha, 1981), 286–293; Shizuko Kōno, *Sohō to sono jidai: Yoserareta shokan kara* (Tokyo: Chūō kōronsha, 1988), 181–224; Utsu, *Saisō yori yori fukaki tamashiini*, 37–98; Reiko Abe, "Sasaki Toyojyu oboegaki; Wasurerareta fujinkaihō undō no ichi senkusha," *Nihonshi kenkyū*, no. 171 (November 1976): 52–65; *Nihon kirisutokyō fujin kyōfūkai hyakunenshi*, 87–90.

49. Among the Kumamoto band, a well-known group of young Japanese students who were converted to Christianity under the influence of their American teacher, L. L. Janes, were Yajima's nephews and nieces. While Janes taught English, science, and social sciences at school and the Bible at home, his wife taught cooking and sewing to a small group of female students at their house. When his wife's girls' class was discontinued, Janes allowed two of the female students to listen to his lectures. These two students were Yajima's nieces, Miya (Yokoi) Ebina and Hatsuko (Tokutomi) Yuasa, who later became active in the WCTU movement in Japan. Hatsuko Yuasa cooperated with Sasaki in breaking the silence of the Tokyo WCTU women in 1887. F. G. Notehelfer, *American Samurai: Captain L. L. Janes and Japan* (Princeton: Princeton University Press, 1985), 130–209.

50. Sasaki was born to a family of Confucian scholars in a pro-Tokugawa domain that became Miyagi Prefecture. Attending Dōjinsha in Tokyo, she met Yoshiharu Iwamoto, who was also studying at Dōjinsha, and her future husband, Motoe Sasaki (1843–1901), who was from the same town and taught at the school. Motoe was the fourth son of a family of doctors, and was married to his father's friend's only daughter to succeed as household head. After his marriage, Motoe moved to

Yokohama to receive Western medical training. Here he encountered Christianity and was baptized in 1872 despite the edict prohibiting the religion. Motoe moved to Tokyo in 1874 to teach at Nakamura's Dōjinsha, and his wife and children joined him at his residence. Presumably Motoe met Toyojyu at Dōjinsha and they started to live together in 1877. Motoe's wife and children returned to her father's home in 1878. For Motoe Sasaki, see Nobuo Itō, "Itō yuken shōden; Purotesutanto jusenshita saisho no tōhokujin no denki," *Tōhoku gakuin daigaku tōhoku bunka kenkyūjo kiyō*, no. 6 (December 1974): 63–73. For Toyojyu Sasaki, see Utsu, *Saisō yori yori fukaki tamashiini*, 46–48; Abe, "Sasaki Toyojyu oboegaki."

51. "Yajima joshi no himitsu," *Fujo shinbun*, 5 July 1925.

52. Azuma Moriya, *Yajima Kajiko* (Tokyo: Fujin shinpōsha, 1923); Kubushiro, *Yajima Kajiko den*.

53. Chiseko Ushioda, "Fujin kyōfūkai to Sasaki Toyojyu fujin," *Fujin shinpō*, no. 34 (25 February 1900): 16–19.

54. *Jogaku zasshi*, no. 62 (30 April 1887): 38.

55. Toyojyu Sasaki, "Fujin bunmei no hataraki," *Jogaku zasshi*, no. 65 (21 May 1887): 86–88.

56. Ōtake, *"Ie" to josei no rekishi*, 247–274.

57. Initially only members of the Imperial family and former lords were granted the peerage by the Meiji government, but the peerage law of 1884 opened the way for Meiji leaders to join the nobility and to qualify for seats in the House of Peers in the Imperial Diet that was expected to open in 1890.

58. Sheldon Garon, *Molding Japanese Minds: The State in Everyday Life* (Princeton: Princeton University Press, 1997), 91–92.

59. Kazuo Kasahara, *Nihon joseishi* (Tokyo: Hyōronsha, 1923), 216–234; Kazue Morisaki, *Karayukisan* (Tokyo: Asahi shinbun, 1976); Sheldon Garon, "The World's Oldest Debate? Prostitution and the State in Imperial Japan, 1900–1945," *American Historical Review* (June 1993): 710–732; Maki, *Jinshin baibai*; Kenichi Tanigawa, *Kindai minshū no kiroku*, vol. 3 (Tokyo: Shin jinbutsu ōraisha, 1971), Judith R. Walkowitz, *Prostitution and Victorian Society: Women, Class, and the State* (Cambridge: Cambridge University Press, 1982); Alain Corbin, *Women for Hire: Prostitution and Sexuality in France after 1850*, trans. Alan Sheridan (Cambridge: Harvard University Press, 1990); Yuki Fujime, *Sei no rekishigaku* (Tokyo: Fuji shuppan, 1997).

60. In 1900, the Ministry of Home Affairs established á new rule under which registration of a woman as a licensed prostitute required the signature of the woman herself. It also recognized a licensed prostitute's right to terminate her business of her own free will. Although advance money was usually paid to a prostitute's family and was a debt to be paid back by the prostitute or her family, the Japanese system of licensed prostitution came to involve the consent of daughters, at least formally. Tamio Takemura, *Haishō undō* (Tokyo: Chūō kōronsha, 1982).

61. Vern Bullough and Bonnie Bullough, *Women and Prostitution: A Social History* (Buffalo, N.Y.: Prometheus Books, 1987).

62. Takemura, *Haishō undō*.

63. *Tokyo fujin kyōfū zasshi*, no. 1 (14 April 1888): 12–13.

64. Ryō Yoshida, "Iminshakai to kirisutokyō: Miyama Kanichi no hawai nihonjin imin dendō, 1887–1889," *Kirisutokyō shakai mondai kenkyū*, no. 31 (March 1983): 141–188; Tarō Andō, "Kinshuron," *Jogaku zasshi*, no. 161 (11 May 1889): 49–54.

65. *Tokyo fujin kyōfū zasshi*, no. 1 (14 April 1888): 12–13.

66. The meeting was conducted by "volunteers" as a project of the "East Department" of the Tokyo WCTU. By March 1889 the Tokyo WCTU had come to be composed of four subunions, namely, the North, South, East, and West unions. Sasaki and her sympathizers belonged to the East Union. *Tokyo fujin kyōfū zasshi*, no. 2 (4 April 1888): 18–19; no. 13 (20 April 1889): 19–21.

67. Ushioda was also born into a former samurai family which rented its house to a Methodist Episcopal missionary, Julius Soper, after the Restoration. As a result of her interactions with him, Ushioda became a Christian in 1882. After she was widowed in 1883, she left her hometown for Tokyo with her five children and began attending a class at Presbyterian Bancho School that trained kindergarten teachers. She also started working as an assistant to Matilda A. Spencer of the M.E. Mission, and then studied at the M.E. Mission's Bible School for Women between 1887 and 1890. After graduating from the school, Ushioda became a Bible woman assisting Spencer in evangelical work. Reiko Abe, "Ushioda Chiseko," ed. Fumiko Enchi, *Kindai Nihon no joseishi*, vol. 8 (Tokyo: Shūeisha, 1981), 47–82; *Nihon kirisutokyō fujin kyōfūkai hyakunenshi*, 309–311.

68. *Tokyo fujin kyōfū zasshi*, no. 1 (14 April 1888): 18–19.

69. *Jogaku zasshi*, no. 110 (19 May 1888): 22; no. 121 (4 August 1888): 25; *Tokyo fujin kyōfū zasshi*, no. 3 (16 June 1888): 80.

70. Toyojyu Sasaki, "Haishō sōnen no netsurui," *Haishō*, no. 2 (15 May 1890): 60–61; *Jogaku zasshi*, no. 121 (4 August 1888): 25; no. 228 (30 August 1890): 81; Ushioda, "Fujin kyōfūkai to Sasaki Toyojyu fujin"; Chiseko Ushioda, "Jiaikan no koto ni tsuite," *Fujin shinpō*, no. 18 (20 October 1898): 10–16; Utsu, *Saisō yori yori fukaki tamashiini*, 58.

71. Frances Willard also believed that a wife was entitled to a share of her husband's income. Sasaki might have read an article in *Union Signal*, which demanded a wife's right to "a reasonable portion" of her husband's income. "A Word to Husbands," *Union Signal*, 18 March 1886.

72. Toyojyu Sasaki, "Dōhō shokei ni nozomu," part 2, *Tokyo fujin kyōfū zasshi*, no. 4 (21 July 1888): 3–6.

73. Chiseko Ushioda, "Kaiko to kibō," *Fujin shinpō*, no. 67 (25 November 1902): 308–311.

74. Saku Asai was a teacher at the Sakurai Women's School before it came under the sponsorship of the Presbyterian Mission, before she opened her own

school in 1883. Masako Katano, "Asai Saku oboegaki," in *Kindai nihon no kirisu-tokyō to joseitachi,* ed. Tomisaka kirisutokyō sentā (Tokyo: Shinkyō shuppan, 1995), 12–50.

75. Saku Asai, "Kyōfūkaiin ni kankoku su," *Tokyo fujin kyōfū zasshi,* no. 3 (16 June 1888): 1–3.

76. Saku Asai, "Fujin kairyō o ronzu," *Tokyo fujin kyōfū zasshi,* no. 4 (21 July 1888): 1–3.

77. Saku Asai, "Kaiin shimai ni tsugu," *Tokyo fujin kyōfū zasshi,* no. 9 (15 December 1888): 1–4.

78. *Tokyo fujin kyōfū zasshi,* no. 5 (18 August 1888): 1. Sasaki had a miscarriage between the birth of her third child in 1885 and the fifth in 1891. This might also have contributed to her resignation.

79. Toyojyu Sasaki, "Indo no joketsu Ramabai fujin," *Jogaku zasshi,* no. 129 (29 September 1888): 4–5; "Ramabai joshi tono mondō," *Jogaku zasshi,* no. 142 (29 December 1888): 7–11; Antoinette M. Burton, "Colonial Encounters in Late-Victorian England: Pandita Ramabai at Cheltenham and Wantage, 1883–1886," *Feminist Review,* no. 49 (Spring 1995): 29–40; Pandita Ramabai, *Through Her Own Words: Selected Works,* ed. and trans. Meera Kosambi (New Delhi: Oxford University Press, 2000): 230–235.

80. Sasaki, "Indo no joketsu Ramabai fujin."

81. Ibid.; Pandita Ramabai, "*Ryōhankyū no hinan,*" part 1–2, *Jogaku zasshi,* no. 129 (29 September 1888): 5–7; no. 130 (6 October 1888): 6–8.

82. "Johakase Ramabai oyobi sono jigyō o hyōsu," *Jogaku zasshi,* no. 143 (5 January 1889): 14–15.

83. "Ramabai joshi tono mondō."

84. "Ramabai gienkin," *Jogaku zasshi,* no. 143 (5 January 1889): 26–27.

85. "Ramabai joshi," *Mainichi shinbun,* 30 December 1888; "Ramabai's Progress in Japan," *Union Signal,* 14 February 1889.

86. Ellen DuBois, *Feminism and Suffrage: The Emergence of an Independent Woman's Movement in America, 1848–1869* (Ithaca: Cornell University Press, 1978).

87. Ueki's father was of the samurai class in Tosa (Kochi). While his father married three times, Emori was the only son believed to be born of an extramarital affair by his mother. When Emori was four years old, his father divorced her. At age sixteen, he was chosen to study at the school of Western learning that was to be built in Tokyo by the former lord of Tosa domain. He left Kochi for Tokyo in 1873, but realizing that the purpose of the school was to produce military cadets, Ueki quit the school and walked back to his hometown. In 1875, Ueki went to Tokyo again to pursue his education on his own. Without enrolling in any school, he spent two years in Tokyo reading widely, including numerous Western books translated into Japanese or Chinese, attending lecture meetings, and contributing his opinions to a variety of newspapers and magazines. During this era, Ueki was a self-proclaimed Christian and enthusiastically attended the services

and meetings of different denominations. After failing the bar exam four times, Ueki returned to Kochi in 1877. He became an organizer and ideologist of the Kochi popular-rights movement. He traveled the country extensively and contributed articles to newspapers both in Osaka and Kochi. Mitsuhiro Sotozaki, *Ueki Emori to onnatachi* (Tokyo: Domesu shuppan, 1976), 13–27; Saburo Ienaga, *Ueki Emori kenkyū* (Tokyo: Iwanami shoten, 1960), 16–27.

88. Sotozaki, *Ueki Emori to onnatachi*, 43–45; Sievers, *Flowers in Salt*, 29–30. For a discussion on the role of women in the popular-rights movement, see Mtoko Ōki, *Jiyū Minken Undō to Josei* (Tokyo: Domesu Shuppan, 2003).

89. Sotozaki, *Ueki Emori to onnatachi*, 49–51.

90. Sotozaki, *Ueki Emori to onnatachi*, 52–54; Ienaga, *Ueki Emori kenkyū*, 308–311.

91. In the book, Ueki argued that the subjugation of Japanese women in daily life, marriage, education, politics, and law was caused by (1) the past three-and-a-half centuries of control by warriors, who valued physical power over all other characteristics; (2) the teachings of Confucianism, Buddhism, and Shintoism; (3) an autocratic political system; and (4) women's self-deprecation as a result of long-time subjugation. Consequently, women came not to pursue an education or to gain knowledge and thus, they were not able to be "good mothers" and produce good children. This in turn stood in the way of society's progress and the prosperity of the state. Ueki suggested that these "evil" conditions should be corrected by (1) revising the property inheritance law to allow women to control their own funds; (2) explaining the logic and merit of equality between men and women; (3) eliminating the teachings of Confucius and Mencius and other "isms" that denied women's rights; (4) promoting female education; (5) creating jobs for women; and (6) releasing women from their confinement in the house and broadening their socialization. After comparing marriage systems in the West and East, Ueki argued that marriage should be a civil contract the terms of which could vary depending on the individuals involved and should be freely agreed upon by a man and a woman, without the intervention of a church. Emori Ueki, "Tōyō no fujo," in *Ueki Emori shū*, vol. 2 (Tokyo: Iwanami shoten, 1990), 187–290.

92. Ueki, "Tōyō no fujo"; Sotozaki, *Ueki Emori to onnatachi*.

93. The content of *Tōyō no fujo* was based on four articles that had been published in *Doyō Shinbun*, the local newspaper of popular-rights activists in Kochi. Ueki completed editing the four articles for the book in June 1887, and intended to have it published by Iwamoto's *Jogaku zasshi* in Tokyo. Ueki asked his friend, Sohō Tokutomi, who was Yajima's nephew and the publisher of a popular magazine at the time, to negotiate with Iwamoto. Since both Iwamoto and Tokutomi were reluctant to publish Ueki's book, Sasaki arranged to print it in her hometown. Shizuko Kōno, "Tōyō no fujo ni matsuwaru Emori, Sohō, Toyojyu no kōyū," *Ueki Emori shū geppō*, no. 2 (March 1990): 1–5.

94. Saku Asai, "Kaitō no jishoku oyobi kōsen," *Tokyo fujin kyōfū zasshi,* no. 13 (20 April 1889): 1–4.

95. "Fujin kyōfūkai fukukai," *Jogaku zasshi,* no. 167 (22 June 1889): 30.

96. Sasaki played a key role in the WWRC, although its organization was first reported by two Japanese teachers of Graham Seminary and the female mission school of the M.E. Mission in Tokyo. Utsu, *Saisō yori yori fukaki tamashiini,* 75; *Jogaku zasshi,* no. 167 (22 June 1889): 29; Toyojyu Sasaki, "Fujin hakuhyō kurabu no seishitsu o nobete sejō no ichigimon ni kotau," *Jogaku zasshi,* no. 186 (9 November 1889): 8–10.

97. Emori Ueki argued that (1) prostitution, like stealing, was against human morality and a woman should not engage in prostitution just because she was poor; furthermore, the system of licensed prostitution caused harm not only by allowing her to be a prostitute but also by registering and labeling her as one, (2) Japan could not deny the existence of prostitution as long as it was publicly licensed, (3) attempts to prevent the spread of venereal disease by regular inspection would never be perfect, and the government's requirement that women's "private parts" be inspected would not only disgrace the nation but also humiliate the women who were inspected, (4) licensed prostitution would not protect women of good families but would create a lewd atmosphere throughout society, (5) it was illogical to license prostitution but to prohibit nonlicensed prostitution, because prostitution was a "shameful" business and should be conducted secretly. The elimination of prostitution was the job of religious and moral activists, and politicians should not involve themselves in this issue, and (6) in Kochi prefecture, the system of liscensed prostitution allowed brothels and prostitutes to take over restaurants and geisha girls, who had more freedom in their lives than prostitutes. "*Kōshō haishi no kengi*" in *Ueki Emori shū,* vol. 6, 319–326. His views are also clearly laid out in his "*Haishōron,*" in *Ueki Emori shū,* vol. 4, 180–196.

98. Ienaga, *Ueki Emori kenkyū,* 71–96.

99. Ueki, "Tōyō no fujo."

100. Emori Ueki, "Rinri no taihon," *Tokyo fujin kyōfū zasshi,* parts 1–5, no. 15 (15 June 1889): 16–20; no. 16 (20 July 1889): 16–19; no. 17 (17 August 1889): 9–12; no. 18 (21 September 1889): 7–11; no. 19 (9 October 1889): 10–14.

101. "Ippu ippusei kenkyū," *Jogaku zasshi,* no. 168 (29 June 1899): 26.

102. *Ueki Emori shū,* vol. 8, 80.

103. Hatsu Yuasa, "Rinri no motoi no yōshi," *Jogaku zasshi,* no. 161 (11 May 1889): 30.

104. In Tokyo, the signatories to Yuasa's petition included Kajiko Yajima, Saku Asai, Emori Ueki, Sen Tsuda, and male Protestant ministers such as Motoichirō Ōgimi, Kajinosuke Ibuka, Masahisa Uemura, and Hiromichi Kozaki. *Jogaku zasshi,* no. 168 (29 June 1889): 26. In Kyoto, Toyoko Shimizu, who later joined Sasaki's group, and Hideko Kageyama, who later became a socialist, gathered signatures

for a petition similar to Yuasa's. *Jogaku zasshi,* no. 170 (13 July 1889): 28; no. 175 (17 August 1889): 27.

105. Hidekichi Ito, *Nihon haishō undōshi* (Tokyo: Kakuseikai, 1931), 140–145.

106. Bullough and Bullough, *Women and Prostitution,* 196; Corbin, *Women for Hire;* Walkowitz, *Prostitution and Victorian Society.*

107. *Tokyo fujin kyōfū zasshi,* no. 32 (20 December 1890): 8–11; *Haishō,* no. 7 (16 January 1891): 18–19; no. 8 (6 March 1891): 13–14, 21–25.

108. Saku Asai, "Teikoku kizoku/shūgi-in giin kakui ni seigansu," *Tokyo fujin kyōfū zasshi,* no. 32 (20 December 1890): 2–4. The movement to abolish the licensed system of prostitution continued, but it was not until 1945 after the Japanese defeat in the Pacific War that the system was nationally abolished by the order of the General Headquarters of the Allied Forces (GHQ), which occupied Japan from 1945 to 1952. The new Japanese Constitution, which was established under the supervision of the GHQ, dropped the criminalization of a wife's adultery and granted women suffrage. The Japan WCTU continually fought hard for the criminalization of prostitution, and prostitution was banned in 1957 by Japan's national law.

109. Fujin Hakuhyō Kurabu, "Zenkoku yūshi konshinkai ni okuru sho," *Jogaku zasshi,* no. 183 (19 October 1889): 23.

110. The queen responded to Sasaki and Ushioda through her secretary, stating that the matter was not in her jurisdiction and that the Secretary of State would reply to them later. *Jogaku zasshi,* no. 183 (19 October 1889): 27; no. 197 (25 January 1890): 24; no. 207 (5 April 1890): 207.

111. Reiko Mitsui, *Gendai fujin undōshi nenpyō* (Tokyo: Sanichi shobō, 1978), 39.

112. Sievers, *Flowers in Salt,* 122.

113. Toyoko Shimizu had married a popular-rights activist in the late 1880s, in accordance with her father's wishes. But she divorced him after four years because of his extramarital relationships. Reiko Yamaguchi, *Naite aisuru shimai ni tsugu: Kozai shikin no shōgai* (Tokyo: Sodo bunka, 1977).

114. Shimizu also briefly taught at the Meiji Women's School where Iwamoto served as principal.

115. Toyoko Shimizu, "Naze ni joshi wa seidan shūkai ni sanchōsurukoto o yurusarezaruya," *Jogaku zasshi,* no. 228 (30 August 1890): 61–64.

116. Toyoko Shimizu, "Naite aisuru shimai ni tsugu," *Jogaku zasshi,* no. 234 (11 October 1890): Appendix 2.

117. Yoshiharu Iwamoto, "Shūgiin fujin bōchō no koto," *Jogaku zasshi,* no. 234 (2 August 1890): Appendix 1.

118. Toyoko Shimizu, "Dōken ni tsuki Itagaki-haku o tou no ki," *Jogaku zasshi,* no. 234 (11 October 1890): Appendix 2–4; "Fujin wa bōchō o yurusazu," *Tokyo fujin kyōfū zasshi,* no. 30 (18 October 1890): 11–12.

119. *Tokyo nichi nichi shinbun,* 24 October 1890.

120. Utsu, *Saiso yori yori fukaki tamashiini,* 79.

121. Toyojyu Sasaki, "Teikoku gikai shūgiin giin shokun ni teisu" *Yomiuri Shinbun*, 17 March 1891, cited in *Nihon kirisutokyō fujin kyōfūkai hyakunenshi*, 80–81.

122. Mitsui, *Gendai fujin undōshi nenpyō*, 39, 63–64, 99.

123. *Union Signal*, 26 August 1886.

124. "Our Round-the-World Missionary," *Union Signal*, 26 August 1886.

125. Mary C. Leavitt, "Shudoku no iden," *Jogaku zasshi*, parts 1–2, no. 28 (5 July 1886): 257–259; no. 29 (15 July 1886): 273–274.

126. "WCTU in Japan," *Union Signal*, 16 May 1887.

127. After West died during her lecture tour in Japan, a number of her lectures were published in Japan to commemorate her. They were entitled "Citizenship," "Sake to tabako no gai" (Harm from Liquor and Tobacco), "Nihon no kōgyō ni oyobosu insyu no heigai" (Evil Effects of Drinking on Japanese Industry), "Kinshu to kōgyō no kankei" (Relationship between Temperance and Industry), "Fujin to kyōfū jigyō tono kankei" (Relationship between Women and Temperance Work), "Koronbia Sekai daihakurankai niokeru beikoku fujin kyōikukai oyobi fujin kyōfūkai no keikaku" (Plan for an American Women's Educational Society and the WCTU at the World Columbian Exposition), and "Bankoku fujin kyōfūkai no undo" (The World WCTU Movement).

128. One *koku* is equivalent to 5.12 bushels.

129. Mary A. West, "Citizenship," *Parmly Billings Leaflets for World's Temperance*, no. 17, trans. and ed. Shō Nemoto (Tokyo: Shūeisha, 1893), 29–41.

130. Ibid.

131. Ackerman, "Our Second Round-the-World Missionary," *Union Signal*, 21 August 1890.

132. Mary Allen West, "Work in Japan," *Union Signal*, 29 December 1892.

133. Jane Hunter, in her study of American Protestant missionary women in China, argues that American missionary women viewed Chinese men as "effeminate" because of their physical and cultural characteristics in comparison with Americans. Hunter, *The Gospel of Gentility*, 204–216.

134. "Our Second Round-the-World Missionary in Japan," *Union Signal*, 24 July 1890.

135. "Our Second Round-the-World Missionary," *Union Signal*, 21 August 1890.

136. "Akkeruman Jō," *Jogaku zasshi*, no. 203 (8 March 1890): 27; "Akkeruman jō: Taizaichū no hataraki no hōkoku," *Jogaku zasshi*, no. 206 (29 March 1890): 28–29.

137. Mary A. Livermore and Frances E. Willard, ed., *A Woman of the Century* (Chicago: Charles Wells Moulton, 1893), 4–5.

138. Ernest H. Cherrington, *Standard Encyclopedia of the Alcohol Problem* (Westerville, Ohio: American Issue Publishing Co., 1926), 1384–1391.

139. Nemoto was born into a samurai family in the domain of a Tokugawa prince. After the Restoration, Nemoto studied at schools in Tokyo and Kobe, including Masanao Nakamura's Dōjinsha, and became a Christian. He went to the

United States in 1879, attended Oakland Public School, and graduated from Hopkins Academy in California and from the University of Vermont in 1889. Nemoto served as a representative to the Japanese Imperial Diet from 1898 to 1923. West, "Work in Japan," *Union Signal*, 29 December 1892; "Hon. Shō Nemoto," *Japan Evangelist* 7, no. 10 (October 1900); *Nihon kirisutokyō rekishi daijiten*, 626.

140. For example, Nemoto visited Willard at her home at Rest Cottage to introduce to her a Japanese Christian journalist and politician, Saburō Shimada, and his wife, who was a member of the Tokyo WCTU, in 1888. "A Visitor from the Orient," *Union Signal*, 17 May 1888.

141. *Union Signal*, 26 May 1887.

142. Among the committee members were Tarō Andō and Kajiko Yajima, president of the Tokyo WCTU. West, "Work in Japan," *Union Signal*, 29 December 1892.

143. Among the people West wrote about were male Christians who founded the Sapporo Temperance Society as well as Sen Tsuda, Tarō Andō, and Shō Nemoto. Mary Allen West, "The Newest Japan," 24 November 1892; "Japan's Welcome," 1 December 1892; "Work in Japan," 22 December 1892 and 29 December 1892. All in *Union Signal*.

144. West, "Work in Japan," *Union Signal*, 22 December 1892.

145. Sasaki became the corresponding secretary and Ushioda the recording secretary of the Tokyo Temperance Society. "Tokyo Temperance Society," *Tokyo kinshukai geppō*, no. 1 (3 December 1890).

146. Saku Asai, "Kurayami no icchi o nasukoto nakare," *Tokyo fujin kyōfū zasshi*, no. 23 (15 March 1890): 2–5.

147. *Jogaku zasshi*, no. 262 (25 April 1891): 27.

148. "Beikoku fujin kinshukai to waga fujin kyōfūkai," *Fukuin Shinpō*, no. 26 (11 September 1891): 14; *Tokyo fujin kyōfū zasshi*, no. 32 (20 December 1890): 12–13; no. 42 (17 October 1891): 4–6.

149. In elections held in December 1891, the Tokyo WCTU officers chose Mrs. Kanamori for president and Mrs. Sekiko Ibuka for vice president. Both were wives of Protestant ministers in Tokyo. However, the election by the Tokyo WCTU members in February 1892 made Yajima president. "Nenkai no moyō," *Tokyo fujin kyōfū zasshi*, no. 44 (19 December 1891): 3–4; "Kaitō, fukukaitō sentei," *Tokyo fujin kyōfū zasshi*, no. 46 (20 February 1892): 2.

150. The Tokyo WCTU bylaws were initially based on those of the World WCTU, which was translated by and published in Iwamoto's *Jogaku zasshi*. The Tokyo WCTU bylaws of December 1886 required its members to make the following pledge, "[I] with the help of God, swear to take appropriate action in order to prohibit and eliminate any object, including all Japanese and Western liquor and tobacco, that would harm [Japanese] manners and customs." However, by the time of West's visit the pledge was revised as follows: "[I], with the help of God, swear to follow appropriate methods based on the principle of each department in order

to achieve the purpose of this union." *Nihon kirisutokyō fujin kyōfūkai hyakunenshi,* 38–39; *Tokyo fujin kyōfū zasshi,* no. 11 (16 February 1889): 17–19; no. 23 (15 March 1890): 10–11.

151. "Uesuto-jyō raiyū no mokuteki," *Tokyo fujin kyōfū zasshi,* no. 53 (31 October 1892): 7–8.

152. West, "Work in Japan," *Union Signal,* 29 December 1892.

153. "Fukani okeru Uesuto-jyō," *Kirisutokyō Shinbun,* 4 November 1892, 2.

154. In the old version, the purpose of the Tokyo WCTU was "to increase the happiness of society in general by rectifying morality, by correcting evil social customs, and by promoting women's dignity," but in the new version it read: "to increase the happiness of society in general by rectifying morality, by correcting evil social customs, and by expanding the work of prohibiting drinking and smoking." As for the pledge, both before and after the revision the Tokyo WCTU made a pledge of total abstinence, but individual members did not. In the old version, article four stipulated that "those who would like to be a member" should make the following pledge: "[I], with the help of God, swear to follow appropriate methods based on the principle of each department in order to achieve the purpose of this union." In the new version, although the pledge included total abstinence from liquor and tobacco, it was moved to the section stating the purpose of the Tokyo WCTU. Because the subject of the sentence is usually omitted in Japanese, in the context of the new version it was the Tokyo WCTU but not the individual member that pledged to abide by prohibition. *Tokyo fujin kyōfū zasshi,* no. 52 (28 September 1892); no. 54 (28 November 1892): 3–4.

155. "Tokyo fujin kyōfūkai sōkai," *Jogaku zasshi,* no. 333 (10 December 1892): 29.

156. "Zenkoku fujinkai no dōmei," *Tokyo fujin kyōfū zasshi,* no. 57 (28 February 1893): 3; "Nihon fujin rengōkai honbu," *Tokyo fujin kyōfū zasshi,* no. 57 (28 February 1893): 5.

157. *Nihon kirisutokyō fujin kyōfūkai hyakunenshi,* 93; *Fujin kyōfū zasshi,* no. 1 (2 November 1893): 52.

158. Ueki had a chronic gastroenteris problem and went to a hospital managed by a retired navy surgeon general from Satsuma in January 1892. He was diagnosed as having intestinal catarrh, but died suddenly at the hospital on 23 January 1892. The cause of his death is the subject of considerable speculation, including the suggestion that Ueki was poisoned to death by his political enemies or by officers of the Satsuma faction in the Meiji government. Ienaga, *Ueki Emori kenkyū;* Sotozaki, *Ueki Emori to onnatachi,* 130–135.

159. Kubushiro, *Yuasa Hatsuko,* 136.

160. In the conservative era of the 1890s, Sasaki's efforts and activism only invited criticism and opposition in the frontier land of Hokkaido. Besides, her daughter's brief marriage with and divorce from a journalist-cum-novelist and an affair on her way to the United States with a married captain of the ship became a scandal. Furthermore, even Toyojyu Sasaki, who endeavored to pursue her activist

agenda in Hokkaido while leaving her husband behind in Tokyo, was suspected of a relationship with her supporter, a Christian progressive man, in Hokkaido. Defeated by the strong backlash against women's and sepecially Sasaki's activism, Sasaki died in Tokyo in 1901. Yasuko Utsu, "Sasaki Toyojyu no Hokkaido ijū saikō," *Seisen joshi daigaku jinbun kagaku kenkyūjo kiyō*, no. 6 (1984): 83–145.

161. Sasaki led two departments of the Tokyo WCTU, first when her friend Chiseko Ushioda served as its president, and next when Sasaki returned briefly to Tokyo.

162. Male popular-rights activists were unrestrained in their sexual relationships. For example, Emori Ueki was known to be a frequent visitor to the pleasure quarters, and others established relationships with their fellow women activists. A well-noted example was the relationship between Kentarō Ōi, a male activist with a wife, and his fellow women activists, Toyoko Shimizu and Hideko Kageyama. Kageyama was bitter about the fact that Shimizu bore Ōi a child; after this the sisterly relationship between the two women turned sour. Yamaguchi, *Naite aisuru shimai ni tsugu;* Hideko Kageyama, *Warawa no hanshōgai* (Tokyo: 1904; reprint, Tokyo: Iwanami shoten, 1958).

163. The professor argued that "eliminating evil customs and bad habits" could not be achieved by personal effort alone but would require cooperation and organizational power. After her recovery from illness in September 1892, Shimizu resumed her work for *Jogaku zasshi*. When her newly wedded husband was away in Europe for a little over five years (from March 1895 to July 1900) for further studies, Shimizu remained in Japan and wrote a number of novels. However, upon her husband's return to Japan in 1900, Shimizu stopped writing forever. Yamaguchi, *Naite aisuru shimai ni tsugu*.

164. Visiting Japan in 1890, Ackerman reported: "There has never been a union formed in Japan among the foreigners: all the work was carried on by the Japanese." "Our Second Round-the-World Missionary in Japan," *Union Signal*, 24 July 1890.

165. Shō Nemoto, "Imperial Temperance Society," *Union Signal*, 22 October 1891.

166. *The Pacific Ensign*, 8 December 1892, 2.

167. Chika Sakurai attended the World WCTU Conference funded by Japan WCTU members. *Nihon kirisutokyō fujin kyōfūkai hyakunenshi*, 93.

168. *Union Signal*, 14 November 1895.

169. Tyrrell, *Woman's World/Woman's Empire*, 197.

170. *Union Signal*, 8 November 1894.

NOTES TO CHAPTER 3

1. For example, key members of the oligarchy were on the Privy Council that functioned as a special advisory body to the Emperor, operating outside the

purview of the Constitution. They also made up an informal group that could meet whenever the need arose to decide upon policies of major importance. Government officials, including cabinet ministers, were responsible to the Emperor, not the Diet. The only subject on which people's representatives could influence government policy was the budget, because a new budget had to pass the two houses.

2. Shobei Shiota, *Nihon shakai undōshi* (Tokyo: Iwanami shuppan, 1982), 1–11.

3. Akiko Fuse, *Kekkon to kazoku: Ningen no rekishi o kangaeru,* vol. 5 (Tokyo: Iwanami shoten, 1993), 60–67.

4. Ryoji Igeta, "Meiji minpō to josei no kenri," in *Nihon joseishi,* vol. 4, ed. Joseishi sōgō kenkyūkai (Tokyo: Tokyo daigaku shuppankai, 1982), 41–76.

5. Fuse, *Kekkon to kazoku,* 60–72; Ōtake, *"Ie" to josei no rekishi,* 274–296; J. E. de Becker, *Annotated Civil Code of Japan,* vol. 1 (London: Butterfield & Co., 1910; reprint, Washington D.C.: University Publications of America, 1979), 8; Igeta, "Meiji minpō to josei no kenri."

6. Under the Meiji Civil Code, a wife could not file for divorce unless a husband's extramarital affair was adjudged a crime, for example if he had an affair with a married woman and was sued and found guilty. Igeta, "Meiji minpō to josei no kenri."

7. Masashi Fukaya, *Ryōsai kenbo shugi no kyōiku* (Tokyo: Reimei shobō, 1990), 123–127.

8. Aoyama, *Meiji Jogakkō no kenkyū,* 463–464.

9. "Hokkaido no Sasaki Toyoju shi," *Fujin kyōfū zasshi,* no. 2 (2 December 1893).

10. *Nihon kirisutokyō fujin kyōfūkai hyakunenshi,* 94–95, 111–112. For example, in 1895 during the Sino-Japanese War the Japan WCTU magazine called upon its members not to devote themselves exclusively to the war effort and not to neglect the daily and "fundamental" effort to correct and reform their society. The government considered this an antiwar statement, and stopped publication of the magazine. Because of government suppression, the Japan WCTU changed the name of its public magazine from *Fujin kyōfū zasshi* to *Fujin shinpō* in 1896. See also "Ichiji no fūha ni mayou nakare," *Fujin kyōfū zasshi,* 15 (20 January 1895): 3–5.

11. *Tokyo fujin kyōfū zasshi,* no. 39 (18 July 1891): 14; no. 55 (28 December 1892): 320.

12. Among the sixteen attendees, fifteen represented the Tokyo WCTU that now became one local union of the Japan WCTU, and one represented a local union in Chiba prefecture. "Nihon fujin kyōfūkai nenkai kiji," *Fujin shinpō,* no. 15 (28 April 1896): 143–144.

13. The Japan WCTU's annual convention in 1895 had received reports from ten local unions in Tokyo, Yokohama, Takahashi, and Kasaoka in Okayama prefecture, Hakodate, Nagoya, Tsu, and Yokkaichi in Mie prefecture, Chiba, and Morioka.

14. "Development of the World's W.C.T.U.," *Union Signal*, 11 July 1895.

15. Ibid.

16. "World's W.C.T.U. Convention," *Union Signal*, 11 July 1895; Tyrrell, *Woman's World/Woman's Empire*, appendix, 292.

17. Before becoming a missionary and a teacher at the female missionary school in Kyoto, Denton, like many other missionary women, pursued a career in teaching. In her teens, while still attending high school, she started to teach summer courses in Nevada County, California. Denton laid the foundation for her lifelong opposition to alcohol during her early years of teaching. Teaching at a county school, she lived with a family on a ranch that employed many men. On late Sunday afternoons, the head of the ranch, his wife, and young Denton went to the nearby village with wagons strewn with straw at the bottom to make the rounds of saloons to pick up drunken workers who were unconscious and semi-conscious. Denton became an ardent worker for the WCTU of Southern California. Frances Benton Clapp, *Mary Florence Denton and the Doshisha* (Kyoto: Doshisha University Press, 1955), 1–14.

18. "Development of the World W.C.T.U.," *Union Signal*, 11 July 1895; *Japan Evangelist* 2, no. 4 (April 1895): 236–237; 3, no. 3 (February 1896): 173–176. See also Tyrrell, *Woman's World/Woman's Empire*, appendix, 292.

19. *Tokyo fujin kyōfū zasshi*, no. 39 (18 July 1891): 14–15. Harris was a missionary wife of the Methodist Episcopal Church. Harris had engaged in evangelical work among Japanese immigrants in California with her husband since 1886, after working in Hakodate and Tokyo from 1871 to 1883. Hatanoshin Yamaka, *Harisu fujin* (Tokyo: 1911; reprint, Tokyo: Ōzorasha, 1995).

20. *Japan Evangelist* 2, no. 6 (August, 1895): 351–352; 11, no. 7 (July 1904): 225–227. See also Jiaikai, ed., *Jiairyō hyakunen no ayumi* (Tokyo: Domesu shuppan, 1994), 13–30.

21. *Japan Evangelist* 3, no. 3 (February 1896): 173–175; 11, no. 7 (July 1904): 225–230.

22. *Japan Evangelist* 3, no. 3 (February 1896): 175–176.

23. Ibid. In 1896, the sites of the five committees were Kyoto, Osaka, Kobe, Nagoya, and Nagasaki.

24. For the relationship between Eliza Spencer-Large, Canadian Methodist missionaries in Tokyo, and the general board, see Rosemary R. Gagan, *A Sensitive Independence: Canadian Methodist Women Missionaries in Canada and the Orient, 1881–1925* (Montreal: McGill-Queen's University Press, 1992), 65–114.

25. Clara Parrish, "Impressions of Japan," *Union Signal*, 28 January 1897.

26. *Japan Evangelist* 5, no. 8 (August 1898): 237; "More Good News from Japan," *Union Signal*, 18 August 1898. The Japanese version includes the Japan WCTU's constitution and brief history. Ukai, trans. and ed., *Bankoku kirisutokyō fujin kyōfūkai annai*.

27. Willard, *Do Everything*, 35–219.

28. *Japan Evangelist* 4, no. 8 (May 1897): 253–254. The other departments were: Evangelistic, Loyal Temperance Legion (children's societies, abbreviated as L.T.L.), Mother's Meetings, Social Purity, Sabbath Observance, Sunday School Work, Work among Young Women in Schools and Colleges (Ys), Press Work, Literature, Work among Soldiers, and Legislation and Petitions. Clara Parrish, "World's W.C.T.U." See also *Nihon kirisutokyō fujin kyōfūkai hyakunenshi*, 136.

29. *Japan Evangelist* 5, no. 5 (May 1888): 153; "Fujin kyōfūkai chuōbu nenkai kiji yōryaku," *Fujin shinpō*, no. 12 (20 April 1898): 26–27.

30. *Japan Evangelist* 4, no. 6 (March 1897): 189; 5, no. 1 (January 1898): 24–27.

31. *Japan Evangelist* 4, no. 7 (April 1897): 221; 4, no. 9 (June 1897): 282; 4, no. 10 and 11 (June and August 1897): 306.

32. *Japan Evangelist* 5, no. 4 (April 1898): 116; 5, no. 10 (October 1898): 321. See also Tyrrell, *Woman's World/Woman's Empire*, appendix, 292.

33. *Japan Evangelist* 11, no. 7 (July 1904): 225–230; Jiaikai, ed., *Jiairyō hyakunen no ayumi*, 13–84.

34. *Japan Evangelist* 5, no. 1 (January 1898): 23–24. For a profile of Parrish, see Frances E. Willard, "Our New Round-the-World Missionary," *Union Signal*, 6 August 1896.

35. *Japan Evangelist* 5, no. 1 (January 1898): 26.

36. *Japan Evangelist* 5, no. 10 (October 1898): 320; "Miss Parrish Leaves Japan," *Union Signal*, 3 November 1898.

37. "A Letter from Miss Parrish," *Union Signal*, 26 August 1897: *Japan Evangelist* 4, no. 8 (May 1897): 253–254.

38. "The W.C.T.U. of the World," *Union Signal* (17 March 1904). Kara Smart made similar efforts in 1904.

39. *Nihon kirisutokyō fujin kyōfūkai hyakunenshi*, 214.

40. *Japan Evangelist* 5, no. 1 (January 1898): 25.

41. *Japan Evangelist* 6, no. 9 (September 1899): 270.

42. Taneko Yamaji, "Yomu hito ni tsugu," *Fujin shinpō*, no. 13 (11 May 1898): 157.

43. Miyama worked as a temperance evangelist until around 1908. His salary and travel expenses were secured by Clara Parrish when she was in Japan. When she left, they were covered by the Temperance Union, the Foreign Auxiliary, some *Japan Evangelist* subscribers, and the Japan WCTU. *Japan Evangelist* 6, no. 8 (August 1899): 244; 6, no. 9 (September 1899): 272.

44. *Japan Evangelist* 4, no. 12 (September 1897): 359–360; 6, no. 2 (February 1899): 53–55; Cherrington, *Standard Encyclopedia of the Alcohol Problem, 1385–1387*; *Kuni no hikari*, no. 66 (29 October 1898): 12–14. Unlike the Japan WCTU or the Foreign Auxiliary, membership in the union was open to national or foreign, Christian or non-Christian temperance societies as long as they required a total abstinence pledge from their members.

45. Tarō Andō became its president. Among its vice presidents were Shō

Nemoto, Sen Tsuda, and Julius Soper. *Japan Evangelist* 6, no. 9 (February 1899): 53–55.

46. *Japan Evangelist* 4, no. 8 (May 1897): 253.

47. "Report of Our Seventh Round-the-World Missionary, Miss Clara Parrish," at the World's Convention," *Union Signal*, 12 July 1900.

48. *Japan Evangelist* 4, no. 8 (May 1897): 252.

49. *Japan Evangelist* 5, no. 5 (May 1898): 152.

50. "Fujin kyōfūkai chuōbu kinenkai kiji yōryaku," *Fujin shinpō*, no. 12 (20 April 1898): 25–31.

51. *Japan Evangelist* 5, no. 5 (May 1898): 155–156.

52. Keigo Kiyoura, "Fujin kyōfūkai no hattatsu ni tsuite," *Fujin shinpō*, no. 16 (20 August 1898): 2–8.

53. "A Letter from Miss Parrish," *Union Signal*, 26 August 1897.

54. "Report of Our Seventh Round-the-World Missionary, Miss Clara Parrish," at the World's Convention," *Union Signal*, 12 July 1900.

55. Ibid.

56. Masanao Shikano, *Ashio kōdoku jiken kenkyū* (Tokyo: Sanichi shobō, 1974); F. G. Notehelfer, "Japan's First Pollution Incident," *Journal of Japanese Studies* (Spring 1975): 351–383.

57. Reiko Abe, "Ushioda Chiseko," in *Kindai nihon no joseishi: Jiyū to kaihō to shinkō to*, ed. Fumiko Enchi (Shūeisha, 1981), 47–82.

58. Shōzō Tanaka was the key figure in this protest against the Ashio mine pollution. In 1891, Tanaka, then a representative of the Tochigi prefecture to the Lower House, first brought the issue before the Imperial Diet. However, after the police attacked thousands of farmers on their way to Tokyo to petition the government in 1900, Tanaka turned his back on the Diet. In 1901, he resigned as representative and attempted to appeal directly to the Emperor, but in vain. The police arrested Tanaka, but soon discharged him labeling him an "insane man." Until his death in 1913, Tanaka devoted himself to Japan's first antipollution movement. Kenneth Strong, *Ox against the Storm: A Biography of Tanaka Shōzō, Japan's Conservationist Pioneer* (Victoria: University of British Columbia Press, 1977).

59. Abe, "Ushioda Chiseko."

60. Abe, "Ushioda Chiseko"; Shikano, *Ashio kōdoku jiken kenkyū*, 387; Eiichi Kudō, *Shakai undō to kirisutokyō* (Tokyo: YMCA shuppan, 1972), 123–177; Chiseko Ushioda, "Kōdoku hisaishi Watarase no tami," parts 1–2, *Fujo Shinbun* 81 (26 November 1901): 4; 82 (2 December 1901): 4.

61. Yajima indicated that she wanted to resign before the 1903 Japan WCTU convention, probably because Kara Smart was rather critical of a single woman dominating the Japan WCTU presidency. The 1903 Japan WCTU convention held in Kobe elected Chiseko Ushioda, then the president of the Tokyo WCTU, as president. Ochimi Kubushiro, *Yajima Kajiko den* (Tokyo: Fujiya shobō, 1935; reprint, Tokyo: Ōzorasha, 1988), 231–235; *Japan Evangelist* 10, no. 4 (April 1903): 137.

62. When socialist women began petitioning the Imperial Diet to repeal the government ban on political participation by women, a few members of the Japan WCTU joined in along with Diet members such as Shō Nemoto. But the Japan WCTU as an organization stayed away, and the socialist women's attempt was discontinued in 1909. In the renewed liberal climate, the government ban on women's political activism was modified in 1922, and women were allowed to join political organizations and attend political meetings. In 1925, male universal suffrage was achieved. *Nihon kirisutokyō fujin kyōfūkai hyakunenshi*, 512; Sievers, *Flowers in Salt*, 114–138; Vera Mackie, *Creating Socialist Women in Japan: Gender, Labor and Activism, 1900–1937* (Cambridge, Cambridge University Press, 1997), 42–69; Katsuko Kodama, "Heiminsha no fujintachini yoru chian keisatuhō kaisei seigan undō ni tsuite," *Rekishi Hyōron*, no. 323 (March 1977): 73–82.

63. Sievers, *Flowers in Salt*, 189–195; Mackie, *Creating Socialist Women in Japan*, 80–85, 131–132; *Nihon kirisutokyō fujin kyōfūkai hyakunenshi*, 513–524; Tsuneko Gauntlett, *Nanajū-nananen no omoimde* (Tokyo: Uemura shoten, 1949; reprint, Tokyo: Ōzorasha, 1989), 113–124; Mariko Matsukura, "Mō hitori no fujin undōka," *Kirisutokyō shakai mondai kenkyū* 51 (December 2002): 85–112.

64. *Japan Evangelist* 5, no. 4 (April 1898): 116–117.

65. Ibid.

66. In 1899, the Foreign Auxiliary started to petition the railway authorities to provide a nonsmoking carriage on each train, and their efforts were supported by both the Temperance Union and the Japan WCTU. As a result, smoking was prohibited in Tokyo electric cars by August 1904, and the government railways bureau decided to attach nonsmoking cars to its local express trains by the end of 1908. See, for example, *Japan Evangelist* 6, no. 11 (November 1899): 336; 6, no. 12 (December 1899): 372; 11, no. 8 (August 1904): 267; 15, no. 11 (November 1908): 428; 16, no. 2 (February 1909): 79.

67. Tyler, *Where Prayer and Purpose Meet*, 225–239. The Young Woman's Branch changed its name to Young People's Branch in 1909 to enlist young men of college-going age as well.

68. *Nihon kirisutokyō fujin kyōfūkai hyakunenshi*, 136; *Japan Evangelist* 4, no. 8 (May 1897) 253–254.

69. *Japan Evangelist* 5, no. 8 (August 1898): 239.

70. *Japan Evangelist* 7, no. 4 (April 1900): 118; "Temperance Legislation in Japan," *Union Signal*, 19 January 1905; "A Bill Prohibiting the Smoking of Tobacco by Minors," *Kuni no hikari/Light of Our Land* 9, no. 9 (October 1901): 11–12.

71. Jessie Ackermann, "The Mission of the W.C.T.U. in Japan," *Union Signal*, 19 December 1901.

72. *Japan Evangelist* 9, no. 11 (November 1902): 368–369.

73. *National WCTU Annual Meeting Minutes* (1905): 194; (1906): 191; (1907): 190, 196–197; (1909): 173. See also, for example, the following articles in *Union Signal*: "The Clara Parrish Fund," 17 February 1898: 10; Margaret Wintringer, "L.T.L.

Conference at Los Angeles," 14 December 1905, 4; J. George Frederick, "Moral Uplift for Japan," 15 February 1906; J. George Frederick, "Progress of the Japan L.T.L. Fund," 13 September 1906, 3; J. George Frederick, "Practical Work for Peace—The Anna A. Gordon Japanese Fund," 9 May 1907; Ada Melville Shaw, "A Successful Japanese Entertainment," 26 September 1907, 3, 15.

74. The Y's Missionary Fund hired Tsuneko Gauntlett, a Japanese woman married to an English national, and Etsuko Sugimoto, as native organizers. The LTL's Anna Gordon Japan Fund secured the service of Azuma Moriya as a native LTL organizer. Gauntlett and Azuma came to play leading roles in the Japan WCTU after the World WCTU stopped sending resident missionaries to Japan in 1913. Gauntlett, *Nanajū-nananen no omoide*, 72–81; *Nihon kirisutokyō fujin kyōfūkai hyakunenshi*, 268–269, 406–407; Mieko Uno, "Shakai kyōiku ni okeru Moriya Azuma no shisō to jissen," *Kyōiku kenkyū* 30 (1988): 85–106.

75. Under the leadership of the World WCTU missionaries, the Foreign Auxiliary, assisted by members of the Japan WCTU and the Temperance Union, translated and published the WCTU's juvenile work materials, such as scientific temperance textbooks, Sunday school lesson books and plans, recitation materials, songs, total abstinence and purity pledge cards, and badges. See, for example, *Japan Evangelist* 9, no. 12 (December 1902): 397; 10, no. 10 (October 1903): 333–335; 10, no. 11 (November 1903): 375; 12, no. 1 (January 1905): 18–20; 15, no. 6 (June 1908): 231; 15, no. 7 (July 1908): 266; 15, no. 12 (December 1908): 461; 16, no. 9 (September 1909): 346–347; 16, no. 12 (December 1909): 495–496; 17, no. 7 (July 1910): 267–268.

76. The first recitation contest with medal awards in Japan was conducted in April 1905 among Japanese children and youngsters whose age ranged from twelve and twenty-five years and who had "signed and kept the total abstinence pledge for six months prior thereto." By the end of 1909, the rules were changed so that anybody, whether total abstainers or not, of any age, could participate in the contest. In 1911, the Japan WCTU started the Temperance Essay Contest with cash awards for middle school students. A full-page announcement of the contest was carried in a magazine the readers of which were mainly nonchurch-going middle school Japanese students. At the first essay contest held in 1911, a student from a school for Buddhist priests in Tokyo won the second prize. *Japan Evangelist* 12, no. 3 (March 1905): 92–93; 12, no. 5 (May 1905): 165–166; 16, no. 9 (September 1909): 346–347; 18, no. 5 (May 1911): 183; 18, no. 7 (July 1911): 278.

77. *Japan Evangelist* 12, no. 3 (March 1905): 92–93.

78. *Japan Evangelist* 10, no. 11 (November 1903): 375. For the WCTU's moral reform movement in the United States, see Alison M. Parker, *Purifying America: Women, Culture, Reform, and Pro-Censorship Activism, 1873–1933* (Urbana: University of Illinois Press, 1997).

79. *Japan Evangelist* 12, no. 1 (January 1905): 18–20.

80. *Japan Evangelist* 16, no. 11 (November 1909): 449.

81. *Nihon kirisutokyō fujin kyōfūkai hyakunenshi,* 395–407. For an account of Japan WCTU activism in Meiji Japan, see Elizabeth A. Dorn, "'For God, Home, and Country': The Woman's Christian Temperance Union and Reform Efforts in Meiji Japan" (Ph.D. diss., University of Hawai'i, 2003).

82. Umeko Tsuda attended Bryn Mawr College from 1889 to 1892. For the life of Umeko Tsuda in Japan and the United States, see, for example, Barbara Rose, *Tsuda Umeko and Women's Education in Japan* (New Haven: Yale University Press, 1992); Yoshiko Furuki, *The White Plum: A Biography of Ume Tsuda, Pioneer in the Higher Education of Japanese Women* (New York: Weatherhill, 1991); Yuko Takahashi, *Tsuda Umeko no shakaishi* (Tokyo: Tamagawa daigaku shuppanbu, 2002).

83. *Japan Evangelist* 2, no. 5 (June 1895): 290–292.

84. Takeyo Takekoshi, ed., *Gunjin no izoku ni okuru sho* (Tokyo: Shūeisha, 1894).

85. *Japan Evangelist* 4, no. 8 (May 1897): 253–254; 11, no. 4 (April 1904): 131–133; Fukiko Shimizu, "Gunjinka ni tsuite," *Fujin shinpō,* no. 82 (25 February 1904): 3–8.

86. *Japan Evangelist* 11, no. 3 (March 1904): 90; 11, no. 4 (April 1904): 131–133; Kara Smart, "An Appeal from Miss Smart," *Union Signal,* 13 April 1905: 12; "Let America Profit by the Lesson," *Union Signal,* 2 May 1907: 3; "Kyōfūkai no nisshin kasuga kaikō kangeikai," *Fujin shinpō,* no. 82 (25 February 1904): 9–10; "Osaka kyōfūkai no shyōbyōhei imon," *Fujin shinpō,* no. 85 (25 May 1904): 8.

87. Mary A. Livermore, *My Story of the War: A Woman's Narrative of Four Years Personal Experience as a Nurse in the Union Army* (Hartford: A.D. Worthington and Co., 1891), 135–142.

88. "Comfort Bags and Pajamas to the Front," *Union Signal,* 16 June 1898; *Japan Evangelist* 11, no. 4 (April 1904): 131–133.

89. *Japan Evangelist* 11, no. 12 (December 1904): 388–391; Shimizu, "*Gunjinka ni tsuite*"; Kara Smart, "Work for Soldiers in Japan," *Union Signal,* 29 December 1904.

90. Smart, "Work for Soldiers in Japan."

91. *Nihon kirisutokyō fujin kyōfūkai hyakunenshi,* 214.

92. One American missionary woman, who fled the danger and confusion in China for Japan, praised Japan's military action in China as an effort to bring "justice." See "Shinkoku bōdō jikkendan," *Fujin shinpō,* no. 41 (25 September 1900): 13–14.

93. *Japan Evangelist* 11, no. 8 (August 1904): 269; 11, no. 9 (September 1904): 292; 12, no. 8 (August 1905): 280; Smart, "Work for Soldiers in Japan."

94. Smart, "An Appeal from Miss Smart."

95. Ibid.

96. Joseph M. Henning, *Outposts of Civilization: Race, Religion, and the Formative Years of American-Japanese Relations* (New York: NYU Press, 2000), 137–164.

97. "Let America Profit by the Lesson," *Union Signal,* 2 May 1907, 3.

98. Frederick, "Moral Uplift for Japan."

99. Flora E. Strout, "Temperance Sentiment Growing among Japanese Young People," *Union Signal,* 12 May 1910: 5.

100. For example, cash awards were used for Ys and LTL recitation and essay contests and to strengthen the tie between Japan WCTU officers and local WCTU workers. In 1909, Flora E. Strout set a precedent by giving cash awards to the Japan WCTU's national superintendent who had turned in the best written report on the departmental work done by the local unions, and to the local union which did the best work at that department. *Japan Evangelist* 16, no. 4 (April 1909): 151–152.

101. "Kankoku to kyōfū jigyō," *Fujin shinpō,* no. 105 (25 April 1906): 4.

102. Tsuneko Watanabe, "Chōsen ryokōki," part 1, *Fujin shinpō,* no. 177 (25 March 1912): 25; Kim Moon-Gil, "Ebina Danjō no Chōsen dendō to nihonka mondai ni tsuite," *Kirisutokyū shakai mondai kenkyū,* no. 46 (1998), 230–265; Yoon Tai Ho, *Nikkan kirisutokyō kōryūshi* (Tokyo: Shinkyō Shuppan, 1968).

103. Kankoku Kirisutokyō Rekishi Kenkyūsho, *Kankoku kirisutokyō no jyunan to teikō,* trans. Han Sokkki and Masahiko Kurata (Tokyo: Shinkyō shuppan, 1995), 239–240.

104. Ruth F. Davis, "Another Link in the Chain of the World's W.C.T.U." *Union Signal,* 11 April 1912; Tsuneko Watanabe, "Chōsen ryokōki," parts 1 and 2, *Fujin shinpō,* no. 177 (25 March 1902): 25–27; no. 178 (25 April 1903): 26–28. Ruth Davis and Tsuneko Watanabe also visited Taiwan together in 1913 to promote Christianity and temperance. For their visit to Taiwan, see Ruth F. Davis, "W.C.T.U. Notes from My Diary," *Union Signal,* 13 March 1913.

105. Ho, *Nikkan kirisutokyō kōryūshi.*

106. Tyrrell, *Woman's World/Woman's Empire,* 6.

NOTES TO CHAPTER 4

1. Yamato Ichihashi, *Japanese in the United States: A Critical Study of the Problems of the Japanese Immigrants and Their Children* (Stanford: Stanford University Press, 1932), 1–15.

2. The founding members included thirty-four Japanese men and one woman, wife of one of the members.

3. In San Francisco, one of the offshoots became founding members of the First Japanese Presbyterian Church of San Francisco and led to the organization of a Young Men's Christian Association (YMCA) in 1885. Others who left the Society became the leading force in commencing the Independent Japanese Congregational Church in Oakland in the early 1900s. Simultaneously, the Gospel Society organized branches in Yokohama and Tokyo in 1885 to assist self-supporting Japanese students preparing to go to the United States. Ryō Yoshida, "Kariforunia no nihonjin to kirisutokyō," in *Hokubei nihonjin kirisutokyō undōshi,* ed. Doshisha daigaku jinbun kagaku kenkyujo (Tokyo: PMC shuppan, 1991), 172.

4. Yuji Ichioka, *The Issei: The World of the First Generation Japanese Immi-*

grants, 1885–1924 (New York: Free Press, 1998), 16–19; Yoshida, "Kariforunia no nihonjin to kirisutokyō," 150–210; *Fukuinkai enkaku shiryō, Shoki no bu A,* 2–11, The Japanese American Research Project Collection at the University of California, Los Angeles (henceforth JARP), Box 291. M.E. Japanese missions were formed in Oakland in 1889, Sacramento in 1891, Fresno in 1894, San Jose in 1894, Los Angeles in 1895, Vacaville in 1896, Riverside in 1902, and so on.

5. *Fukuinkai enkaku shiryō, Shoki no bu B,* 20; *Niki no bu A,* 20, JARP, Box 291.

6. *Fukuinkai enkaku shiryō, Shoki no bu A,* 16–17; B, 21; *Niki no bu A; Niki no bu C,* JARP, box 291. After the initial record of Gospel Society female members' efforts to organize the Female Charitable Society in March 1883, the Female Charitable Society is not mentioned again until March 1889 when it held its third meeting.

7. *Fukuinkai enkaku shiryō Shoki no bu A,* 29, *Niki no bu B,* JARP, box 291; "Kawaguchi Masu shi no shojō," *Tokyo fujin kyōfū zasshi,* no. 28 (16 August 1890): 6–7.

8. Tel Sono, *Tel Sono; The Japanese Reformer, an Autobiography* (New York: Hunt and Eaton, 1892). Sono later attended the M.E. Deaconess Training School in Chicago and the Missionary Training Institute in New York to become a Christian worker. Then, after raising funds in the United States to build a female Christian school in her home country, Sono returned to Japan. She helped World WCTU missionary Flora Strout deliver a temperance lecture at a Buddhist university in 1908. *Jogaku zasshi,* no. 303 (6 February 1892): 716; *Japan Evangelist* 15, no. 6 (June 1908): 231.

9. Sono, *Tel Sono,* 51–56.

10. Alexander Saxton, *The Indispensable Enemy: Labor and the Anti-Chinese Movement in California* (Berkeley: University of California Press, 1971); Lucie Cheng Hirata, "Free, Indentured, Enslaved: Chinese Prostitutes in Nineteenth Century America," *Signs* 5, no. 11 (1979): 3–29; Ichioka, *The Issei,* 1–6; Sucheng Chan, *Asian Americans: An Interpretive History* (New York: Twayne, 1991), 45–61.

11. The first group of Japanese contract laborers to the Hawaiian islands ended their term in 1887.

12. "Rekishi inmentsu no tan: onna no tobei jijō," JARP, box 134, folder 6; Kazuo Kasahara, *Nihon joseishi* (Tokyo: Hyōronsha, 1923), 216–234; Kazue Morisaki, *Karayukisan* (Tokyo: Asahi shinbun, 1976); Ichioka, *The Issei,* 28–39.

13. Zaibei Nihonjinkai, ed., *Zaibei nihonjinshi,* vol. 1 (San Francisco: Zaibei nihonjin kai, 1940; reprint, PMC shuppan, 1984), 64–65; Ryō Yoshida, *Amerika nihonjin imin to kirisutokyō shakai: Kariforunia nihonjin imin no haiseki, dōka to E. A. Stōji* (Tokyo: Nihon tosho sentā, 1995), 63–64.

14. Chinda to Okabe, June 13, 1891, enclosure, "Fuseigyō fujoshi torai kinshi seigan," 16 May 1891, *Japanese Foreign Ministry Archival Document,* reel 1, JARP. Translated and cited in Ichioka, *The Issei,* 39.

15. M. C. Harris, "The Japanese Woman's Home," *Woman's Home Missions*

(1894): 6; F. B. Harris, "Editor Woman's Home Missions," *Woman's Home Missions* (1894): 140.

16. "Kawaguchi Masu shi no shojō."

17. "Gaikoku ni okeru Nihon fujo hogo hōan," *Tokyo fujin kyōfū zasshi,* no. 35 (21 March 1891): 8–9.

18. See, for example, the following three articles, all of which appeared in *Tokyo fujin kyōfū zasshi,* no. 48 (31 May 1892): "Hitan subeki ichidaimondai," 4–6; "Kaigai shūgyōsha torishimari no kenpaku," 6–7; "Kanashimubeki hōdō: Kaigai shūgyōsha no arisama," 14–17.

19. For example, in 1900 the Japanese in Siberia remitted about one million yen, of which 63 percent was sent by Japanese women engaged in the prostitution business who were called *rōshigun* (troops of daughters and children). Kasahara, *Nihon joseishi,* 216–234.

20. "Shūgyōfu torishimari no kunrei," *Tokyo fujin kyōfū zasshi,* no. 57 (28 February 1893); 15–16; Mitsui, ed., *Gendai fujin undō nenpyō,* 42.

21. "Gaikoku ni okeru nihon fujin," *Fujin kyōfū zasshi,* no. 2 (2 December 1893): 30–31; "Kaigai shūgyōsha torishimari no kenpaku," *Fujin kyōfū zasshi,* no. 3 (2 January 1894): 20; *Nihon kirisutokyō fujin kyōfūkai hyakunenshi,* 71–80.

22. See, for example, "Hitansubeki ichidai mondai."

23. Ichioka, *The Issei,* 35. In San Francisco, Japanese brothels were located in or near Chinatown on Dupont Street (present-day Grant Avenue) and on St. Mary's Street.

24. "Oriental Work: A Historical Sketch," *Woman's Home Missions* (May 1924): 9–11; Wesley S. Woo, "Protestant Work among the Chinese in the San Francisco Bay Area, 1850–1920," Ph.D. diss., Graduate Theological Union, 1984, 154–155.

25. The original purpose of the California Branch was to assist with missionary work in Shanghai. But this was soon dropped in favor of work among Chinese women on their shores. The California Branch changed its name to the Occidental Branch in 1877 and to the Occidental Board in 1881, while remaining an auxiliary of the Woman's Foreign Missionary Society of the Presbyterian Church, Philadelphia. In 1899, however, the Occidental Board established a direct relationship with the general foreign missionary board and became the Woman's Occidental Board of Foreign Missions (WOBFM) of the Presbyterian Church, U.S.A. Mrs. H. B. Pinney, et al., "Story of the Decades: A Historical Sketch of the Woman's Occidental Board of Foreign Missions," *The Occidental Board of Woman's Foreign Missionary Society of Philadelphia Annual Report* (henceforth *WOBFM Annual Report*) (1920): 8–20. For Cameron House, see also Pascoe, *Relations of Rescue;* Mildred C. Martin, *Chinatown's Angry Angel: The Story of Donaldina Cameron* (Palo Alto, Calif.: Pacific Books, 1977).

26. They were under the appointment of the Missionary Society of the M.E. Church.

27. Upon its formation, the Woman's Missionary Society of the Pacific Coast

sought to unite with the Woman's Foreign Missionary Society of the M.E. Church in New York, but the Woman's Foreign Missionary Society was unwilling to engage in any work within the United States. As a result, the Pacific Coast Society remained a direct auxiliary of the general Missionary Society of the M.E. Church until 1893. That year the Pacific Coast Society was merged with the WHMS of the M.E. Church, founded in 1880. Thus the Oriental Bureau of the M.E. WHMS came to take charge of Methodist women's work for Asian women on the Pacific Coast and in Hawaii. See "Oriental Work: A Historical Sketch."

28. M. C. Harris, "Report of the Japanese District, California Conference, for the Year 1893–1894," in *Gospel in All Lands* (1894): 577.

29. F. B. Harris, "Editor Woman's Home Missions," 140.

30. M. C. Harris, "Report of the Japanese District, California Conference, for the Year 1893–1894," 577.

31. "Home Missions on the Pacific Coast," *Woman's Home Missions* (1903): 63; Herbert B. Johnson, "Japanese Women: Opportunities of Work among Them on the Pacific Coast," *Woman's Home Missions* (1906): 306–307; *Annual Report of the California Conference, Woman's Home Missionary Society of the Methodist Episcopal Church* (henceforth *WHMS—CC Annual Report*) (1903): 8; (1905): 5.

32. Stella Wyatt Brummitt, *Looking Backward, Thinking Forward: The Jubilee History of the Woman's Home Missionary Society of the Methodist Episcopal Church* (Cincinnati, 1930), 99–100; *WHMS—CC Annual Report* (1905): 20–23; (1906): 18–20.

33. F. B. Harris, "Editor Woman's Home Missions," 140.

34. Flora B. Harris, "Iro Iro," *Woman's Home Missions* (1903): 65–66.

35. Margarita Lake, "Japanese Woman's Home," *California Christian Advocate*, 28 April 1904: 17.

36. Rev. Harris left San Francisco for Japan with his wife to become the Bishop of Japan and Korea in 1904.

37. Johnson, "Japanese Women," 307.

38. *WOBFM Annual Report* (1905): 66–68.

39. *WOBFM Annual Report* (1900): 80–81; (1902): 44.

40. Hirata, "Free, Indentured, Enslaved."

41. Toyoko Yamazaki, *Sandakan hachiban shokan* (Tokyo: Chikuma shobō, 1972); Toyoko Yamazaki, *The Story of Yamada Waka: From Prostitute to Feminist Pioneer,* trans. Wakako Hironaka and Ann Kostant (Tokyo: Kōdansha International, 1985).

42. Pascoe, *Relations of Rescue*; Judy Young, *Unbound Feet: A Social History of Chinese Women in San Francisco* (Berkeley: University of California Press, 1995), 34–37.

43. *WOBFM Annual Report* (1905): 66–68.

44. Yamazaki, *The Story of Yamada Waka*. Waka Yamada later became a noted advocate for the state protection of motherhood in early-twentieth-century Japan.

45. *WOBFM Annual Report* (1904): 57.

46. *WOBFM Annual Report* (1905): 66–68.

47. Yamazaki, *The Story of Yamada Waka.*

48. *WOBFM Annual Report* (1905): 66–68.

49. *WOBFM Annual Report* (1909–10): 60; (1911–12): 50.

50. Ichihashi, *Japanese in the United States,* 228–242; Ichioka, *The Issei,* 51–56. As for prostitutes, the U.S. government passed the Page Law in 1875 to prohibit their entry, and the Japanese Foreign Ministry issued an ordinance in 1893 to control the overseas migration of Japanese women for the purpose of prostitution.

51. Ichioka, *The Issei,* 156–164.

52. "Shashin kekkon ni tsuite," *Ōfu nippō* (Sacramento Daily), 22 June 1915; "Shashin kekkon yurai," *Ōfu nippō,* 27 June 1915; "Shashin kekkon mondai," *Ōfu nippō,* 29 February 1916.

53. Ichioka, *The Issei,* 164–175.

54. "Shashin Kekkon," parts 1–2, *Shin sekai* (New World), 11 and 12 June 1909; "Shashin kekkon shōrei ron," *Ōfu nippō,* 28 February 1915: "Shokuminchi ni onna o okuranu kyōkoku wa nai," *Ōfu nippō,* 28 April 1916.

55. Dr. E. A. Sturge, "Japanese Picture Brides and Picturesque Japanese Children," *Assembly Herald* 18 (June 1912): 301–303.

56. Margarita Lake, "Work for Japanese Women and Children," *Woman's Home Missions* (1907): 68; "Oriental Missions on the Pacific Coast under the Care of the Woman's Home Missionary Society," *Woman's Home Missions* (February 1909): 4.

57. *Abiko Family Papers,* JARP, Box 11, Folder 6. For Japanese and Issei YWCA activism for Japanese immigrant women, see Eiichiro Azuma, "Interstitial Lives: Race, Community, and History among Japanese Immigrants Caught Between Japan and the United States, 1885–1941" (Ph.D. diss., UCLA, 2000), 119–122.

58. Ichioka, *The Issei,* 156–173; *Nihon gaikō bunsho, taibei iminmondai ni kansuru nichibei kōshō keika* (Tokyo: 1972), 576–582.

59. In America, until 1917 a man and his picture bride who had completed the marriage procedure under the Japanese legal system were required by U.S. law to solemnize their marriage after the bride's arrival in America.

60. Ichioka, *The Issei,* 164–173; Nakano, *Issei, Nisei, War Bride,* 42–50; Nakano, *Japanese American Women;* Valerie J. Matsumoto, *Farming the Home Place: A Japanese American Community in California, 1919–1982* (Ithaca: Cornell University Press, 1993); Linda Tamura, *The Hood River Issei: An Oral History of Japanese Settlers in Oregon's Hood River Valley* (Urbana: University of Illinois Press, 1993); Akemi Kikumura and Michiko Tanaka, *Through Harsh Winters: The Life of a Japanese Immigrant Woman (as Told to Akemi Kikumura),* (Novato, Calif.: Chandler and Sharp, 1981).

61. Ichioka, *The Issei,* 164–173.

62. For example, "Iwayuru Fūchan mondai no rakuchaku," *Shin sekai,* 22 July 1908; "Otto o kirau indarame," *Shin sekai,* 22 April 1909.

63. Mary M. Bowen, "Report of Evangelist to Japanese," *Minutes of the State Convention of the California Woman's Christian Temperance* (henceforth *California WCTU Minutes*) (1910): 91.

64. Bowen was born in 1849 near Morgantown, West Virginia, as the daughter of the Hon. Lot Garrison Bowen, a military officer and statesman, and Cassandra Vance (Wright) Bowen. "Rev. Mary M. Bowen," Jesse W. Wooldridge, ed., *History of Sacramento Valley,* vol. 2 (Chicago: Pioneer Historical Publishing Co., 1931), 270–276; John W. Leonard, ed., *Woman's Who's Who of America* (New York: American Commonwealth Co., 1914), 118–119.

65. Bowen to President Wilson, 30 January 1907.

66. Before becoming a missionary, Bowen worked for women's educational institutions, including Western Reserve Seminary in Ohio and Beaver Woman's College in Philadelphia. At Beaver Woman's College, a Methodist institution south of Pittsburgh, Bowen was an "assistant lady principal." See "Rev. Mary M. Bowen," 270–276; Leonard, *Woman's Who's Who of America,* 118–119.

67. Bowen's name was listed as a missionary of the M.E. WHMS in its official publication from February 1891 to August 1892. As a WHMS missionary, she worked first at the Haven Industrial Home in Savannah, Georgia, and then at the newly opened Glenn Home in Cincinnati, Ohio. At the Glenn Home, she worked among colored people. *Woman's Home Missions* (1891): 3, 14; (1892): 25, 70, 110.

68. For example, Bowen's reports on the parish work of the First Church in Oakland appear in a Methodist Episcopal newspaper, *California Christian Advocate* on 18 January, 22 February, and 15 March 1893.

69. "Social Purity Convention," *Pacific Ensign,* 1 June 1893: 2.

70. Ryō Yoshida, *Amerika nihonjin imin to kirisutokyō shakai,* 58.

71. Mary M. Bowen, "Among the Japanese," *California Christian Advocate,* 4 January 1899, 4.

72. M. C. Harris reported on the work of the M.E. Japanese Mission in the California *Christian Advocate.* His reports talked about the efforts of male Japanese preachers and sometimes touched upon the work of American women as teachers and matrons, but never referred to Bowen.

73. F. B. Harris, "Japanese Missions," *California Christian Advocate,* 10 May 1899, 5.

74. *Sacramento Bee,* 6 May 1908, 5.

75. *United Brethren Yearbook* (1916): 87.

76. "California Conference, Quest. 22," *Minutes of the Annual Conferences of the M.E. Church* (Fall 1924).

77. After establishing themselves, some of the beneficiaries supported Bowen in her projects and personal life. Zaibei Nihonjinkai, ed., *Zaibei nihonjinshi,* vol. 2, 374–375.

78. "Ōfu no bussō," *Shin sekai,* 16 March 1900; "Ōfu ōda kokuso jiken no

jijitsu," *Shin sekai,* 19 March 1900; "Nagai dokutā no sainan yobun," *Shin sekai,* 20 March 1900.

79. Kie arrived in the United States in 1906, and received a marriage certificate in the state of Washington. "Hakuhatsuō no tōsho ni tsuite," parts 1–3, *Shin sekai,* 5–7 March 1908; "Tsunoda Yoshi no torishirabe no jijō," *Shin sekai,* 2 May 1908; *The Sacramento Superior Court Record, #12503 Urabe v. Urabe,* Sacramento Archives and Museum Collection Center, Sacramento, Calif. (henceforth SAMCC).

80. "Dokuritsu kyōkai no fujin shūyō," parts 1–2, *Shin sekai,* 28 and 29 February 1908.

81. "Hakuhatsuō no tōsho ni tsuite," parts 1–3.

82. "Fujin mi o kyōkai ni tōzu," *Shin sekai,* 26 November 1908; "Fujiwara fūfu no rikon mondai," parts 1–4, *Shin sekai,* 5–6, 8, 11 March 1908; *General Index of the Sacramento Superior Court, 1907–1908,* Case #13004, SAMCC.

83. *Nichibei nenkan* (1905): 160; (1915): 113, JARP, Box 358.

84. Sacramento Supreme Court General Index, 1899–1904, 1904–1907, 1907–1908; Sacramento Supreme Court Civil Index, Plaintiffs, 1909–1936, SAMCC. Gary Y. Okihiro and Timothy J. Lukes reported that Issei divorce cases were initiated mainly by women between 1900 and 1942 in Santa Clara Valley, California. Gary Y. Okihiro and Timothy J. Lukes, *Japanese Legacy: Farming and Community Life in California's Santa Clara Valley* (Cupertino, Calif.: California History Center, 1985), 75.

85. "Rikon no ōi genin," *Shin sekai,* 16 March 1909.

86. *Ōfu nippō* reported seventy-two marriages and forty-three divorce suits in the city of Sacramento in March 1917, and a decreasing rate of marriage and an increase in divorce. "Kekkon to rikonsū," *Ōfu nippō,* 4 April 1917.

87. "Rikon no ōi genin."

88. "Rikon taikoku nihon," *Ōfu nippō,* 16 December 1916.

89. "Rikon no ōi genin." In Japan, women were first allowed to file for divorce under the emerging Meiji legal system in 1873, during the liberal period. The Meiji Civil Code of 1898, which stipulated divorce by suit and consent, enabled a wife to file for divorce in cases of intolerable abuse, insult, desertion, or when a husband was found guilty of a crime and sentenced. Ōtake, *"Ie" to josei no rekishi,* 289–296.

90. "Rikon zōka no hanei," *Shin sekai,* 7 June 1909; "Dōhō fujin no beika," 24 June 1909; "Fujin dōtoku no taihai," *Ōfu nippō,* 1 September 1909.

91. *"Inpu Yoshino,"* parts 1–6, *Ōfu nippō,* 12, 15–16, 18–19, 21 March 1911; "Dokuritsu kyōkai towa nani," parts 1–4, *Ōfu nippō,* 1, 4–5, 7 April 1911.

92. *California WCTU Minutes* (1883): 11–12; (1885): 35–36. After the formation of the WCTU of Southern California in 1886, the state of California contained two WCTU unions directly affiliated with the National WCTU: the WCTU of California (comprised of counties in the northern and central regions) and the WCTU of

Southern California. For an overview of the WCTU of California's activism, see Debra L. Larsen, "The History of the Woman's Christian Temperance Union of Northern California, 1879–1900" (Master's thesis, California State University, Hayward, 1977). For an account of the WCTU of Southern California's activism, see Betty Jane Woods, "A Historical Survey of the Woman's Christian Temperance Union of Southern California" (Master's thesis, Occidental College, 1950).

93. *Fukuinkai enkaku shiryō, Shoki no bu A*, 15–16, JARP.

94. Yoshida, "Kariforunia no nihonjin to kirisutokyō," 162.

95. For example, Flora B. Harris visited Frances E. Willard at the Rest Cottage with Shō Nemoto and Saburo Shimada in 1888. "A Visitor from the Orient," *Union Signal*, 17 May 1888.

96. Tel Sono was affiliated with the North San Francisco WCTU for a few months in 1889. Mrs. L. M. Carver, "Miss Tel Sono, the Japanese Kaishinsha Reformer," *Union Signal*, 13 June 1889, 4.

97. Carver, "Miss Tel Sono"; Sono, *Sono Tel*, 65–66; *California WCTU Minutes* (1889): 95.

98. "San Francisco County Report," *Minutes of the National Woman's Christian Temperance Union* (henceforth *National WCTU Minutes*) (1894): 258.

99. *California WCTU Minutes* (1894): 108–109.

100. Mrs. Dorcas J. Spencer, *A History of the Woman's Christian Temperance Union of Northern and Central California* (Oakland: West Coast Printing Co., n.d.), 123–124; *California WCTU Minutes* (1896): 60–61.

101. *California WCTU Minutes* (1897): 51. In 1896 and 1911, there were massive campaigns to amend the California State Constitution to realize woman suffrage. For WCTUs in northern and southern California and the woman suffrage movement, see Gayle Gullett, *Becoming Citizens: The Emergence and Development of the California Women's Movement, 1880–1911* (Urbana: University of Illinois Press, 2000); and Rebecca J. Mead, *How the Vote Was Won: Woman Suffrage in the Western United States, 1868–1914* (New York: NYU Press, 2003).

102. Judging from the writing of L. P. Williams, it seems that Chinese sons and the California WCTU became allies over the woman suffrage issue in 1896. In 1911, however, the Chinese Six Companies of San Francisco, a leading Chinese organization, sent out an order to all native-born Chinese in California to vote against the woman suffrage amendment at the elections that year. See "California Suffrage Campaign Notes," *Union Signal*, 28 September 1911, 12.

103. The main people behind the anti-Chinese movement were white laborers, while Republicans and Protestant clergymen defended Chinese labor. Saxton, *The Indispensable Enemy*.

104. *National WCTU Minutes* (1880): 63–64; (1881): appendix l xii; (1886): lxxxviii–lxxxix.

105. *California WCTU Minutes* (1896): 60–61.

106. Chan, *Asian Americans*, 92.

107. *California WCTU Minutes* (1896): 60–61; (1898): 66–67; (1904): 67.

108. *California WCTU Minutes* (1898): 66–67.

109. *California WCTU Minutes* (1897): 51; (1898): 66–67.

110. Chiyoko Kozaki traveled to the United States with her husband, a Congregational minister who was invited by Issei churches for the moral reform and evangelization of Issei communities. Utako Hayashi came to the United States to raise funds for her orphanage project in Osaka, Japan.

111. Chiyoko Kozaki, "Beikoku junkai nikki," part 1, *Fujin shinpō*, no. 104 (25 December 1905): 14–15.

112. *Fujin shinpō*, no. 101 (25 September 1905): 29–30; no. 104 (25 December 1905): 27–28; no. 105 (25 January 1906): 35; no. 106 (25 February 1906): 74; no. 108 (25 April 1906): 25–26. Responding to the invitation from American WCTU women, Issei unions in Los Angeles and Riverside were affiliated with the WCTU of Southern California in 1906. But among the highly mobile immigrant communities of the early twentieth century, many of the Issei unions formed in 1905 did not last long and other unions also came and went, except the Oakland Japanese WCTU which lasted until 1941.

113. According to Kozaki, brothels located in the Issei community in San Francisco disguised their businesses as air-gun shops, just as unlicensed brothels in Japan disguised theirs as archery shops.

114. Kozaki, "Beikoku junkai nikki," parts 2, 6, *Fujin shinpō*, no. 105 (25 January 1906): 14–19; no. 109 (25 May 1906): 16–19.

115. This statement was first published in an Issei community newspaper in San Francisco, and then in Japan WCTU's official magazine. "Zaibei fujin to Yajima kaito," *Fujin shinpō*, no. 114 (25 October 1906): 7.

116. Kozaki wrote, "I would like to create [Japan WCTU unions] in Seattle, Portland, Oakland, Los Angeles, and especially in San Francisco." Chiyoko Kozaki, "Beikoku tsūshin," *Fujin shinpō*, no. 103 (25 November 1905): 21. Female members of the (Japanese) Pine Methodist Church in San Francisco had formed a women's society before Kozaki's visit in August 1905, but they did not join the Japan WCTU's network. Although Clara Johnson, who took charge of the California WCTU's Japanese Department between 1913 and 1926, was the wife of the superintendent of the M.E. Japanese Mission, the women's society of the Pine Methodist Church did not associate with WCTU. In 1920, when Yajima made her second trip to San Francisco, a former student of Yajima's, who was living in San Francisco, organized an Issei WCTU in the city.

117. "Zaibei fujin to Yajima kaitō." The devastation of San Francisco caused by the earthquake, which hit the city in April 1906, might also have had an effect.

118. Yajima's nephew-in-law was a Congregational minister who came to Oakland in 1904 in response to the call of an offshoot of the Gospel Society to establish a Japanese church, financially independent of American missions. Yajima's grandniece, Ochimi, then attending the Pacific School of Religion in Berkeley, was

a graduate of the Presbyterian female mission school in Tokyo where Yajima was the acting principal. Ochimi Kubushiro, *Chichi to ryōjin* (Tokyo: Tokyo shimin kyōkai shuppanbu, 1936); Ochimi Kubushiro, *Haishō hitosuji* (Tokyo: Chūō kōronsha, 1981), 50–99.

119. "Ōfu fujin kyōfūkai," *Fujin shinpō*, no. 117 (25 January 1907): 19–20; *California WCTU Minutes* (1907): 29.

120. The Oakland Issei WCTU's bimonthly newsletter was first called *Hakuhyō fujin* (White Ribbon Woman), then renamed *Zaibei fujin shinpō* (Japanese Woman's Herald in America). This newsletter was probably the oldest publication for Issei women by Issei women. Kubushiro, *Haishō hitosuji*, 78–79; *California WCTU Minutes* (1907): 29.

121. *Union Signal*, 7 November 1907, 1–2.

122. *California WCTU Minutes* (1916): 74.

123. In 1917, the newsletter was sent to different parts of California, and to Japan, Hawaii, Utah, Oregon, Washington, New York, and Alaska. *California WCTU Minutes* (1913): 77; (1917): 82.

124. In 1910, Mary Bowen organized an Anglo-Japanese WCTU in Sacramento. In 1920, when Kajiko Yajima at age eighty-eight made the second trip to California, three additional Issei unions were formed in northern California in San Francisco, Loomis, and Sacramento. *California WCTU Minutes* (1910): 91; (1920): 79–80.

125. See, for example, *California WCTU Minutes* (1907): 29; *Fujin shinpō*, no. 126 (25 October 1907): 23; no. 128 (25 December 1907): 23; no. 154–55 (15 May 1910): 33.

126. After their creation, Japan WCTU's official magazine, *Fujin shinpō*, carried reports from each union for a short while. Reports from the Portland and Riverside unions appeared only a few times. There was one account of the Seattle union in 1906 and a few more between 1911 and 1913. In 1911, Yajima's grandniece, Ochimi (Okubo) Kubushiro, moved to the city after her marriage to a Congregationalist minister, but they returned to Japan in 1913. The Los Angeles union was active for some time, but their reports disappeared from *Fujin shinpō* in 1908. Both Japanese and American WCTU records reported that the Issei unions in Los Angeles and Riverside were affiliated with the WCTU of Southern California in 1906. However, the minutes of the 1924 Southern California WCTU Convention, the earliest minutes to which I had an access, did not list these two unions. According to the Southern California WCTU Convention minutes, one Issei union was formed under the L.A. City Federation in 1930, and another under the L.A. County Young People's Branch/Youth Temperance Council in 1934. *Fujin shinpō* (1906–1913); *National WCTU Minutes* (1906): 207; *Southern California WCTU Minutes* (1924–1941).

127. The Issei Oakland Union remained on the list of local unions in the *California WCTU Minutes* until 1941, when Issei and their children were relocated.

128. Until then, the Oriental Work Department took charge of work among both the Chinese and the Japanese.

129. Spencer, *A History of the WCTU of Northern and Central California,* 123–124. Smart returned to the United States in 1906 due to her illness, and moved to California after her marriage in 1907.

130. Smart secured the cooperation of Rev. Herbert B. Johnson of the M.E. Japanese Mission and of Dr. H. H. Guy, the Pacific Coast Superintendent of Japanese Work at the Christian Church Mission. *California WCTU Minutes* (1908): 46–47.

131. Spencer, *A History of WCTU of Northern and Central California,* 122–124; *California WCTU Minutes* (1910): 91; (1911): 69–70; (1912): 72–73; (1913): 77.

132. *California WCTU Minutes* (1915): 81–82; (1916): 74; (1921): 82; (1925): 125. After Clara Johnson, Mrs. Rose Baker took charge of the department in 1927.

133. Kubushiro, *Haishō hitosuji,* 78–79.

134. "Zaibei fujin to shūyō," *Ōfu nippō,* 7 February 1912.

135. Ochimi Kubushiro, "Dōtokujō no jōbihei," *Fujin shinpō,* no. 213 (28 March 1915): 4–7; Kubushiro, *Haishō hitosuji,* 67–71.

136. *Fujin shinpō,* no. 126 (25 October 1907): 21–22; no. 134 (25 June 1908): 26–27.

137. Otowa Okubo, "Kashū ni okeru dōhō," *Fujin shinpō,* no. 198 (25 December 1913): 16–19. Otowa Okubo was also active in the Japanese YWCA that was founded in San Francisco in 1912.

138. The number of Japanese women in America increased from 985 (4 percent of the total Japanese population) in 1900, to 9,087 (14 percent) in 1910, and to 38,303 (35 percent) in 1920. Glenn, *Issei, Nisei, War Bride,* 245.

139. Matsumoto, *Farming the Home Place,* 25.

140. Ichioka, *The Issei,* 173–175.

NOTES TO THE EPILOGUE

1. This contrasts with the situations in the countries that came under Anglo-American colonial rule. See, for example, Patricia Grimshaw, *Paths of Duty: American Missionary Wives in Nineteenth-Century Hawai'i* (Honolulu: University of Hawai'i Press, 1898).

2. East Lawn Record, no. 16330. East Lawn Memorial Cemetery in Sacramento, Calif.

Index

About the Author

Rumi Yasutake studied at Doshisha University, University of Texas at Austin, and UCLA, where she received a Ph.D. in history. She has taught at UCLA, California State University Long Beach, and Konan University in Kobe, Japan, where she is an associate professor of American Studies.